AF839982

IMPROVING EQUITY THROUGH FISCAL POLICY

Improving Equity through Fiscal Policy: Dashed Dreams explores the delivery of key services to the public and to what extent equity is considered when government allocates resources. Authors Marc K. Fudge and Marc Holzer examine the key topics in a typical public budgeting, finance or policy course including taxation, public choice and political economics from an equity-based lens. They then offer a deep dive into the development of US public policies, tackling a complex history of policies written expressly to undermine or suppress the advancement of Blacks and people of color. The result is a timely supplement to public budgeting and finance courses that encourages readers to recognize and reckon with the persistence of deep disparities—and the ways in which contemporary public budgeting cannot be understood without considering equity.

The book begins with a discussion of the value of social equity and how it emerged as a critical component of public administration and policy. It then provides coverage of the economic role of government in society, taxation and its distributional effects, voter suppression, as well as inequities in housing, education and health. It further explores the racial wealth gap as well as positive examples of strategies that have helped to support a fairer and more equal allocation of resources. *Improving Equity through Fiscal Policy: Dashed Dreams* offers instructors, students, policymakers, elected officials, managers and leaders a critical and necessary re-examination of this important topic.

Marc K. Fudge is a professor in the Department of Public Administration at California State University, San Bernardino. His research focuses on public finance, equity and justice, and performance management. His work appears in the *Journal of Public Budgeting, Accounting & Financial Management, Public Financial Management*, the *Journal of International Finance and Economics*, and several other publications. He currently serves on the California State University President's Diversity, Equity & Inclusion Board and he is the director of the Center on Fiscal Policy & Innovation. He is a former President of the Conference of Minority Public Administrators (COMPA) and the former Chair of the Section on Public Performance and Management.

Marc Holzer is Distinguished Research Professor at Suffolk University, Boston. He is Emeritus Professor and was Founding Dean of the School of Public Affairs and Administration at Rutgers University-Newark. Professor Holzer is extensively published, is a Past President of the American Society for Public Administration and is a Fellow of the National Academy of Public Administration.

Routledge Public Budgeting and Finance

Editor Bruce D. McDonald III
Professor of Public Budgeting and Finance and Director of the School of Public Service, Old Dominion University, Norfolk VA

Public budgeting is a core function of public administration. Regardless of the level of government, size of government, type of management, or the socio-economic and political characteristics of the government, the execution of policies and programs requires the expenditure of resources, and important funding decisions must be made. Yet public officials are faced with policy and program implementation in an environment of limited resources. The Routledge Public Budgeting and Finance series explores issues related to effective, ethical, and equitable budgeting and financial management in the context of public administration. Topics of interest to the series include, but are not limited to:

- Budgeting for times of uncertainty
- Sales taxes
- Budget and revenue forecasting
- Management of local government debt
- Public pensions
- Financial analysis of public budgets
- Social equity budgeting
- Financing of subgovernment structures
- Financials of economic development
- Law enforcement budgeting
- Managing and organizing budget offices
- Transportation and infrastructure finance

Authors interested in discussing book project ideas on these and other public budgeting topics are encouraged to contact series general editor Bruce D. McDonald, III, Old Dominion University, at bmcdona@ncsu.edu.

RECENTLY PUBLISHED BOOKS

Improving Equity through Fiscal Policy
Dashed Dreams
Marc K. Fudge and Marc Holzer

IMPROVING EQUITY THROUGH FISCAL POLICY

Dashed Dreams

Marc K. Fudge and Marc Holzer

Routledge
Taylor & Francis Group
NEW YORK AND LONDON

Designed cover image: Davide Zanin, Getty Images

First published 2026
by Routledge
605 Third Avenue, New York, NY 10158

and by Routledge
4 Park Square, Milton Park, Abingdon, Oxon, OX14 4RN

Routledge is an imprint of the Taylor & Francis Group, an informa business

© 2026 Marc K. Fudge and Marc Holzer

The right of Marc K. Fudge and Marc Holzer to be identified as authors of this work has been asserted in accordance with sections 77 and 78 of the Copyright, Designs and Patents Act 1988.

All rights reserved. No part of this book may be reprinted or reproduced or utilised in any form or by any electronic, mechanical, or other means, now known or hereafter invented, including photocopying and recording, or in any information storage or retrieval system, without permission in writing from the publishers.

Trademark notice: Product or corporate names may be trademarks or registered trademarks, and are used only for identification and explanation without intent to infringe.

Library of Congress Cataloging-in-Publication Data
Names: Fudge, Marc author | Holzer, Marc author
Title: Improving equity through fiscal policy : dashed dreams / Marc Fudge and Marc Holzer.
Description: New York, NY : Routledge, 2026. | Series: Routledge public budgeting and finance | Includes bibliographical references and index.
Identifiers: LCCN 2025009097 | ISBN 9781032670843 hardback | ISBN 9781032670829 paperback | ISBN 9781032670850 ebook
Subjects: LCSH: Fiscal policy—Social aspects—United States | Finance, Public—Social aspects—United States | Income distribution—Social aspects—United States | Equality—Economic aspects—United States | African Americans—Economic conditions—21st century | Minorities—United States—Economic conditions—21st century
Classification: LCC HJ257.3 .F84 2025
LC record available at https://lccn.loc.gov/2025009097

ISBN: 978-1-032-67084-3 (hbk)
ISBN: 978-1-032-67082-9 (pbk)
ISBN: 978-1-032-67085-0 (ebk)

DOI: 10.4324/9781032670850

Typeset in Sabon
by Apex CoVantage, LLC

I would like to dedicate my contributions to this book to my parents Robert and Janice Farley. My parents have continued to be among my greatest supporters and instilled in me a relentless drive to seek educational, social and economic freedom regardless of the situation we have been placed in.

Marc K. Fudge

This book is dedicated to my doctoral students in the field of public administration, an exceptionally diverse group whom I have had the privilege of mentoring. They have changed the face of the professoriate in our field, been recognized for the quality of their published research, have risen to positions of academic and professional leadership, and are serving as role models for their own students.

Marc Holzer

CONTENTS

FIGURES

TABLES

INTRODUCTION

The allocation of resources continues to be a critical component of service delivery, sustainability and growth, for communities around the world. The manner in which services are delivered to the public and precisely how those decisions are made provide a foundation for this book. Building upon that framework, however, is the vital and critical endeavor of ensuring that equity is firmly entrenched and built within the foundation. In particular, we aim to better understand to what extent equity is considered when government delivers services to the public. Furthermore, we examine key topics in public management and policy from an equity-based lens. These topics include education, healthcare, housing, voting and taxation. History shows us that the equitable delivery of services has not occurred with great frequency and as a result we see an enormous disparity in wealth between Whites, Blacks and people of color. Of paramount concern in this book is the belief that historically many US public policies have not been developed in a manner that was fair and equitable for Blacks and people of color. On the contrary, we believe the majority of those policies were written in an effort to suppress the advancement of Blacks and people of color. Our examination of equity is framed from the perspective of public budgeting and finance, in part because we believe that one of the primary goals of government is to ensure that services are delivered equally and fairly. While some may view the relationship between equity and public budgeting and finance to be unique or interesting, we feel as if it is necessary and logical. Due to the fact that government is forced to deal with the issue of scarce resources, and other fiscal challenges, it becomes even more critical to examine equity in this context.

DOI: 10.4324/9781032670850-1

As V.O. Key once famously inquired, "On what basis shall it be determined to allocate X resources to activity A, instead of Activity B?," we are curious to learn more about the fiscal decision-making process governments choose as it relates to equity. We simultaneously explore the historical aspects of equity from various topics and how they began inequitable practices of service delivery, thus leading to the racial wealth gap we see today. We believe that *Improving Equity through Fiscal Policy: Dashed Dreams* will force instructors, students, policymakers, elected officials, managers and leaders to begin re-examining why equity has not been a more prominent topic in all subjects.

Prior to delving into the contents of the book, we would like to clarify our position on a few key terms used in *Improving Equity through Fiscal Policy: Dashed Dreams.* We identify people of color (POC) as those who do not identify as White or Black, but who may identify as other racial/ethnic groups. For example, we realize that the terms Hispanic and Latino are often used interchangeably in the United States. This may be, in part, because in the United States the terms "Hispanic" and "Latino" were originally not used to classify individuals on the US Census Survey. In the 1960 US Census, the term Hispanic, Latino or Chicano did not even appear on the survey. White, Negro, Aleut, Eskimo, American Indian, Chinese, Japanese, Filipino, Hawaiian and Part Hawaiian were the terms used so that individuals could self-identify themselves. The narrow list made it impossible for someone of Hispanic or Latino ethnicity to appropriately identify themselves. Hispanic and Latino, in fact, have different meanings where Hispanic refers to individuals from Spain or are descended from Spain. Latino, on the other hand, refers to individuals who are descendants of Latin America or have Latin American heritage but live in the United States. To illustrate one difference, Brazilians, for example, would be considered Latinos but not Hispanic. Professor Dr. Cristina Mora, from the University of California, Berkeley, states that she may interchangeably use the terms Chicana, Latina or Latinx depending on the context. "We create preferences and we still understand ourselves" (Campos, 2021). In recent years, two gender-neutral terms have emerged to refer to Latinos: Latinx and Latinè (OSIC, 2020). These terms are gender-neutral and non-binary and are similar to how the terms "Black," "White" and "Asian" refer to both men and women. There is some "push-back" however to the term Latinx. According to Dr. Christina Sisk, a sociology professor at the University of Houston states, "One of the arguments against Latinx is that it doesn't sound like Spanish at all. You can't say Latin . . . X . . . You know?" (Hurtado, 2022). In an effort to be more inclusive, we use the terms Latinè along with Latina and Latino. As such, we capitalize the first letter when talking about the race of individuals or their ethnicity. For example, we capitalize "B" in Black when referring to individuals who identify as Black. We use the term Black to encapsulate African-Americans, Africans and descendants of Africa who live in the United States, unless otherwise referred to as African. Similarly, we choose to capitalize the "W" in White to fairly treat those who identify as that racial group. According to the Center for the Study of Social Policy, "To not name 'White' as a race is, in fact, an anti-Black act which frames Whiteness as both neutral and the standard" (Nguyen & Pendleton, 2020). Di'Angelo and Dyson (2018) similarly state, "White people get to be just people," and oftentimes do not have their race named to describe them, whereas non-Whites are often described with their race. Thus, we choose to capitalize the first letter when discussing any individual's race or ethnicity.

Our book takes an in-depth analysis of the relationship between equity and public budgeting and finance. We explore some of the topics a student would typically learn in upper-division or graduate budgeting, finance or public policy classes such as taxation, public choice and political economics and take this opportunity to explore topics such as housing, educational and healthcare disparities that you may find in a public policy, sociology or an urban studies course. We believe the result of this text is broad in scope, yet one that also includes specific material that will foment continued exploration in the subject-matter ultimately resonating with the reader in an effort to develop introspection and further questions about our society. A particular aim is to help inform students in a way that will lead to further exploration and inquisitiveness that ultimately results in a more informed resident in our society.

Chapter 1, *An Equity Perspective,* begins by discussing the value of social equity and how it emerged as a critical component of public administration and policy. Three questions that will be addressed in this chapter are as follows:

1. In what ways does government address social equity from the perspective of one of the chapters from this book like taxation, housing, healthcare, etc.
2. In what way(s) could socially equitable outcomes be improved?
3. How will Social Equity be measured?

It is important for readers to continue to pose these questions in each chapter of *Improving Equity through Fiscal Policy: Dashed Dreams* to understand the relationship equity has with other important topics.

In Chapter 2, *Government and the Economy,* we examine the economic role of government in society. On a macro level, the decisions government makes in terms of the allocation of resources to its residents help us to understand the extent that equity is a factor and even considered. A question to ponder is, how critical is the implementation of equity principles in communities that are more homogeneous? Why, or why not? Should equity be attended to with greater urgency in more diverse communities? And if so, at what point does equity become more important? Ultimately, we believe the implementation of equity principles should be introduced, implemented and practiced in all communities all of the time. If we are to pursue the goal of a fair and just society for all, then the ideals of equity should travel with us wherever we go and can then be applied in every community for all to benefit.

In our chapter on *Taxation*, we discuss the theory of taxation, the various types of taxes and the distributional effects of taxes on various groups of people, including the marginalized and the disenfranchised. In this chapter, it becomes acutely clear that taxes and other types of consumption fees adversely impact the traditionally marginalized and disadvantaged, along with the poor, those with less discretionary income and racial minorities than those with more income to spare.

We use the chapter on *Voter Suppression* to introduce public choice theory and the relationship it has to voting. In 2020, several US states passed what many consider restrictive voting laws built upon the assumption that recent elections had become wrought with fraud and were otherwise rigged in favor of one party (or person) over another. We cover what we believe to be the genesis of this line of thinking, the rationale for such legislation and how it ultimately influences the services that are delivered to the public.

Our chapter on *Healthcare* explores the varied quality of care individuals of various races and ethnic groups receive. Particular attention is paid to infant and maternal morbidity and mortality rates across races. We also explore the outcome of healthcare and the relationship between physicians and patients based upon their races.

Some of the biggest disparities among people in the United States exist in the area of housing. In this chapter, we discuss housing disparities that have occurred, in large part, from government organizations such as the Federal Housing Authority (FHA). Racist policies, including "redlining," have led to, among other things, educational and socioeconomic disparities in the United States.

Following our chapter on housing disparities, and strongly related, we explore educational inequity along with the Supreme Court's ruling on the use of Affirmative Action, higher education underrepresentation of minority students, student loan debt and the impact they have on expanding the racial wealth gap.

Relatedly, the next chapter examines the *Racial Wealth Gap* and how systemic racism has led to huge economic and social disparities between Whites and non-Whites in the United States. The racial wealth gap is a prominent factor negatively impacting equity, and it is the resultant effect of inequitable and racist education, housing and healthcare policies in the United States.

In the final chapter, *Advancing the Equity Needle Forward,* we examine the topic of Reparations along with identifying various strategies that have been successful in terms of improving equity. Our book would be incomplete without an exploration of the topic of Reparations. While many see this as a contentious and sensitive topic that draws ire, we believe it is a necessary and important conversation to have especially as we present strong evidence of a continued racial wealth gap in the United States. It is also vital that we identify organizations and places where policies, procedures and activities that support equity are being implemented. There are many successful initiatives occurring across the globe in cities, government and nonprofit organizations, and firms that are worth emulating and applauding. While many of the examples in this book show where disparities exist and are prevalent, we use the final chapter to highlight the positive examples that others can look to as goals for the future and to ultimately move the equity needle forward.

References

Campos. (2021). *What's the difference between Hispanic, Latino and Latinx?—On navigating identity, language and community from a scholarly and first-person perspective.* https://www.universityofcalifornia.edu/news/choosing-the-right-word-hispanic-latino-and-latinx

Di'Angelo, R., & Dyson, E. (2018). White fragility: Why it's so hard for White people to talk about racism. Boston: Beacon Press.

Hurtado, D. (2022). Latino vs. Hispanic: Experts explain the difference between these umbrella terms. *ABC13.com.* https://abc13.com/what-is-the-difference-between-latin-and-hispanic-culture-does-mean-heritage-month/12324390/

Key, V. O. (1940). The lack of a budgetary theory. *American Political Science Review*, *37*(4), 1137–1144.

Nguyen, A. T., & Pendleton, M. (2020). *Recognizing race in language: Why we capitalize "Black," and "White."* Center for the Study of Social Policy. Retrieved February 21, 2023, from https://cssp.org/2020/03/recognizing-race-in-language-why-we-capitalize-black-and-white/?gclid=CjwKCAjw-rOaBhA9EiwAUk-LV4gxRvdJb4scUQmw9809_SLhzq6YWX44ntfxGT0VgOF8AWqzc1pHe-jBoCFbwQAvD_BwE

OSIC—Department of Organizational Strategy, Initiatives, and Culture. (2020). *Hispanics v. Latino v. Latinx explained.* https://www.yesprep.org/news/blog/featured/~board/blog/post/hispanic-vs-latinos-vs-latinx-explained

1

AN EQUITY PERSPECTIVE

This chapter begins our exploration by examining equity from a broad, generalist perspective. Various concepts and ideas about equity are discussed before the working definition, that will be used throughout this book, is presented. Over the course of the remaining chapters, the working definition is applied to the specific area of study it is applied. *An equity perspective* also introduces us to the relationship between equity and public budgeting and finance. It then moves along to discuss the different perspectives scholars have espoused regarding equity. After reviewing the various definitions of equity, this chapter introduces students to the definition developed by the authors. The chapter concludes with challenges and opportunities to infuse equity into public budgeting and finance topics and courses.

Importance of equity

The delivery of services to the public is an essential component of what government does for the residents of a jurisdiction. In many ways, we not only expect government to protect us from general harm but we also expect our governments to afford us opportunities to prosper. And certainly, we do not expect our government to stand in the way of our prosperity for any reason. Prosperity can take on different forms such as economic prosperity, educational prosperity, health prosperity and many other areas. As a result, the US government provides free education for children from kindergarten through high school. It is the hope of all residents that the

DOI: 10.4324/9781032670850-2

public education one child receives will not be significantly different from the public education received by another child. We know this is not the case, however. The amount of resources a school district has at its disposal varies based upon several factors including tax base, the percentage of federal government funding received, political and community interest and how well, or poorly, those funds are allocated by school administrators. Despite these differences, and notwithstanding educational funding equalization laws in all states, great levels of disparity still exist across school districts. Historically, we have also seen many examples where the US government has actively worked against allowing all students to gain educational prosperity. Another area that government is responsible for delivering services to the residents of a jurisdiction is public safety. Police departments and their respective public safety officials are expected to ensure the safety and well-being of all of its residents. Indeed a great deal of discretion is required of the police because they are often faced with making critical, potentially life-altering decisions in a matter of seconds. Similarly, one of the most recognizable duties of fire departments is to extinguish fire to protect buildings, individuals and their belongings from destruction.

The US federal government provides free healthcare to individuals who meet certain income requirements or are 65 years of age or older. It would be naive to think that the services local governments provide to their residents are the same throughout a state. Furthermore, it would be equally as unlikely to expect each of the 50 states to provide the same level of services as each other. What is expected, however, is that service provision is done in a fair manner. In other words, the decisions made in one city or state should allow one resident to have the same ability to receive equitable services as another resident. Collectively, the fair and equitable distribution of public services should be afforded to all residents. Again, historically and currently, we see examples of enormous disparities in healthcare and healthy outcomes among various groups.

The term equity is usually understood differently by individuals depending on several factors. First, prior professional experience (employment or organizations) and an individual's educational preparation regarding equity commonly afford an individual with a baseline context that is likely to be higher than someone who is unfamiliar, or vaguely familiar with the topic of equity. Second, oftentimes when first learning about equity, many tend to think the term equity has the same definition as equality. The two terms, however, are vastly different. Equality refers to the idea of treating everyone the same, or equal. The term emanates from the concept of egalitarianism which is "a belief in human equality especially with respect to social, political, and economic affairs" (merriam-webster.com). When the term equal is applied to governance, it is easy to see how it can be confused with the definition of equity because it espouses a similar idea.

The term equity refers to the idea of treating all people fairly. Equity is an attempt to ensure that all people are able to achieve the same, or similar, results if afforded fair treatment. Figure 1.1 captures the subtle but critical differences between equality and equity. In the *equality* picture, each of the fans is standing on a box, of equal size, so that they can look over the fence at a baseball game. The sizes of the boxes are the same, or equal, so one may surmise that since everyone has been treated the same that the issue has been resolved. Unfortunately, the kid with the purple shirt still cannot see the game. The same-size boxes provide an equal solution to each fan, but do not treat them each fairly. In the *equity* picture, we see that an adjustment has occurred so that the kid with the purple shirt can now watch the game too. As it turns out, the fan with the blue shirt did not need a box to see the game anyway. The fan in the red shirt still needs, at least one box to see the game, but not more than that. With just one box his needs are still met without impacting the fan with the blue shirt. The fan in the purple shirt, however, now has two boxes placed under him and he can now adequately see the game without impacting either of the two other fans. In this case, equity is achieved because a fair outcome is the result.

Key to a firm understanding of equity also includes a keen background into a term that has been gaslit to mean something demonstrably different than its original definition. The term Woke refers to the state of an individual being aware and *awake* to social injustices and finds its origins from the Jamaican philosopher, Marcus Garvey, who in the early 20th century calls for Black's in America, Jamaica and other parts of the world to "wake up" and join his Pan-African movement (Robinson, 2022). In 1938, Blues musician Lead Belly recorded the song *Scottsboro Boys* that tells the story of four Black youths who were falsely accused of raping a White woman in Alabama and ultimately sentenced to death. Fortunately, through multiple appeals, their sentences were overturned and they were not executed. In the song, Lead Belly warns of Blacks travelling to Alabama, "I advise everybody to be a little careful when they go down there. Stay woke. Keep your eyes open" (Robinson, 2022). The term was also used in the play *Garvey Lives,* where an actor extorts, "I been sleeping all my life. And now that Mr. Garvey done woke me up, I'm gon' stay woke. And I'm gon' help him wake up other black folk" (Beckham, 1972). Today, woke is often used as a pejorative term, thus obfuscating its original and true meaning in an effort to minimize the goal of the word. According to author Michael Harriot in an interview with the National Association for the Advancement of Colored People the Legal Defense Fund, "When you look at the long arc of

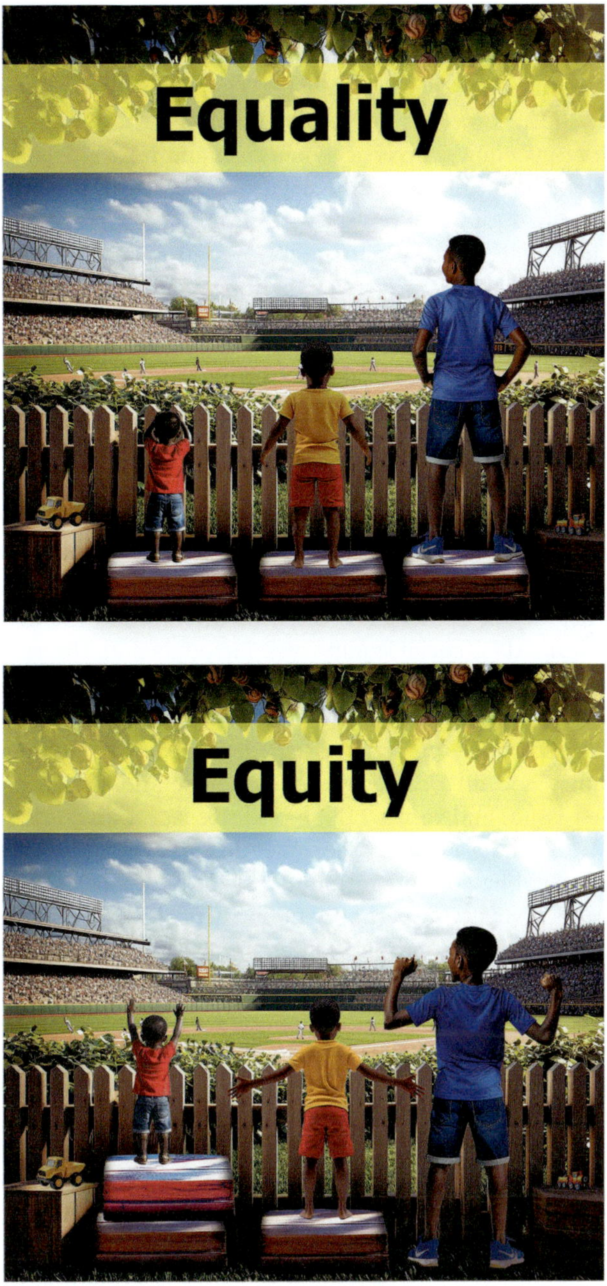

FIGURE 1.1 Equality Versus Equity.

Source: Original creation

history and America's reaction to the request for Black liberation – every time Black people try to use a phrase or coin a phrase that symbolizes our desire for liberation, it will eventually become a cuss word to white people" (Robinson, 2022). Indeed, there has been a significant amount of opposition to the terms equity, diversity, inclusion and now also a reframing of the term Woke to mean something negative. The work towards achieving equity is long, arduous and replete with those who strive towards the cessation of the social progress many seek. A great part of the work towards achieving equity includes proactively fighting against blatant attempts that actively work to undermine social and economic justice.

Emergence of equity principles

In the fall of 1968, with the backdrop of the Civil Rights Movement, social unrest and the assassinations of Dr. Martin Luther King, Jr. and Robert F. Kennedy, Dwight Waldo organized the Minnowbrook Conference. Waldo wanted to bring a group of leading scholars together to discuss the current state of public administration in the United States. At the conference, the term social equity began to gain increased attention in the field of public administration. Also, social equity was introduced as the third pillar of public administration (Frederickson, 2010). "Through conversation that was sometimes heated, the participants formulated the beginnings of New Public Administration—an action-oriented perspective that embraced normative inquiry and advocated for social equity and citizen participation among other issues and values" (Nabatachi & Carboni, 2019, p. 12). As a result, for nearly half a century, social equity has been seen as an integral component of public administration theory and practice.

The lack of diversity is perhaps the most problematic issue surrounding the original Minnowbrook Conference with participants only being White males. Despite the extremely noble attempts by the attendees, the fact remained that no people of color, nor any women, were among the participants and any study that aims to address inequity in society should include those who are most likely to be the most profoundly impacted. It is difficult to imagine that the conversations would not have been significantly different if women, Blacks, Hispanics/Latinè and people of color had been in attendance. Certainly today, there would be questions raised regarding the attendees of such a conference. Despite the shortcomings of the first Minnowbrook Conference, it did set the stage for equity to be critically examined and included in the fabric of public administration, the US government and society, in general. Since then, an increased emphasis on scholarly research has focused on explaining what social equity is (Gooden & Portillo, 2011; Johnson & Svara, 2011) along with empirically testing the extent of its presence in public-sector organizations.

A common theme that has emerged in later studies has been the challenge of developing a generally accepted definition of what social equity is. According to Frederickson (1990), "[s]ocial equity is a phrase that comprehends an array of value preferences, organizational design preferences, and management style preferences" (p. 228). Frederickson (2014) goes on to say that social equity emphasizes: Equality in government services; Responsibility for decisions and program implementation for public managers; Change in public management; Responsiveness to the needs of citizens rather than the needs of public organizations; and An approach to the study of and education for public administration that is interdisciplinary, applied, problem-solving in character, and sound theoretically. Guy and McCandless (2020) say that social equity refers to the need for public services to be fair for everyone in terms of access, process, quality and outcomes. "Its reach is broad and its dimensions are many, requiring equitable management of all institutions serving the public" (p. 1). Important questions that they pose in terms of understanding the implications of equity are:

- What does fairness mean in *X* circumstance?
- Who decides what is fair?
- Besides understanding problems of social equity, what are promising solutions?

According to Johnson and Svara (2011), "social equity is the active commitment to fairness, justice, and equality in the formulation of public policy, distribution of public services, implementation of public policy, and management of all institutions serving the public directly or by contract" (p. 282). While the above definition is inclusive and broad, it does not address precisely who benefitted as a result of the increased sales tax revenue. What were the monies used for? Who made the decisions to allocate the resources in the manner in which they were used? Or as Frederickson (1990) poses: Well managed for whom, efficient for whom, economical for whom? How do we go about addressing concerns regarding "fair to whom" because developing and implementing laws and policies that demonstrate fairness is obviously important in the administration of government? Moreover, what is the basis of us determining what is fair, equitable, just and accessible? It becomes critically important that we understand "fair" policies and laws are developed based, in part, upon the perceptions of those actually implementing the laws and policies.

Another challenging element associated with defining social equity has been creating methods to appropriately measure it. This creates a contemporaneous issue: how do we define and then accurately assess when social equity has effectively been implemented into the structure of an organization? Campbell (1976) stated that the issue of equity and what it refers to is not new but "the current effort to give it operational meaning in concrete policy areas is" (p. 556). He posed this dilemma nearly 50 years ago, yet public and nonprofit organizations are still trying to apply social equity to specific policy areas. According to Campbell, "At the heart of these concerns will be defining equity, developing measures of it, collecting and interpreting relevant data, and developing policies responsive to it" (p. 558). So how do public and nonprofit organizations move the needle forward? It is not an easy proposition even for scholars who have expertise in creating mechanisms to improve government performance. When we rely simply on efficiency and effectiveness as ways to assess the performance of government, it does not answer several critical questions of importance. First, how are we determining whether, or not, an organization or a department is performing well? How do we assess poor performance? *Performance Scholars* (those who study performance measurement, performance management, performance budgeting, resident-centered performance improvement, etc.) have continuously tried to effectively and accurately measure organizational performance. Performance scholars have moved from using output measures to determine program or agency success to using the more difficult outcome measures. Outcomes can be defined as measurable items that help managers determine how well, or poorly, an organization is performing. Outcomes are the results of the human resource and financial capital used by an organization. For example, as a result of the sanitation department increasing trash and waste removal by 3.4% from last fiscal year to this fiscal year, retail sales in downtown increased by 6%, resulting in over $80,000 in sales tax revenue. This example shows how the field of public administration has moved beyond using output measures to assess performance, but it does not address the prevailing issue of social equity. Specifically, how is social equity addressed in the context of the performance of an organization?

Creating yet another obstacle towards defining and measuring social equity is an individual's contextual understanding of the topic. Certainly, what one person considers fair is likely to be different from what another person thinks. Furthermore, if the idea of fairness is indeed actually supported by managers, elected officials and decision-makers, it is also likely based upon each individual's sensibility to what fairness means. Psychologists would define *sensibilities* as the ability of one to react to different situations or circumstances. According to Pam (2013), there are four components of sensibility:

1. The capacity to respond to an emotional situation with a refined feeling.
2. The ability to receive sensory input.

3. Having reason and sound judgment.
4. Feeling or perceiving a thing to be real.

In terms of organizations and how individuals behave within organizations, our sensibilities are influenced by our experiences, interactions or lack thereof. Our sensibilities then shape how we act and react to certain situations and ultimately our policy preferences. If we have had limited experience interacting with individuals from disadvantaged groups, then the manner in which we act towards them may be significantly different than how we would act towards them if we would have had a great deal of previous experiences and interactions with them.

Beyond sensibilities, another important component that impacts our policy preferences is having a general understanding of the groups of individuals in the jurisdiction whom you serve. Frederickson (2010) says that social equity is a term that requires individuals to include their own particular value, organizational design and management style preferences. It is the responsibility of the public decision-maker to become aware and *culturally competent* about your constituents. DeAngelis (2015) defines cultural competence as an individual's relative ability to understand, appreciate and interact with people from cultures or belief systems different from one's own. Cultural competence also requires that one does not conceptualize a concrete definition of another person, or group of individuals, based upon a limited interaction or experience with others. As we continue to learn more about people from groups that we are not familiar with, then our cultural competence broadens. Taken together, the concepts of sensibilities and cultural competence are important to understand for public managers, policymakers, elected officials and public administrators as they develop and implement laws and legislation designed to assist the public. It is likely that our management style and overall interactions with others are greatly influenced by our sensibilities and the extent of our cultural competence. Most importantly, decisions regarding public policy, our political preferences and the manner in which resources are allocated to the public are influenced by our sensibilities and cultural competence.

Working definition of social equity

In the previous section, we discussed some of the commonly used and referred-to descriptions of what social equity is. A recurring theme shared among these descriptions is the idea of fairness. We also shared the challenges of relying upon the term *fairness* in a definition of social equity. Specifically, who is the program fair to? Blessett et al. (2017) developed a more explicit definition of social equity that while including the idea of fairness also provides measurable items that can assist one in determining the extent to which social equity is actually being achieved in public and nonprofit organizations:

> *Social equity, in public administration, refers to policy formulation and implementation, public management practices, the provision of public goods and services, and administrator/resident interactions that reduce (and ultimately eliminate) disparity, marginalization, and discrimination while increasing social and political inclusion.*

The above definition provides specific items that public and nonprofit managers may use to address social equity. Moreover, each of the specific items can be quantified in such a way as to assess the existence of social equity. Furthermore, if we use *administrator/resident interactions* as an example in cases where individuals have been required to complete a court-ordered probation term, then we can potentially look at the number of times that the probationer has met with their probation officer to determine if a particular number of meetings changes the likelihood that the probationer will remain in good standing in the community and avoid future arrest and incarceration. Taken a step further, we can also examine the demographic and socioeconomic characteristics of the probationer and the probation officer to see if a relationship exists between them. For example,

The number of interactions/meetings and:

- The percentage change in rearrest/incarceration
- The percentage change in graduating from school (high school, college, postsecondary training, etc.)
- The percentage change in securing gainful employment
- The percentage change in annual income
- The percentage change in owning a home

Essential social equity question

Attempting to achieve socially equitable results is a challenging task because of the reasons we have mentioned. Furthermore, it requires discretion based upon the situation and is likely to change and be different in various jurisdictions along with the organization and the population served. Three questions immediately emerge as we attempt to address social equity from a fiscal perspective. The first question, specifically related to public budgeting and finance, asks:

1. How is social equity addressed in terms of expenditures and revenues?

When we begin to think about the relationship between social equity and public budgeting and finance, we must first consider what government spends its money on. That is, what services does government decide are important to provide to its residents? Aside from education, public safety and healthcare, what are the primary services delivered by government in a jurisdiction? For instance, how does a city provide care for the elderly? Is housing seen as a priority? What about parks and recreation? Transportation? In many ways, these services may be a response to the mobilization of residents and the respective responses to that mobilization by elected officials. V. O. Key (1940) famously asked, on what basis shall it be decided to allocate *X* resources to Activity A instead of Activity B? The areas that a government chooses to place a higher priority on give us a glimpse into what they feel are important issues. Education, healthcare and public safety at the local level of government receive funding from federal and state governments. The manner in which funds are allocated to specific areas within the jurisdiction, however, helps us to understand the level of priority government places on each. For example, if we were to look at these three key areas of service delivery among local governments, we could calculate the percentage of expenditures on each relative to total governmental expenditures:

- % of public education expenditures/total expenditures
- % of public safety expenditures/total expenditures
- % of public healthcare expenditures/total expenditures

The percentage spent in each of the three areas is influenced by a variety of factors. Cities and jurisdictions with larger populations tend to receive more funding for education to meet the needs of their residents than those that are less populated. These locations will have larger budgets for teacher, administrator and staff salaries and benefits. There also may be a greater need to provide a wider range of educational services that include subsidized before- and after-school care, and or, free and reduced lunches. Another area that may require additional attention by a government is funding for public safety. Funding in this area may be borne out of the idea to help make the community safer. Funding may also be necessary to continue the safe feeling residents have about living in this community. As healthcare and the need to provide, at least, an adequate amount of healthcare to the public continuously increases, jurisdictions are increasingly being tasked with this public service. Increased funding for healthcare may be resultant of a growing and simultaneously aging population. Ultimately, public funding for each of these areas is different depending on the needs of the respective jurisdictions. Further, revenue generation capacity (taxation, service charges, and user fees) is also different by jurisdiction. Indeed, some areas are able to generate more revenue than others because they simply may be tourist destinations. Some cities offer more desirable retail shopping opportunities, and some are more economically developed. In these cases, the jurisdiction is in a better position to add streams of revenue that other areas may not be able to do as easily, thus influencing the amount of revenue spent on public services. Perceived need by residents or elected officials may also impact the amount of money spent on services.

The second critical question that needs to be addressed as we examine public budgeting and finance through the lens of social equity is.

2. In what way(s) could socially equitable outcomes be improved?

Put another way, based upon the particular topic we are referring to, whether that is user fees and service charges, capital budgeting, or taxation, we should determine how social equity can be improved for individuals and groups. Examining social equity from this perspective forces public managers, elected officials and those involved in the decision-making process to adopt and implement the specific public budgeting and finance activity into action and to consider the broad range of results that are likely to occur. This may be seen as a holistic approach towards achieving social equity because we are not just thinking about the efficiency and effectiveness of achieving a goal but we are also refocusing our approach to now thinking about the marginalized and traditionally disadvantaged. Framing social equity through the lens as it applies to marginalized and disadvantaged individuals and groups may change the focus of the activity and it may also change what we think is a successful outcome.

Developing flexible strategies that lead to socially equitable outcomes is a critical component towards success. If we understand that departments, programs and units within government differ, we also must be cognizant of the fact that departments, programs and units in various cities and states will also differ. Implementation of a social equity initiative in one city may not be completely mimicable in another city. Understanding that success can be achieved in one place, however, does give us an opportunity to explore a similar initiative or plan in another place. The flexibility and awareness that the initiative may need to be tailored to fit the jurisdictional needs is critical towards achieving success.

Another key component of social equity is the ability to actually measure its existence. Specifically:

3. *How will social equity be measured?*

Simply put, how do we know when social equity has been achieved in a particular setting? Referring back to one of the definitions of social equity, a broad and inclusive definition that will afford the opportunity to effectively measure its existence or lack thereof was developed by Blessett et al. (2017). If we parse their definition:

> *Social equity refers to policy formulation and implementation, public management practices, that reduce disparity, marginalization, and discrimination.*

This definition clearly identifies measurable components. Policy formulation allows us to closely examine any public policy and or public management practice that has been implemented by an organization. Does the policy or practice address and or eliminate disparity, marginalization or discrimination? If so, how can we prove it? For example, a councilwoman found that a large percentage of her constituents face undue financial hardships when they file their taxes. As a result, a local college has decided to create a program where students majoring in accounting assist low-income residents with preparing and filing their federal and state income taxes. The program aims to help residents keep their earnings while also following the required laws in terms of filing personal income taxes on an annual basis. One way to measure the overall success of this program would be to calculate the percentage change in the number of residents who participated in the service last year, as opposed to this year. Another way to measure its effectiveness would be to survey residents who had their taxes done elsewhere in the past and now participate in the new program and obtain their feedback. What are the benefits of the program? Have their been cost savings and have they been beneficial to you and your family? Are you likely to continue using this service in the future? By applying the concepts of the definition to a specific plan, or initiative, it allows organizations the ability to identify areas of disparity, marginalization, discrimination, and social and political inclusion. Further, it allows organizations to work to strengthen areas in need, potentially improve engagement with the public, and aid in the identification and development of effective strategies to serve constituents. If reported appropriately, it also increases the degree of transparency of the organization and the amount of accountability it has with residents. Martin and Lewis (2019) discuss the importance of understanding that measuring equity is multifaceted and cannot be minimized to a single construct. Moreover, there is no one-size-fits-all model to measure equity and there is not a single metric to measure its existence, or lack thereof. "In some cases, descriptive disparities are sufficient while others require multivariate statistical regressions that control for other potentially contributing or intervening factors to determine whether a disparity is present" (Martin & Lewis, 2019, p. 4). Depending on the context of the situation, along with the specific area of equity that is under examination, will determine the most appropriate methods of measurement. Martin and Lewis (2019) go on to say that for government, or service providers, various measures of equity will be applicable depending on the target population and the specific interventions that are sought. One may think of measurement of equity in a similar manner as one who is conducting a quantitative research study. Identifying the dependent variable will determine what type of regression analysis is used. Thus, the importance of measurement flexibility is essential to pinpointing and ultimately achieving socially equitable results.

Antecedents of social equity

As we begin to closely examine social equity and its relationship to resource allocation by government and nonprofit organizations, it becomes increasingly evident that social equity is not developed in isolation. That is, while social equity specifically refers to equity being infused within the framework of public-sector service delivery, outcomes and measurable results, along with concepts of social equity emanate from principles of equity. Some may view this as a chicken-egg conundrum where we ponder which came first. It is more likely that those who espouse principles of equity are more inclined to work in areas, and for the benefit of individuals who require equitable treatment. It is less likely that an individual who begins working for a government organization such as the Department of Health and Human Services was not already inclined to view equity as, at least, mildly important. As we reflect back on the chapters in this book, we see several examples of individuals who support ideas of equity and either fought hard to achieve it or were summarily dismissed, who have not worked in government. This is important to note because it means that we develop an equity-minded framework and focus, *prior* to working for government or at a nonprofit organization. In the final chapter of this book, *Moving the Equity Needle Forward*, we will discuss equity initiatives that have been developed by private-sector firms and individuals who work there. Since they do not work for government, does it mean that they are not working towards social equity? Or is it sufficient to state that equity is the most important result sought and social equity is a byproduct of that goal? If the latter is the case, then we may be able to eliminate the term social equity and simply refer to related activities simply as equity initiatives, programs, etc. It is a nuanced perspective and it does not necessitate the elimination of the term social equity, in general. But for the purposes of this book and since our aim is to examine the relationship between equity and housing, voting, education, healthcare and other topics, it becomes more important to remove the barrier that the term social equity creates and simply refer to these activities as equity. As a result, we may define equity as *fairly distributing opportunities and resources to individuals and organizations that effectively provide the measurable prospect for independence, growth and sustainability*. For these purposes and for the remainder of the book, we will simply use the broader term equity.

Conclusion

The value of equity continues to grow in all facets of society. Long after the first Minnowbrook Conference where (social) equity emerged as a "pillar" of public administration, scholars continue to discuss the importance of equity specifically in the delivery of services and in public administration overall. We have never seen the need for equitable practices to be applied as we have with the recent Covid-19 pandemic. Historical inequities throughout the United States have exposed structures, policies and practices leading to social vulnerability (Gaynor & Wilson, 2020). A specific example of those who were left most vulnerable as a result of the pandemic was seen in the employment sector where low-income Black, Hispanic/Latiné and other people of color were disproportionately more likely to lose their jobs (Lund et al., 2020).

While various definitions are used to describe equity, the prevailing theme centers around the idea of fairness. Key questions to ask regarding fairness, are fair to whom? And, who ultimately decides what is fair? The definition that is used in this book to define equity encompasses fairness and provides us with a framework to answer the questions regarding fairness to whom, and decided by whom. Furthermore, this definition allows us to appropriately measure the extent to which equity exists, in a given situation, or not.

When equity is not addressed in a given situation, we are left to deal with the status quo of that condition. Not only does inactivity towards achieving equity exacerbate problems in our communities, it has the potential to lead to reactions that are much more drastic and perhaps problematic, if issues had simply been addressed in the first place.

References

Beckham, B. (1972). *Garvey lives!* University of Virginia Press.

Blessett, B., Fudge, M., & Gaynor, T. (2017). *Moving from theory to practice: An evaluative assessment of social equity approaches*. Center for Accountability and Performance.

Campbell, A. (1976). Approaches to defining, measuring and achieving equity in the public sector. *Public Administration Review, 36*(5), 556–562.

Deangelis, T. (2015). In search for cultural competence. *American Pyschological Association, 46*(3). https://www.apa.org/monitor/2015/03/cultural-competence

Frederickson, H. G. (1990). Public administration and social equity. *Public Administration Review*, *50*(2), 228–238.

Frederickson, H. G. (2010). *Social equity and public administration—Origins, developments and applications*. M.E. Sharpe.

Frederickson, H. G. (2014). Introduction to new public administration. In R. Box (Ed.), *Public administration in society—Critical issues in American governance*. Third edition. M.E. Sharpe.

Gaynor, T. S., & Wilson, M. E. (2020). Social vulnerability and equity—The disproportionate impact of COVID-19. *Public Administration Review*, *80*(5), 832–838.

Gooden, S., & Portillo, S. (2011). Advancing social equity in the Minnobrook tradition. *Journal of Public Administration Research and Theory, 21*, 61–76.

Guy, M. E., & McCandless, S. (2020). *Achieving social equity: From problems to solutions*. Melvin and Leigh Publishers.

Johnson, G., & Svara, J. (2011). *Justice for all – Promoting social equity in public administration*. Routledge.

Key, V. O. (1940). The lack of a budgetary theory. *The American Political Science Review*, *34*(6), 1137–1144. https://doi.org/10.2307/1948194

Lund, S., Ellingrud, K., Hancock, B., & Manyika, J. (2020). *COVID-19 and jobs: Monitoring the US impact on people and places-A clearer picture is emerging of the sectors, regions, and demographic groups at risk across the United States*. McKinsey Global Institute.

Martin, C., & Lewis, J. (2019). *The state of equity measurement—A review for energy-efficiency programs*. The Urban Institute.

Merriam Webster. (n.d.). Egalitarianism definition. *Merriam-Webster.com*. https://www.merriam-webster.com/dictionary/egalitarianism

Nabatachi, T., & Carboni, J. (2019). *Assessing the past and future of public administration*. IBM Center for Business and Government. http://www.businessofgovernment.org/sites/default/files/Assessing%20the%20Past%20and%20Future%20of%20Public%20Administration%20%20Reflections%20from%20the%20Minnowbrook%20at%2050%20Conference_0.pdf

Pam, M. S. (2013, May 11). Feeling. In *PsychologyDictionary.org*. Retrieved March 16, 2021, from https://psychologydictionary.org/feeling/

Robinson, I. (2022). *How Woke went from "Black" to "Bad."* Legal Defense Fund. www.naacpldf.org/wok-black-bad/

2

GOVERNMENT AND THE ECONOMY

This chapter introduces students to the role government plays in a market economy. Students will learn when government intervention in the economy may be necessary and under what conditions. Students will also learn of the potential outcomes and the results of government intervention.

In 1974, 36% of the US energy consumption was obtained from the oil reserves of foreign nations. At the same time, the United States experienced a severe gasoline shortage, which resulted in long lines of cars at gas stations across the country. And since there were no electric cars then, consumers still needed to purchase gas for transportation. The increased reliance on gas, coupled with a significant decline in supply, caused problems for gas stations because it was not uncommon for them to simply run out of gas at a given point in a day which left many frustrated and unable to travel freely. One strategy gas stations often used was to simply impose limits on the amount of gas that could be purchased.

The gas shortages that occurred stemmed, in part, from an oil embargo imposed on the United States as a result of its involvement in the October War. In 1973, President Nixon requested that Congress make available over $2 billion in emergency aid to assist Israel in its war with Egypt and Syria. As a result of the US involvement, the Organization of Arab Petroleum Exporting Countries (OAPEC) implemented an oil embargo on the United States (Reich, 1995). OAPEC nations refused to export oil to the United States and also began to cut production which dramatically increased the price of oil around the globe. The price of oil quadrupled going from $2.90 per barrel to $11.65 per barrel (Corbett, 2013). As a related policy measure, the United States adopted a national

DOI: 10.4324/9781032670850-3

FIGURE 2.1 Sign Reading "Gas shortage! Sales limited to 10 gallons of gas per customer" Posted at a Connecticut Filling Station During the Energy Crisis.

Source: Original creation, adapted from Owen Franken/Corbis Historical/Getty Images https://www.federalreservehistory.org/essays/oil-shock-of-1973–74

speed limit of 55 miles per hour (mph), in part, to reduce dependence on foreign oil. The speed limit legislation not only decreased the US foreign oil dependence from 36% to 28%, it also proved to be safer for motorists (Castleman, 2009). It has been estimated that the speed limit being reduced to 55 mph nationally saved over 4,000 lives annually (Castleman, 2009).

Government intervention, or regulation in this case, decreased foreign oil dependence, served as a measure to allow gas stations to end limits on the amount of gas an individual could purchase at a given time and made communities safer. The example of decreasing the national highway speed limit to 55 mph, the decline in foreign oil dependence and the decrease in highway fatalities shows the relationship between government and the economy, or what is referred to as public finance. Public budgeting and finance studies of the relationship between government and the economic implications of those decisions is known as the branch of economics that deals with the revenues and expenditures of a government. As we will learn throughout this book, government plays an essential role in how the economy operates and how government action, or lack thereof, ultimately impacts the residents of a community.

Furthermore, public budgeting and finance requires that elected officials work to meet the needs of their residents by delivering services that ultimately benefit the community. Their commitment to service delivery helps to ensure that each resident is afforded the same opportunities for quality education, healthcare, safety and housing. In terms of the national highway speed limit, the 55 mph limit was repealed in 1996 and the US dependence on foreign oil increased to more than 60% of the US consumption (Castleman, 2009). While we have seen a significant increase in the cost of oil and gas in the United States, there seem to be less discussions on returning to a 55 mph national speed limit.

Understanding the economic role of government

Adam Smith, a Scottish philosopher often referred to as the father of modern economics, defined public finance as the investment into the nature and principles of state expenditure and state revenue. More recently, Gruber (2019) defines public finance as the study of the role of government in the economy. Similarly, Hyman (2014) says that public finance "is the field of economics that studies government activities and alternative means of financing government expenditures" (p. 7). A popular belief during the 18th century, among those referred to as Mercantilists, was that government should promote trade and industry, thus having a larger role in the economy (Stiglitz & Rosengard, 2015). As Smith wrote *The Wealth of Nations* in 1776, perhaps in response to the view of Mercantilists, he wondered if society could ensure that those entrusted with governing could actually pursue the public interest. Smith believed that the public interest is maintained best when each individual simply does what is in her or his own self-interest. Further, he believed that individuals are able to tell what is in their best interest more effectively than they are to ascertain what is in the public's or everyone's own interest, and as a result government should take a smaller role in the economy. Key components in Smith's beliefs were the concepts of competitiveness and profit motives. As Smith saw it, only firms that produced goods that were wanted, at the lowest possible price, would be successful.

Recently, other methods have been used to balance government and firms' roles in the economy. Since the 1980s, **privatization** has emerged as a trend in both Europe and the United States. Privatization refers to when a government-owned business, operation, or property becomes owned by a private, nongovernment party. A **Public–Private Partnership (PPP)** is a collaborative effort between government and the private sector to deliver public services. Many local governments "outsource" or privatize certain responsibilities such as trash collection. Both privatization and PPPs aim to balance government's role in the economy without inhibiting economic growth and innovation. For example, in a **mixed economy**, the private sector has primary responsibility for production but the government also plays a broad economic role. In a mixed economy, government alters the behavior of the private sector through regulations, taxes and subsidies. Achieving the most appropriate balance is delicate and the various approaches to government's role in the economy come with positive and negative unintended consequences. As Hyman (2014) ponders, "How much should governments do, and how much should be left to private enterprise and initiative through market sale of goods and services?" (p. 27). This issue has become more prominent as the question "How heavily should our financial institutions be regulated?" continues to be posed. We have recently seen the collapse of Silicon Valley Bank and Signature Bank and many speculate that deregulation was a contributing factor. As a result of these banks shutting down, many wonder whether, or not, this will lead to another recession and or will it be more difficult to obtain credit? Where does government step in? The fallout from the collapse of the two banks has left many investors, including those who use other institutions, to wonder what may happen to their money. From an equity standpoint, it would not appear to be fair for all residents to pay a portion to make those investors whole. Unlike the financial crisis from 2008 and 2009 when taxpayers *did* foot the bill to bail out Wells Fargo and other banks, the Federal Deposit Insurance Corporation (FDIC), through their Deposit Insurance Fund (DIF), will be used to make investors "whole" in these cases.

The field of economics aims to better understand how changes in our economy occur as the result of another variable or factor. **Positive Economics** describes the economy and constructs models that predict either how the economy will change or the effects of different policies (Stiglitz & Rosengard, 2015). For example, when the US Federal Reserve increases interest rates in an effort to minimize inflation. Positive economics is a model of the economy that attempts to depict the basic features of the economy. **Normative Economics** is a model of the economy that attempts to evaluate alternative policies, weighing the various benefits and costs. Whereas positive economics is concerned with how the economy functions, or what is, normative economics examines how things should be and makes value judgments. Normative economics would ask whether, or not, reducing the speed limit to 55 mph nationally is a good thing. In addition to decreasing US foreign oil dependency, the policy also proved to be effective at reducing motor vehicle fatalities on highways, so the answer would be "yes," this is a good policy. **Welfare Economics** is a part of normative economics that evaluates different situations of a given economic system, in order to choose the best one. Questions that welfare economics seeks to answer are: what products should be produced, for whom should they be produced, and ultimately, who should make these decisions (Stiglitz & Rosengard, 2015). Welfare economics evaluates alternative policies and analyzes costs and benefits. As one considers who benefits from a particular policy, and who may not, another key concept is important. **Pareto efficiency**, or **Pareto optimality**, is an economic state where resources cannot be reallocated to make one individual better off without making at least one individual worse off. In other words, Pareto efficiency is when an economy has its resources and goods allocated to the maximum level of efficiency, and no change can be made without making someone worse off. Pure Pareto efficiency exists only in theory though the economy can move towards Pareto efficiency. This model is often used to make economic policy as it is difficult to make any change that will not make any individual worse off. Consider the fee that is imposed on an individual to register an automobile. If the vehicle purchased was model year 2022 and cost $45,000, the registration fee would be approximately $587, according to the California Department of Motor Vehicles (dmv.ca.gov). The $587 fee is nominal in relation to the total cost of the vehicle (amounting to less than 1%), but it is a fee that must be paid or the driver runs the risk of being ticketed if pulled over by a police officer. Since the fee does not take into consideration the income of the individual, it is equally applied to all based on the above criteria. All things being equal, those who make $50,000 per year are more likely to have the registration fee adversely impact them financially compared to an individual who earns $100,000.

While Smith has been very influential in the field of public finance, many economists, and others today, support the belief that the private sector has certain limitations when attempting to produce efficient and equitable outcomes while meeting the social needs of residents in a constantly evolving society (Stiglitz & Rosengard, 2015). In fact, scholars such as Karl Marx, Jean Charles Leonard de Sismondi and Robert Owens thought the evils in society were due to the private ownership of capital. The challenge facing local and state government is what is the precise investment or role that government should play in that environment or economy? Gruber (2019; Schick, 1998) states that there are four predominant questions that should be addressed when attempting to understand the role government plays in our economy: When should government intervene in the economy? How might the government intervene in the economy? What is the effect of those interventions on economic outcomes? Why do governments choose to intervene in the way(s) they do? As we delve deeper into the role government plays in our economy, we should then consider four general stages of analysis, for each of the "when," "how," "what" and "why" questions:

1. Describe what government does
2. Analyze the consequences of government action
3. Evaluate alternative policies
4. Interpret the political forces that underlie the decisions government makes

Going back to the example at the beginning of the chapter regarding the adoption of a national speed limit of 55 mph, we can apply the first predominant question of government's role in the economy through the four stages of analysis. First, what government does? The federal government can set national highway speed limits through an emergency measure as we saw in 1974.

General speed limits apply to all roads in a class, such as rural interstates or local streets. They are set by State, municipal, or even at times by Federal law based on trade-offs between safety, travel efficiency and community concerns, taking into account the design characteristics of each road class (Venkatraman et al., 2021). Second, in analyzing the consequences of action, government realizes that the benefits of this policy will decrease foreign oil dependency while also reducing motor vehicle accidents and deaths. Other alternative policies at the time would have included negotiations with OAPEC, seeking cheaper sources for foreign oil, and tapping into their own oil reserves. Finally, the key political forces that underlie governmental decisions include the members of the US House of Representatives and the US Senate, state legislatures and the major oil companies, such as Exxon-Mobile, Shell and Chevron. Another key force is the American Petroleum Institute (API). The API is one of the United States' most powerful trade organizations and has a significant impact on what congress does (McGreal, 2021). As we consider the general stages of analysis, it is apparent that policy decisions are complex and include a variety of factors from diverse sources. In this case, where do considerations regarding equity come into play? And if equity is at all considered, to what extent is it considered, and by whom? It is easy to narrow down the focus of important issues onto the financial or budgetary considerations, as they relate to everyone affected. It becomes much more challenging to think about the financial and budgetary considerations at hand, as they impact the most vulnerable and disenfranchised. Should not the impact on these groups be at the forefront of the political forces' thoughts? It is likely that the percentage of those adversely impacted by governmental decision-making is greater than the percentage of those who are not adversely affected at all.

As we delve deeper into the notion of the market correcting itself so that the economy can function at the highest capacity possible, we are still left with the question of how to help make our society more equitable. While Smith and perhaps other economists may not view the role of government in the economy expanding to address inequities, the problem would still exist without a reasonable solution. This is a considerable dilemma, in particular for proponents of a smaller role for government in the economy. In reality, it is difficult to believe that those who support less government involvement in the economy would simultaneously support addressing equity directly. It is more likely that the topic of equity would be left to nonprofits and organizations outside of government to deal with, while *inequality* would be a subject tackled by economists.

Equality–equity dichotomy

As we discussed in Chapter 1, equality refers to the idea of giving the same, or equal, amount, whether it is benefits, treatment, access, etc. to everyone. Equity, on the other hand, refers to ensuring that everyone is treated fairly and given the same opportunities for success.

If our society were truly equal, there would be less need to focus on the topic of equity because everything would be the same for all individuals. Education, healthcare and employment opportunities would be same for women as they would be for men. Furthermore, the *types* of educational, healthcare and employment opportunities would be the same. Unfortunately, this is not the case. According to the Bureau of Labor Statistics (2023), since 1979 when salary data began to be collected, women have consistently earned less than men. Women earned 82% of what men earned in 2016. If we look further, we see further evidence of pay disparities between women and men. Table 2.1 shows the median weekly salary in 2016 for women and men, by their respective age groups.

TABLE 2.1 Median Weekly Salary for Women and Men—2016

Age	*Women*	*Men*	*% Difference*
16–24	$486	$512	5%
25–34	$700	$820	17%
35–44	$839	$1,000	19%
45–54	$836	$1,075	29%
55–64	$830	$1,102	33%

Source: Bureau of Labor Statistics, US Department of Labor, The Economics Daily, Women's median earnings 82% of men's in 2016 at https://www.bls.gov/opub/ted/2017/womens-median-earnings-82-percent-of-mens-in–2016.htm

The pay disparities between women and men only grow larger as individuals grow older. The prime earning years for most individuals fall between the ages of 45 and 64. As you can see, women earn 29% less between the ages of 45 and 54 and even less (33%) between the ages of 55 and 64. What makes the data more perplexing is that it is recent (2016) and not from 1960. While pay disparities at any point in time are disturbing, seeing them reflected today simply means that equity is a goal that has yet to be attained.

Similar to the issue of unequal wages being earned by women and men, the problem of lack of employment, or unemployment, affects women and men in various ways as well. Since women, in general, earn less than their male counterparts, they will also earn less in unemployment benefits should they lose their jobs. Because individuals and groups vary in the amount that they may need, equity levels the playing field. Inequality, therefore, would refer to various individuals receiving unequal benefits. The allocation of unequal benefits is an idea that can be rectified by an oversight agency or a government fairly easily. For example, qualified individuals receive unemployment benefits based upon a percentage of their salary, the amount that they have contributed towards unemployment insurance or the number of weeks an individual has worked in the base period (usually up to 26 weeks). As a result, the amount of unemployment benefits each individual receives will be different and unequal. Yet, the payments are equitably distributed to ensure that each individual receives an amount relative to what they have contributed. If we look at the unemployment rates by employment sector and gender, we see that in 2020 women had a higher total rate of unemployment and also higher rates in each of the specific areas. Table 2.2 shows the unemployment rate by job sector, or type of job, and gender for the years 2020 and 2021.

TABLE 2.2 Unemployment Rate by Sector and Gender (2020 and 2021)

	2020		*2021*	
	Men	*Women*	*Men*	*Women*
Total	7.8	8.3	5.5	5.2
Management, professional and related occupations	4.2	4.9	2.8	2.9
Professional and related occupations	4.6	5.1	2.9	2.8
Service occupations	12.6	13.3	7.9	7.7
Sales and office occupations	7.2	8.5	4.9	5.5

Source: www.censusbureau.gov

The unemployment rate represents the number of unemployed as a percent of the labor force. Unemployment data also are available by *demographic characteristics*. See also *Labor force* and *Employment*.

For 2020 and 2021, we see that the unemployment rates between women and men were either the same or that women had higher unemployment rates for jobs in the same sectors. This fact is exacerbated when coupled with median weekly earnings between women and men.

Unemployment is not simply a gender issue in the United States. Blacks, Asians and Hispanics/Latinés generally have higher rates of unemployment than Whites. We acknowledge that the unemployment rate can be influenced by various factors in the economy, as we witnessed after the Great Recession. Other common factors leading to unemployment include technological improvements which may leave untrained workers displaced or not needed altogether (think self-checkout lines at the grocery store), industry consolidation or simply voluntarily leaving the workforce. When a person chooses to leave a job and becomes unemployed, that is obviously their choice. Other factors, however, such as education, race, gender and sexual orientation are not. Are we to believe that "the market" will simply correct itself and socioeconomic factors leading to unemployment will eventually become equitable? The unemployment rate by race also reveals interesting results. According to the US Bureau of Labor Statistics (BLS), between 2016 and 2021, the unemployment rate for Blacks has been the highest in comparison to Whites, Hispanics/Latinés and Asians. In fact, both Black and Hispanic/Latiné residents in the United States have had higher unemployment rates than both Whites and Asians during that time period.

The results of the data beg the question, "Why is this the case?" and more importantly, "What can be done to address this issue and create equity?" The answer certainly is not an easy question to solve and is resultant of various factors including educational background and access which ultimately impact where one is able to find employment. As a result of employment opportunities, or a lack thereof, an individual is often "forced" to

TABLE 2.3 Unemployment Rate by Race (2016–2021)

Year	*White*	*Black*	*Hispanic*	*Asian*
2021	4.8	9.2	6.7	4.9
2020	7	12.1	10.2	7.8
2019	3.3	6.6	4.3	2.7
2018	3.5	7	4.6	3
2017	3.8	8.1	5	3.4
2016	4.4	9.1	5.7	3.5

Source: The US Bureau of Labor Statistics https://www.bls.gov/cps/tables.htm

live in a certain community. Perhaps because one has had a poor educational background, in comparison to others, they are not as prepared to attend college or may decide to forgo that opportunity entirely so that they can begin taking care of themselves and their family. The relationship between education, employment and housing are all related and likely have an influence not just on that one person and their family but also on future generations. How does government address these inequities if at all?

One way for government to address inequities is to pose questions regarding equity at the time when they are planning large-scale improvement efforts in communities. Oftentimes projects that have a high critical value also have the most profound impact on communities because they create jobs, decrease unemployment, provide tax revenue, and lead to other revenue-generating efforts (commercial and individual real estate, additional transit lines, and visitors/tourists to buy goods). Projects that are designed to make significant improvements to a community and that will take longer than one year to complete are referred to as **capital projects.** Thus, when projects take longer than one year to be completed, funds to support those projects must be allocated on a multi-year basis which is known as a capital budget. A **capital budget** is an expenditure list of high-cost items that are expected to provide benefits and services over a considerable period of time. The capital budget is an essential component of public budgeting and finance at all levels of government, but at the local level perhaps its value is heightened because local governments typically have less sources of revenue to draw upon to pay for capital projects. Differing from the operating budget, the capital budget shows budgetary information by the project. The information shown usually includes expected expenses, areas of revenue generation and a qualitative description of the project. Further, the capital budget details what the expected expenditures will be over a multi-year period of time. The importance of capital budgeting cannot be overstated because the projects that are funded by them contribute to the economic development and growth of communities. Thus, the value of budgeting for capital projects is based upon the impact it will have on improving fiscal choice (Mikesell, 2017). Capital budgeting also supports projects that are in need of modernization and refurbishment. Whether the project is the construction of a new highway, or an extension of an existing one, commercial and residential real estate are likely to be enhanced because there are now more ways for individuals to gain access to them. Another common example of a project that requires capital budgeting is new school facilities that meet the needs of a growing community. They may also provide better and more innovative services such as smart classrooms, concert halls, science and technology laboratories and sports fields and arenas. "Although capital investment decisions are often made among analysts, engineers, and asset managers, they have real social impacts: raising local property values, reducing injury, and developing public spaces that provide a wealth of community benefits" (Karl, 2021, p. 16). Absent a careful consideration of the impacts of equity in capital budgeting "threatens to perpetuate inequality," and does not allow for communities to effectively remove themselves from generations of inequity (Karl, 2021). Due to the potentially enormous breadth of scope of capital projects, they typically require a much more exhaustive analysis of their viability. Capital projects are also expected to have longer life expectancies in that their usefulness will carry on for many years. Because of the expensive nature and the expected longevity of capital projects, increased thought, planning and preparation are required prior to committing to such projects.

References

Bureau of Labor Statistics. (2023). *BLS reports. Highlights of women's earnings in 2021*. https://www.bls.gov/opub/reports/womens-earnings/2021/#:~:text=In%202021%2C%20women%20who%20were,62%20percent%20of%20men's%20earnings

Castleman, T. (2009). 55 MPH speed limit makes economic, political, and environmental sense. *US News and World Reports*. https://www.usnews.com/opinion/articles/2009/07/27/55-mph-speed-limit-makes-economic-political-and-environmental-sense#:~:text=Generally%2C%20the%20faster%20a%20driver,to%204%2C000%20lives%20per%20year

Corbett, M. (2013). Oil shock of 1973–74. *Federal Reserve of Boston*. Retrieved March 14, 2023, from https://www.federalreservehistory.org/essays/oil-shock-of-1973-74

Gruber, J. (2019). *Public finance and public policy* (6th ed.). Worth Publishers.

Hyman, D. (2014). *Public finance – A contemporary application of theory to policy* (11 ed.) Cengage.

Karl, E. (2021, June). Prioritizing community values in capital budgeting – A case study from the city of Oakland. *Government Finance Review*.

McGreal. (2021). https://www.theguardian.com/environment/2021/jul/19/big-oil-climate-crisis-lobby-group-api

Mikesell, J. (2017). *Fiscal Administration*. Cengage Leaning.

Reich, B. (1995). *Securing the covenant: United States-Israel relations after the cold war*. Greenwood Publishing Group, Inc.

Schick, A. (1998). *A contemporary approach to public expenditure management*. World Bank Institute.

Stiglitz, J., & Rosengard, J. (2015). *The economics of the public sector* (4th ed.). W.W. Norton & Company.

The US Bureau of Labor Statistics. (2025). *Unemployment by race: 2016–2021*. https://www.bls.gov/cps/tables.htm

Venkatraman, V., Richard, C. M., Magee, K., & Johnson, K. (2021, July). *Countermeasures that work: A highway safety countermeasures guide for State Highway Safety Offices* (10th ed., 2020, Report No. DOT HS 813 097). National Highway Traffic Safety Administration. https://www.nhtsa.gov/book/countermeasures/countermeasures/11-speed-limits

3

TAXATION

One of the ways for a community to effectively deliver services to its residents is for a fee to be assigned to organizations, companies and individuals when they make transactions or purchases. That fee, better known as a tax, helps to support the growth, economic development and sustainability of a community. The tax price refers to the additional amount an individual must pay when government expenditures increase by one dollar. Specifically, the tax price is the cost to the taxpayer of a one-dollar increase in tax-financed public spending (Kenton et al., 2024). Most people, however, do not view the tax as something that positively helps their community nor improves their personal situation. Taxation is often met with disdain by residents, in part, because they believe the value of services delivered does not always correlate or match the amount they actually pay in taxes. Taxes are often referred to as a "forced extraction" because taxes are required to be paid even if they do not directly benefit the individual or business. For example, families who do not have school-aged children are still required to pay property taxes, of which a portion is used to finance public education. While governments use the funds acquired through taxation to support economic development, infrastructure, education and public safety, tax revenue is not directly related to the *value* of the services provided to the public. Thus, there is not always a clear and direct relationship between taxation and the quality of services received.

This chapter begins by discussing the Tax Cuts and Jobs Act of 2017, along with the inequities associated with the legislation. We will then discuss the theory of taxation and precisely what are the objectives government aims to achieve by taxing those who reside in the jurisdiction. Next,

DOI: 10.4324/9781032670850-4

we turn our attention to the impact of taxation on equity. Finally, we examine user fees and service charges which have increasingly been relied upon by government for revenue. With this increased reliance, however, are deleterious effects that only augment inequities. While the impact of taxes on various groups of people, based on income, has received a great deal of attention, less extensively examined has been the effect of these taxes on individuals and groups based upon their race or ethnicity. We will present specific examples of the inequitable impact tax policies have on Hispanics/Latinés, Blacks and people of color. The chapter will conclude with recommendations on how the tax system in the United States can be improved in an effort to become fairer and more equitable to all residents.

Tax cuts and jobs act

The Tax Cuts and Jobs Act (TCJA) was passed in 2017 and was the most significant change in tax law in nearly 30 years. At the time, it was touted that the TCJA would provide $3.2 trillion in tax cuts for all American families. That figure has since been disputed because it does not take into account the amount that is offset, showing only one side of the tax ledger. In other words, tax changes that cut taxes are stated, but changes that will increase taxes are ignored (Durante et al., 2021). For example, doubling the standard deduction results in $720 billion less in tax revenues over ten years, but repealing personal exemptions increases tax revenues by more than $1.2 trillion (Farley, 2017). Furthermore, it is estimated that of $275 billion within the TCJA, approximately $200 billion goes to the top 20% of households who earn over $110,000 annually. The new tax law gives the top 20% of the nation's highest-income-earning households more than two-and-a-half times the tax cuts it gives to the bottom 80% of households, $77 billion (Wiehe et al., 2018).

Figure 3.1 shows the average tax benefit from the Tax Cuts and Jobs Act by household income group. What we find is that wealthier households reap the largest share of the benefits of the TCJA.

As we dig deeper into the TCJA, we see further evidence of its inequity when it is examined across ethnic and racial lines. For Black, Hispanic/Latine and Asian taxpayers, the share of the tax cut from the TCJA amounts to 5%, 6.7% and 5.5%, respectively (Wiehe et al., 2018). White taxpayers, on the other hand, see their overall share of tax cuts from the TCJA stand at nearly 80%, and the top 5% of White taxpayers see their share of tax cuts amount to 43.5% (Wiehe et al., 2018). These inequitable figures are important to note because while the top 5% of White households only comprise 3.9% of all tax filers, this small group is set to receive nearly 44% of the total tax cuts as a result of the new legislation (Wiehe et al., 2018).

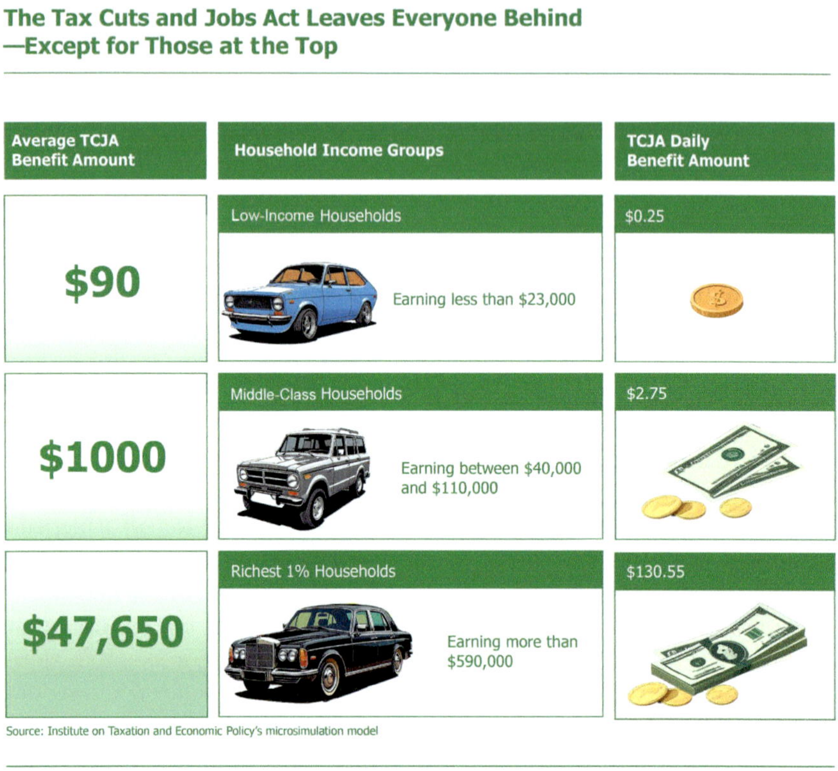

FIGURE 3.1 The Tax Cuts and Jobs Act Leaves Everyone Behind—Except for Those at the Top.

Source: Adapted from Institute on Taxation and Economic Policy's microsimulation model

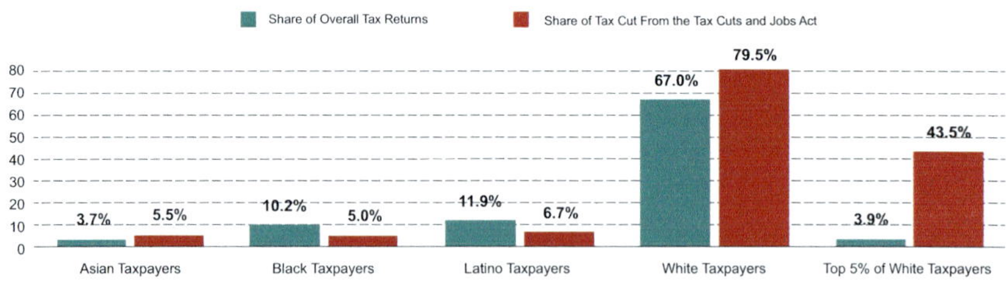

FIGURE 3.2 Communities of Color Are Especially Overlooked by the Tax Cuts and Jobs Act Share of Overall Tax Returns Compared to Share of Total Tax Cuts From the Tax Cuts and Jobs Act.

Source: Adapted from Institute on Taxation and Economic Policy's microsimulation model

Another example of the inequity of the TCJA can be seen in how Pass-Through Entities (PTEs) are taxed. In the United States, the majority of businesses are not subject to the corporate tax but rather their profits are taxed under the individual income tax (taxpolicycenter.org). The four types of PTE are Sole proprietorships, Partnerships, Limited Liability Companies (LLCs) and S-Corporations. PTEs claim a credit on state individual income tax returns for the amount of their share of the pass-through entity tax paid by the partnership, S-Corporation, sole proprietorship or LLC.

They also do not require the partner or shareholder to report income on their personal tax return and are not subject to the corporate income tax rate (Cooper et al., 2016). The corporate income tax rate traditionally has been higher than the individual, or joint couple income tax rate. The provision that PTE report income based upon the individual tax returns of the owners allows them to avoid the corporate tax rate (Cooper et al., 2016). A supply-side economics approach to improve monetary policy includes lowering the corporate tax rate to help spur business growth, development and investment. At times, the corporate income tax rate in the United States has been as high as 35% and many view that rate as hindering business development and investment. The thought follows that if the corporate income tax is lower it will lead firms towards greater investment and those investments will then lead to economic growth. This is a spurious line of thinking because there is scant evidence suggesting that lower corporate income tax rates lead to increased business investment and thus a stronger economy. In fact, it is more likely that decreasing the corporate income tax rate will simply increase the divide among the wealthy and everyone else.

In addition to the benefits accrued under the TCJA, the federal government also provided PTEs with a 20% deduction in qualified business income (Davis et al., 2021). The 20% deduction included in the Tax Cuts and Jobs Act of 2017 is in addition to PTE already paying a lower share in taxes than other businesses.

The share of business activity characterized as PTE along with income from partnerships and S-corporations has continued to rise. According to the Tax Policy Center (2024) in 2020, individuals reported approximately $1.04 trillion in net income from all types of PTEs which accounted for 8.3% of total adjusted gross income (AGI) reported on individual income tax returns. Furthermore, PTE income primarily rests among those who earn the most. According to the Urban-Brookings Tax Policy Center (2023) in 2022, approximately 91% of net pass-through income will come from the top 20% of income earners with 57% represented by the top 1% of taxpayers.

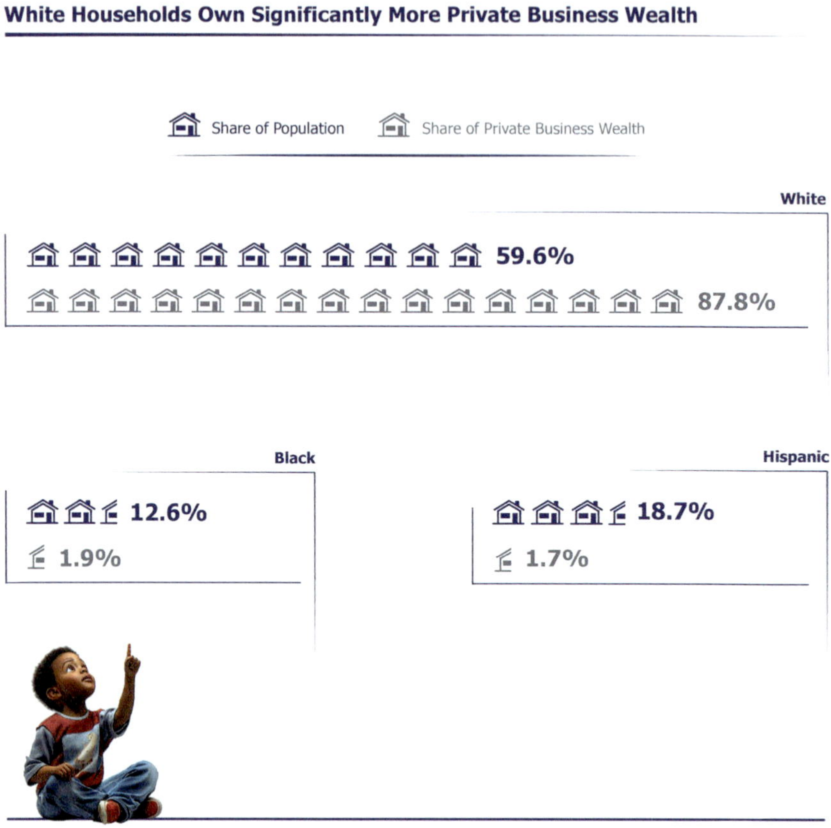

FIGURE 3.3 White Households Own Significantly More Private Business Wealth.

Source: Original creation, adapted from ITEP compilation of data and projections from the Federal Reserve and US Census Bureau. Population shares are as of February 2021 while asset ownership shares are for the entire first quarter of 2021. The Hispanic category includes people of any race while the Black and White categories include only non-Hispanic people

Equitable taxation of PTE is a critical step in achieving income and wealth fairness because the share of business wealth owned by Blacks and Hispanics/Latines in the United States is significantly lower than that of Whites. The overall growth in PTE income has continued to exacerbate the racial wealth gap and has simultaneously accounted to an increased share of income by the top 1% of all earners in the United States (Cooper et al., 2016).

Colorado recently eliminated the ability of single taxpayers with PTE incomes over \$500,000 and married couples with PTE incomes over \$1,000,000 to be eligible for a partial exclusion from income or a special set of lower tax rates (Davis et al., 2021). In President Biden's 2021 Build Back

Better proposal, he sought to expand the base of the 3.8% of Net Investment Income Tax (NIIT) to apply to active business income for S-Corporations, LLC or Pass-Through Entities. Repealing the 20% deduction afforded to Pass-Throughs, who earn more than $400,000 annually, would raise $143 billion over the next ten years. The additional revenue would almost exclusively be derived from the top 1% of earners (Davis et al., 2021).

Requiring these types of businesses to be taxed equitably would be a step in the right direction of achieving equitable tax reform. It also indicates that progressive taxation is one of the goals of the economy and that the wealthy are required to pay their fair share in taxes.

Other way that the TCJA exacerbates economic inequities is by changing the Alternative Minimum Tax (AMT). The AMT was originally created to ensure that wealthy individuals paid their fair share in taxes. High-income taxpayers who use large tax breaks may owe a smaller percentage of taxable income under the standard tax laws. In these cases, those taxpayers are required to recalculate their tax liability using the AMT guidelines. The AMT eliminates some of those tax breaks so that the taxpayer owes the amount that is higher (Ross, 2023).

While the AMT already does not apply to realized and unrealized income on capital gains, the TCJA further weakened it by increasing the amount of income exempt from the tax from $86,200 to $109,400 for married taxpayers and from $55,400 to $70,300 for individual, or single, taxpayers and the AMT increases in 2023, 2024 and 2025 (Probascu, 2024; Ross, 2023). A logical next question thus becomes, "*How much revenue does the AMT actually generate?*" The answer in 2019 was $4.7 billion, but that is significantly less revenue than was generated in previous years. Prior to the TCJA, the AMT generated $37.7 billion, or 2.6% of income tax revenue (Tax Policy Center, 2024). Figure 3.4 shows the amount of tax revenue generated from the AMT from 1970 through 2018.

Tax revenue generated from the AMT has steadily increased over time culminating in 2010 when it represented nearly 4.5% of individual income tax revenue. The percentage of AMT as a share of individual tax revenue dropped to 1988 levels (less than 0.5%) after the enactment of the Tax Cuts and Jobs Act. Tax revenue from the AMT will begin to increase in 2025 if the TCJA expires. Figure 3.5 shows the expected amount of AMT revenue and the projected amount from 2025 through 2030.

Theory of taxation

The slogan "no taxation without representation" is commonly used when someone is displeased with their *political voice* and the value of services received from government, relative to what they must pay as a tax,

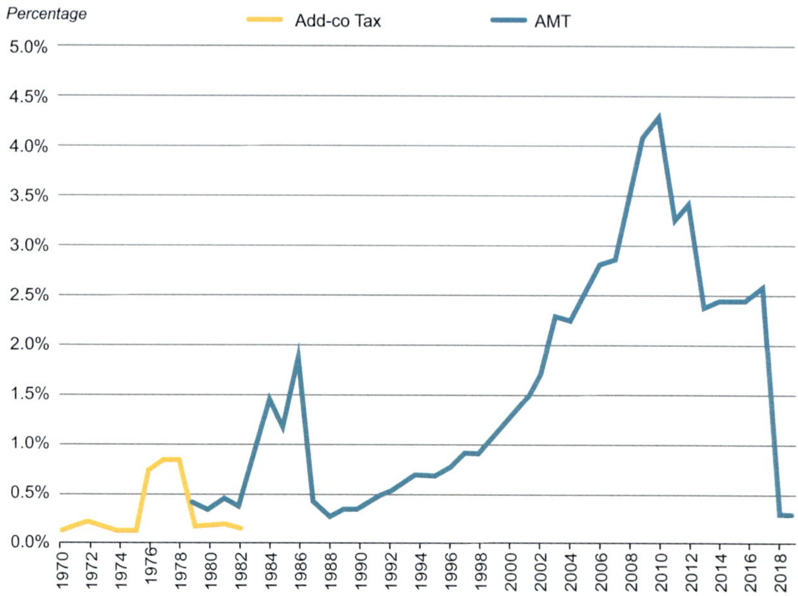

FIGURE 3.4 Alternative Minimum Tax Revenue Share of Total Individual Income Tax Revenue, Calendar Years 1970–2018.

Source: Adapted from Urban-Brookings Tax Policy Center Microsimulation Model (versions 0304–4, 0308–4, 1006–1, 0613–1, 0319–2); Harvey and Tempalski (1997); private communication with Jerry Tempalski; and SOI Division of Internal Revenue Service

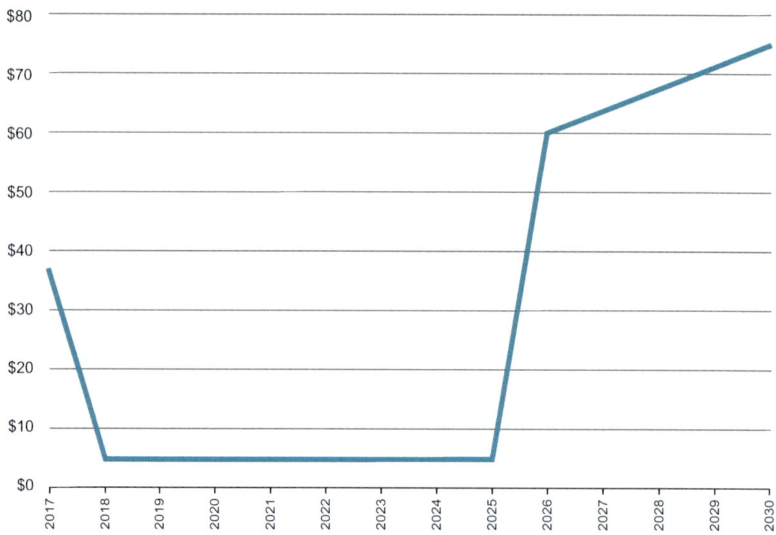

FIGURE 3.5 Projected Alternative Minimum Tax Revenue in Billions of Dollars, Calendar Years 2017–2030.

Source: Adapted from Urban-Brookings Tax Policy Center Microsimulation Model (Version 0319–2)

emanates from the colonial period in the United States. During that time, American colonists felt as if the taxes being imposed by the British Parliament were unfair because the colonialists were not permitted to serve in the parliament, among other reasons. Since their voices and opinions were not "heard," they felt as if any tax imposed on them was not justified. Today, many people still feel as if their voices should be "heard" and their opinions taken into consideration by government. While residents today have the opportunity to organize politically and US citizens can vote in elections, some still feel as if the amount they are taxed is unfair. Taxation ultimately has a direct impact on consumers and producers. Whereas, consumers are most concerned with the total cost of a product; producers of goods are most concerned with how much money they receive as a result of the transaction (Stiglitz & Rosengard, 2015). It thus becomes very important for government to express the reasons for taxation and for individuals to become familiar with those reasons. From a theoretical perspective, there are numerous goals of taxation for a jurisdiction (federal, state or local government) to achieve, including: raising revenue to deliver services, wealth redistribution, price stability, economic growth and full employment of the workforce.

Types of taxes

State and local governments in the United States primarily rely upon five mechanisms to raise revenue through taxation. The most commonly used types of taxation governments use to raise revenue are the payroll tax, the income tax, the corporate income tax, wealth taxes and consumption taxes. Each of the following types of taxes is necessary for a city, county or state to effectively deliver services to its residents. The manner in which those taxes are implemented, whether progressive or regressive, can have a significant impact on the economic outcomes of those same individuals.

The **payroll tax** is a tax that is levied on earnings of workers and is the main source of funding for social insurance programs such as Medicare, Medicaid, Social Security, and unemployment insurance (Gruber, 2019).

The US Federal Government is granted the ability to tax individual income on wages, salaries, investments or other forms of income an individual or household earns as per the ratification of the 16th Amendment to the Constitution in 1913. "The Congress shall have power to lay and collect taxes on incomes, from whatever source derived, without apportionment among the several States, and without regard to any census or enumeration" (National Constitution Center, 2023). The **Income tax** is based upon the income individuals accrue during the year and a portion of that income is subject to the individual income tax. While labor earnings include income for tax purposes, the tax is different than the payroll tax for several reasons. First, the income tax applies to additional income sources, such as interest earnings from household savings, investments or rental income. It also applies to the entire household, not just one individual like the payroll tax. The income tax is a progressive tax in that the more an individual earns, the higher the amount they will be taxed. On the other hand, the payroll tax does not adjust, and high-income individuals pay the same amount as low-income individuals thus making it a regressive tax. There are states where implementation of the income tax tends to be more regressive than progressive. In Virginia, for example, the income tax rates range from 2% to 5.75%. The top bracket applies to taxable income above $17,000, thus resulting in a flatter tax bracket structure where the majority of residents are subject to the top income bracket on a portion of their income (Davis et al., 2021). In an era where many believe that government only cares about the wealthy and that the poor and less advantaged are taken for granted, Virginia's income tax does not appear to be fair. One of the goals of equity, particularly as it relates to taxation, is that it is not just fight for fairness among racial, ethnic groups and genders but for fairness between economic classes.

The corporate income tax levies a tax on corporations in an effort to capture earnings of owners of capital resources that may not ordinarily be taxed by the government (Gruber, 2019). The corporate income tax has fluctuated over time with it currently being set at a flat rate of 21%, as per the Tax Cuts and Jobs Act (TCJA) of 2017.

Wealth taxes are those taxes levied on the value of physical assets that an individual or family may own and are paid through the property tax and estate taxes. Items in this category include real estate, land, stocks, jewelry and artwork. Equitable taxation of investment income, for example, is a contributing factor leading to racial inequity in state income tax law.

An area where tax inequity is present is in capital gains. **Capital gains** refer to profits from the sale of items like stocks, bonds, real estate, jewlery and cryptocurrencies. While not considered a wealth tax, capital gains taxes apply when these capital assets are sold, and in 2017, less than 9% of US households reported net capital gains on profit from sale of stocks, bonds, antiques and real estate (Guzman, 2020). Despite representing approximately 2% of all tax returns, taxpayers with federal adjusted gross incomes (AGI) higher than $200,000 annually reported nearly 84% of taxable capital gains in 2017 (Guzman, 2020). Further, filers with AGI above $2 million, 0.1% of Americans, received more than 54% of capital gain income (Guzman, 2020). Conversely, households with AGI less than $75,000 received less than 6% of all capital gain income (Guzman, 2020). Interestingly, the lower-income filers who earn less than $100,000 annually make up over 80% of all federal income tax filers. As Guzman (2020) notes in the inequity and unequal distribution of capital gains, "any across the board capital gain tax cut will dramatically reduce the share of income taxes paid by the very wealthiest taxpayers – and shift the tax system's impact more heavily onto lower and middle-income taxpayers (p. 2). What we are seeing is that those who are wealthier are taxed the least and can further supplement their income with capital gains. It is important to note that those who are wealthier should not feel negatively stigmatized. No one is faulting individuals who have built wealth for their families, or who are fortunate to have been born into a wealthy family. Similarly, it is important to note that the poor and disadvantaged should also not be stigmatized or considered lazy, because it is more likely that various public policies have played a large role in the economic class many individuals find themselves in. Later in this book, we closely examine such polices. Overall, it is important that those who earn higher incomes, through investments or otherwise, should pay a higher share of their income and investment incomes.

Raising revenue to deliver services

As with any accumulation of resources, the more you have, the better position you are to meet the needs of individuals and businesses. While there is not a direct relationship between taxation and service delivery, the additional tax revenue earned allows government to have greater financial flexibility in delivering services. Service delivery among governments is often the result of the financial management capacity of the jurisdiction. If a jurisdiction, for example, is keenly focused on managing its resources and strategically positions itself to be fiscally strong over the short and long terms, then it is more likely that it will provide better services to meet the needs of its residents. Further, jurisdictions that do not generate a great deal of tax revenue can still effectively deliver services without going bankrupt, even in economic downturns. Take, for example, the two following cases in California. In July 2012, Standard & Poors (S&P) downgraded the city of San Bernardino's credit rating from a BBB+ to a CC. At the time, S&P stated that San Bernardino did not have sufficient funds to meet its obligations with an expected shortfall in the amount of $450 million (https://www.reuters.com/article/sanbernardino-downgrade/update-1-sp-cuts-san-bernardino-calif-refunding-debt-to-cc-idUKL2E8IBG7020120711). As we know, a short time later on August 1, 2012, San Bernardino filed for bankruptcy. During the Great Recession, the US credit rating declined to an AA+ status according to the S&P Index. And while San Bernardino County's rating also dipped to AA+ status that was more of a reflection of the general economic uncertainty as a result of the Great Recession. Despite these economic worries that surrounded the United States and the city of San Bernardino, San Bernardino County still maintained higher credit ratings in comparison to the cities in its jurisdiction (https://www.redlandsdailyfacts.com/2011/08/09/standard-poors-lowers-credit-rating-of-san-bernardino-county-governments-investment-pool/). In 2012, Moody's gave San Bernardino County's issuer rating an Aa2, its pension obligation rating an Aa3 and lease obligations a rating of A1. According to the rating agency, "The stable outlook on the county's ratings reflects Moody's belief that the county will manage through the coming years' challenges and maintain its credit position over the long term, continuing to adhere to its conservative budgeting practices and emphasize structural balance. The county's sound financial position and management through the economic downturn are also reflected in its ratings, as is its moderate and notably simplified debt portfolio" (https://www.moodys.com/research/Moodys-assigns-MIG-1-rating-to-San-Bernardino-Countys-2012–13-Rating-Action—PR_246991?cy=aus&lang=en). Conversely, even fiscally strong cities and jurisdictions can mismanage their finances, thus making service delivery efforts more challenging. A prime example of government financial mismanagement occurred in the county of Orange, California. Despite being known for affluent wealth, desirable beaches and multimillion-dollar homes, Orange County California suffered a financial crisis in 1994 when it was forced to file for bankruptcy because of overzealous investments by the county treasurer at the time. The point of this comparison is that sound financial management practices can overcome environments and communities where the relative tax revenue is weak. Moreover, strengthening socioeconomic indicators may very well lead to an improved financial outlook for local governments. According to Moody's report on San Bernardino County's fiscal outlook, one of the areas that they indicated that could better their rating and ultimately lead to an improved financial position was by "improving their socioeconomic indices" (https://www.moodys.com/research/Moodys-assigns-MIG-1-rating-to-San-Bernardino-Countys-2012–13-Rating-Action—PR_246991?cy=aus&lang=en).

Such an approach is likely to have the impact of attracting individuals and families to the area, or region, which will create an environment of sustainable economic growth. The ability of a city or county to increase its relative economic growth gives government greater financial flexibility to address issues that it is concerned with. Eventually, economic growth and financial flexibility can result in the capacity of government to enhance opportunities of equity through improved service delivery.

The impact of taxation on equity

The term "socioeconomic" is viewed by many to be nebulous, unclear and without a clear definition, yet the term primarily refers to material living conditions, education, unemployment, income, housing and health. Other terms that may be included in defining socioeconomic include participation, trust, safety, social relations and the environment. Many of these terms or indicators are what is included when we discuss equity in a community. What is the per capita difference in income between men, women, Blacks, Latines/Hispanics, Whites, Asians and Native Americans and Indigenous people? What are the health, housing and education disparities that exist among the groups of people listed earlier? Ultimately, improving socioeconomic conditions and addressing equity are extremely closely related. The benefits of addressing equity and its outcomes by government not only improve the lives of its residents but also have the distinct potential to enhance the economic effects for that jurisdiction as well and this can be achieved through taxation.

The manner in which taxes are implemented in the United States generally falls into two categories: progressive and regressive. A **progressive tax** refers to one where individuals who earn higher incomes are taxed at a higher rate. That is, as income increases, so does the tax rate. The progressive tax system is based on the ability to pay principle, or the wherewithal to pay principle. Both principles have foundations in the assumption that those who earn a higher level of income should pay a greater proportion of their income to support the government (Dennis-Escoffi & Fortin, 2005).

A **regressive tax**, on the other hand, refers to one where individuals pay a decreasing proportion of their income in taxes as their income increases. As a taxpayer's income moves from one bracket to the next higher tax bracket, their average tax on total income decreases along with their marginal tax rate (Dennis-Escoffi & Fortin, 2005). Most support the idea that a regressive tax system is unfair to those who perhaps need the most financial assistance. It does not appear inherently just to tax those with lower incomes at the same rate or *more* than those with higher incomes. Some have gone as far as to argue that if you tax millionaires more, or at least their "fair" share, they will move from a high-taxing state to one with lower taxes, but this is an uninformed opinion that is not based in fact. Young et al. (2016) found that while individuals who earn over $1 million annually may move across state lines to seek residences in states with lower taxes, the actual number or percentage is far lower than what one may assume. In 2005, of the 500,000 individuals who filed tax returns exceeding an income of $1 million, only about 12,000 or 2.4% actually fled to a lower-taxing state. The percentage of millionaires who sought to live in states with lower taxes was lower than the number of non-millionaires (2.9%) who fled from one state to another (Young et al., 2016). In fact, the majority of the US residents who moved from one state to another were low-income tax filers (annual income of approximately $10,000) which represented 4.5% of the population. Moreover, "the migration rate drops steadily with income, and migration

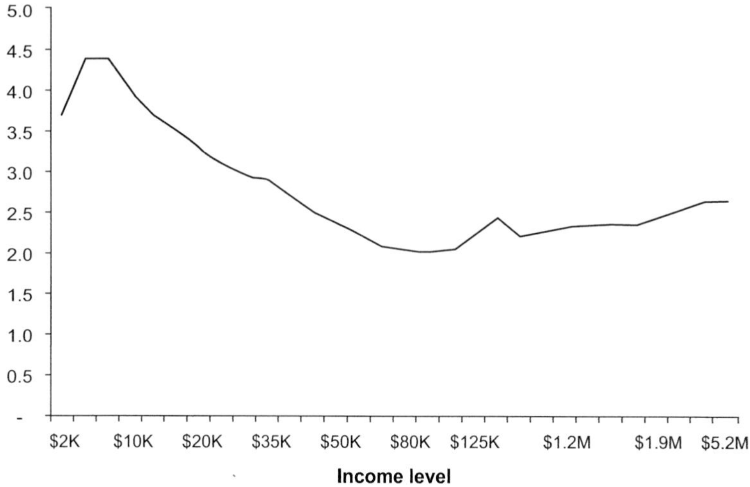

FIGURE 3.6 The Percentage of the US Population Migrating.

Sources: Adapted from US Department of the Treasury, IRS microdata, 1% sample of all tax filers (N = 24 million) and 100% sample of people making $1 million or more (N = 45 million). Adapted from Young et al. (2016)

is lowest (2.0%) for people making around $90,000" (p. 427, Young et al.). Figure 3.6 shows the percentage of the US households who moved from one state to the next in 2016.

As you can see, the percentage of migration declines as income increases. And, in general, the rate of migration based upon income shows that lower-income households are the most mobile. Where you see a slight increase is among households who earn around $100,000 to $125,000 annually. It is also important to note that as income increases, the population earning that income decreases. Young (2018) found that households who earn around $10,000 annually have 4.5% migration rate compared to millionaires (2.4%) migration rate. "These folks are struggling, and migration seems to be part of their survival strategy and their search for work. People are more likely to move when things are not working out for them where they live" (Young, 2018, p. 22). Further, according to Mazerov (2023), while California has the highest marginal tax rate out of all 50 states, over the past ten years, it has the second lowest out of state migration among households earning $200,000 or more.

Table 3.1 shows migration rates by socioeconomic group. In addition to the majority of all millionaires moving from one state to the next in favor of lower taxes, millionaires who were married and filed joint returns, with one child or more, with no children and who were under the age of 65, moved with less proclivity than the rest of the population.

TABLE 3.1 Migration Rates by Socioeconomic Group

	Millionaires		All Population	
	Migration Rate	**Share of Sample**	**Migration Rate**	**Share of Sample**
Overall	2.4%	100%	2.9%	100%
Married, filing jointly	2.2%	90%	2.3%	58%
Single/non-joint filer	4.1%	10%	3.7%	42%
Difference	-1.8%**		-1.4%**	
One child or more	2.0%	50%	2.5%	40%
No children	2.9%	50%	3.3%	60%
Difference	-0.9%**		-0.8%**	
Age 65+	2.2%	20%	1.6%	15%
Under age 65	2.5%	80%	3.1%	85%
Difference	-0.2%*		-1.4%**	
Business owner	2.0%	23%	1.6%	4%
Not a business owner	2.6%	77%	2.9%	96%
Difference	-0.5%**		-1.4%**	

Source: Adapted from Young et al. (2016) Migration Rates by Socioeconomic Group

Note: One percent sample of all tax filers (N= 24 million), and 100 percent sample of people making $1 million or more per year (N = 45 million).

Source: Office of Tax Analysis microdata, 1999 to 2011.

*$p < 0.05$ **$p < 0.01$ Using robust standard errors clustered by state (two-tailed tests)

As governments aim to improve their respective communities, there are several ways that equity could be improved from the perspective of taxation, in particular the income tax. The progressive tax structure, where individuals and families who earn more income are also subject to higher tax rates, is largely viewed as the most effective manner to decrease economic inequity. Some states, such as Arizona, California, Connecticut, Hawaii, Maryland, New Jersey and New Mexico have implemented a more progressive and equitable tax structure over the past several years. This tax structure can raise substantial revenue with which to fund public

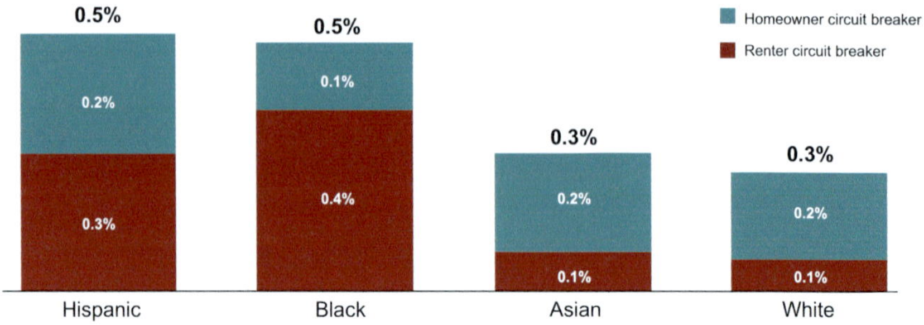

FIGURE 3.7 Renter Portion of Minnesota's Circuit Breaker Is Particularly Important to Black and Hispanic Families Circuit Breaker Credit as a Share of Overall Family Income.

Source: Adapted from Institute on Taxation and Economic Policy, October 2021. Analysis is for Tax Year 2019

investments that directly combat inequity. Moreover, progressive income taxation has the ability to minimize inequality and "it is also a powerful tool for advancing racial equity because an outsized share of top earners' income flows to white families" (Davis et al., 2021, p. 14). Minnesota, for example, has a renter tax credit that increases family income by 0.4% annually ($234) for Black households, 0.3 ($178) for Hispanic/Latine households, 0.1% ($88) for Asian and 0.1% ($70) White households (Davis et al., 2021). "These are statewide averages (that) include both eligible and non-eligible households and for benefiting households, the average income boost is much larger than these amounts" (Davis et al., 2021, p. 29). In Figure 3.7, we see the tax credit for Minnesota's circuit breaker tax program as a share of overall family income.

Additionally, California has implemented an income tax bracket structure that affords greater equity among lower- and middle-income groups, who tend to be overwhelmingly people of color. In California, this can be seen through the state levying marginal tax rates between 1 and 13.3%, with the top bracket applying to taxable income over $1 million for individuals and $1.2 million for married couples (Davis et al., 2021). Furthermore, California also provides income tax equity for low- and middle-income families through a refundable Earned-Income Tax Credit (EITC), a Young Child Tax Credit and a nonrefundable low-income renter's credit. Other states have passed similar legislation aimed to assist low-income individuals and families. For example, New Mexico increased its surcharge on health insurance premiums which will raise approximately $153 million annually to assist nearly 200,000 residents below the age of 65 to afford health coverage (Tucker, 2021). The state of Washington passed a measure that imposes a 7% tax on capital gains above $250,000 annually. The measure is expected to raise over $500,000 annually and will be used to provide additional funding for childcare, early learning and public schools while simultaneously creating tens of thousands of new jobs (Tucker, 2021). Conversely, Virginia with its regressive, flatter tax bracket structure does not offer any refundable tax credits in excess of personal income tax liability (Davis et al., 2021). In order to implement these policy changes, local governments need to make achieving equity a priority. Additional solutions that can lead to equitable outcomes include providing renters with tax credits, using tax credits to improve child well-being, supporting single parents with the head of household filing and balancing local income tax implementation while decreasing reliance on sales taxes and user fees (Davis et al., 2021). The Earned Income Tax Credit (EITC) has proven to be an effective tool in this regard and those states that do not afford residents the option of an EITC should strongly consider implementing its use. Further, states could also expand it by offering EITC to low-income workers without children and to immigrant workers (Davis et al., 2021).

Public perception of taxation

Many people do not view the US tax system positively, in part, because it creates a gap in wealth and income between people of color and the White majority. It is argued that the wealth and income gap continues to lead to economic inequity and an overall system of inequality. A significant body of research has been conducted on the equity of taxation among various groups of individuals based upon their race (Davis et al., 2021; Kitson, 2021). This particular line of research states that tax policies should be reviewed and changed because they inherently impact Blacks and Hispanic/Latine individuals more adversely than Whites. Specifically, because of the history of racist housing, and educational and employment policies and practices in the United States, Blacks and Hispanic/Latine individuals are not able to significantly decrease the wealth gap, thus making any seemingly neutral tax policy unduly favor Whites.

Even beyond tax policies that have shown not to be neutral, we are also learning that tax administration can also be discriminatory and biased. According to a study conducted by Stanford University's Regulation, Evaluation and Governance Lab, Blacks were, at least, three times more likely to be audited by the Department of Internal Revenue Services (IRS) than other tax filers (Tankersley, 2023). These results even occurred after differences in the types of tax returns various groups of people are likely to file. While the results of the study did not indicate implicit bias from independent IRS agents, they did suggest that discrimination existed in the computer algorithms used by the IRS when determining whom to audit. Specifically, the results found that discrimination occurs that flags tax returns with potential errors in the claiming of certain tax credits, like the EITC, which supplements low-income workers' incomes in an effort to alleviate poverty (https://

www.nytimes.com/2023/01/31/us/politics/black-americans-irs-tax-audits.html). Interestingly, tax returns that include business income are far less likely to be audited, and in this case, Black taxpayers are less likely than others to report business income. What will need to occur to eliminate discrimination and bias when determining whom to audit? The IRS will need to change the algorithms in their computer systems that unfairly target Blacks and others who file taxes while claiming specific tax credits that are available to assist lower-income individuals and families.

User fees

Another key type of taxation is based upon the amount an individual or family consumes by enjoying various goods and services. Consumption taxes are typically levied during the sale of a good or service and the tax on the sale or consumption of goods is applied to a broad array of goods. When the tax is applied to certain goods (cigarettes, alcohol, cars and gasoline) however, the tax is referred to as an excise tax (Gruber, 2019). Relatedly, another form of consumption goods that are not taxed but instead monies are collected at the time of utilization for the opportunity to use the particular item (toll roads, admission to state and national parks, and parking meters) are known as service charges and user fees. States reliance on user fees and service charges has continued to significantly increase over the past 25 years.

User fees and service charges are monies that are directly paid by residents and or organizations to government for the ability to utilize a particular service or item. Such services include highways and roads that may reduce the time it takes to travel from one distance to another. Other examples where a state or local government may impose a user fee/service charge include obtaining a driver's license, automobile registration, marriage license, highway tolls, plans for new construction, attending recreation classes, and the use of public pools and parks (Institute on Tax and Economic Policy). Additionally, charges may be assessed for services related to planning for subdivisions and zoning, healthcare and air travel. According to Propheter, Levine and Fudge (2017, p. 261), "User fees are different from conventional taxes in that they take the form of a direct payment to government for a specific service rendered to a specific taxpayer, usually made at the same time that the service is rendered". In most instances however, the amount of a fee may not exceed the cost of providing the service, granting a benefit or a privilege, which may include costs associated with overhead, capital improvements and debt service (Institute on Tax and Economic Policy). The economic efficiency effect of user fees is obvious: Since taxpayers pay only for those publicly provided goods and services that they use, scarce resources are better allocated to their most highly valued uses (Duff, 2004). In addition to economic efficiency, user fees and charges have been viewed as a popular method to increase government revenue primarily because they are politically acceptable. Elected officials are more likely to support the introduction of a new user fee or charge as opposed to a tax increase (Jang & Kwon, 2014). Whereas the imposition of taxes requires legislative approval by a majority, or a supermajority, user fees and service charges face far less scrutiny. In fact, user fees and service charges often only require that a local government council approve their utilization prior to implementation. Local governments have the ability to apply and impose user fees at their discretion. The lack of voter approval affords cities the opportunity to get aboard the free cash cow that user fees represent. Further, the majority of residents do not voice significant opposition to the fee or an increased fee. It is rare that you see something similar to the Straphangers Campaign as we saw in New York City in 1979. Without groups of individuals voicing their disdain for user fees, then government is left to feel as if their implementation is not a significant financial burden to most. An important question to address is *if the public were more aware of the implications of user fees, would we be more or less acceptable of their utilization?* Because the public typically does not voice a great deal of opposition to them, it makes their implementation more politically palatable than simply raising taxes.

After the adverse fiscal impacts of Proposition 13 had been felt by California residents, many still were in favor of the tax and expenditure limitation (TEL). Most residents continue to embrace Proposition 13 in spite of the many issues associated with it, such as reduced spending (and lower outcomes) in public education. Nearly 60% of Californians still supported Prop 13 and actually *preferred* it to the ambiguity surrounding the previous version of property tax fluctuations (Hoene, 2004). Moreover, increasing taxes for just about any reason seemed to be generally opposed by residents of the Golden State. In 1987, a *Los Angeles Times* poll found that 67% of voters disagreed with raising taxes to cut the federal deficit (Skelton, 1991).

The utilization of user fees and service charges has steadily increased over the time (Fudge, 2018) and Bartle et al. (2011) found that as a percentage of total government revenue, user fees and service charges have increased from 10.4% in 1975 to 15.7% in 2007. Since the tax revolts of the late 1970s and early 1980s, municipal user fees and service charges have increased year over year on average faster than other revenue sources in real terms (Lincoln Institute of Land Policy, 2015). Figure 3.8 shows the percentage change in per capita revenue average for 112 fiscally standardized cities between 2007 and 2012.

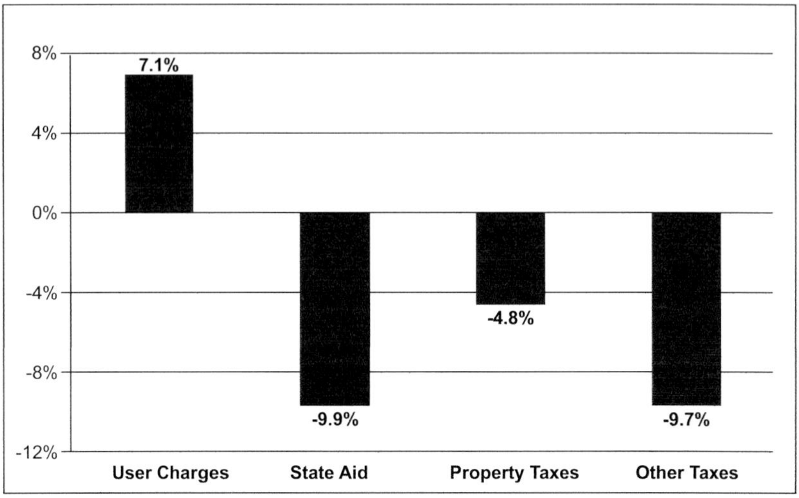

FIGURE 3.8 Percentage Change in Per Capita Revenue, 2007–2012 (Adjusted for Inflation). Average for 112 Fiscally Standardized Cities.

Source: Adapted from Lincoln Institute of Land Policy, 2015

Recently, other external economic factors have led to elected officials and public managers relying more heavily upon user fees as a practical matter to effectively deliver services. During the Great Recession, user fee reliance among US local governments increased significantly as a means for them to continue to function. Next, we examine two types of user fees that can be challenging to avoid paying: driver's licenses and toll roads.

Driver's licenses

Perhaps the most compelling issue confronting user fees and service charges is their ability to "force" residents to utilize them because there are *no other viable options*. For many, there may not be a practical alternative to paying a user fee or a service charge. Wagner (1991) asserts that "while a fee for a driver's license can be avoided by choosing not to drive, this is a practical option for precious few" (p. 7). Accordingly, it may be easier to avoid paying income or property taxes than it may be to avoid paying some user fees. The legal provision to operate a motorized vehicle with a driver's license also comes with equity concerns. While it is understood and rather important for individuals to possess a certain aptitude and level of understanding in order to be permitted to drive, charging a fee for that privilege appears to be more closely related to a tax rather than a fee for use. This is especially the case in US cities where public transit use is not a distinct possibility. For many places, whether rural or suburban, public transportation often is a less efficient option than driving a car. Whereas cities and urban environments typically provide effective public transportation options, many suburban and rural locations do not. Undoubtedly, not having a car is simply not an option for a lot of individuals, thus the requirement to pay a driver's license "fee" is not an option either. "User charges do not necessarily reflect the interplay of supply and demand in markets, but are a reflection of political and other forces" (Hyman, 2014, p. 389).

Toll roads

Charging a fee to travel on certain roads also poses similar negative outcomes as driver's license fees. Toll roads, or express lanes, provide the consumer the ability to travel to and from locations quicker than the non-toll road comparators. Choosing to drive on a highway that charges a toll becomes a balanced choice as long as the non-toll road is adjacent, or near the toll road. In this case, drivers can actually see the benefit of paying the fee, or not, because of what traffic looks like on the other highway. If the highway is not closely located to the toll road, then such comparisons cannot easily be made. Aside from individuals using a GPS device, one is left to surmise and assume that the free highway is more crowded than the toll road. Also, highway patterns and the amount of people travelling on a particular road, or highway, can change rapidly due to accidents or construction. Further, the free highway is likely to be a less efficient means of traveling for the drivers. The extent to which the inefficiency makes it prohibitive to travel on the free highway is less certain and drivers are making a decision on whether to pay the fee, or not, based on a lack of information. The lack of public information available affords the toll roads, and those who receive revenue as a result of their location, to act as monopolistic entities. In a monopoly market, the seller faces no competition, as she or he is the sole seller of goods with no close substitutes. Essentially, they enjoy the power of setting the price for their goods. Roads with tolls possess the characteristics of being a monopoly because they afford driver's poor substitutes, and there may not be alternative roads that provide similar starting and exit points for the driver. A common belief associated with user fees is that it is a charge by government that restricts competition from the private sector. Another belief about user fees is that they induce coercive restriction of public options and they have continued to grow at a high rate.

Identifying public policies and legislation, through taxation, that will lead to successful equity outcomes can easily be tracked and measured

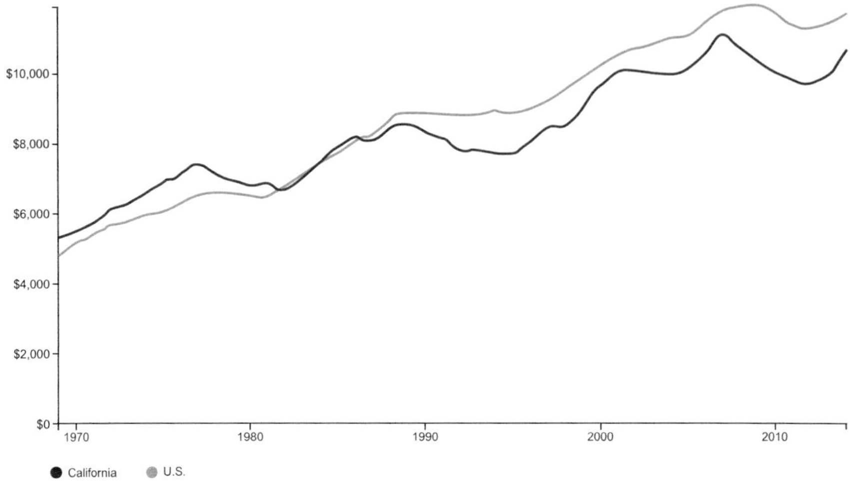

FIGURE 3.9 Per Pupil Spending for Fall Enrollment, California Versus the US Average, 1969–1970 Through 2014–2015.

Source: Adapted from National Center for Education Statistics

through socioeconomic data. As a result, when equity is not addressed, we are also easily able to identify the deleterious impact that inaction can lead to. For example, in 1978, the state of California passed the notorious Proposition 13 which, among other things, capped the amount property tax could increase on a home at 2% annually. While this legislation was hailed as a fight against rising home prices and the significant increase in property taxes associated with those homes, the legislation had an extremely negative impact on K-12 education. California went from being ranked among the best public schools in the nation to among the worst (Fensterwald, 2022; Rancano, 2018; Saxton et al., 2002).

Further, increased reliance upon user fees and service charges to make up for the shortfall in property tax revenue soon followed. If lawmakers, at the time Proposition 13 was passed, strongly considered the consequences of their actions, Proposition 13 could have been implemented differently. For example, perhaps a 2.5–3% annual property tax max may have been more appropriate. Another way to pass Proposition 13 and yet avoid the unintended, inequitable consequences associated with it may have been to create a formula where the percentage of property tax revenue had to stay above a particular threshold and if it did not then the property tax rate could be adjusted. Instead, California has shifted reliance away from wealthier property owners to those less wealthy thus decreasing equity and exacerbating racial disparities in the state.

The inequity of user fees

In Alabama where revenue from income taxes stands at 7%, the lowest in the United States, reliance on user fees as a form of revenue has expanded (Kasier-Shatzlein, 2022). User fees are commonly assessed for things such as boat and driver's licenses, golf courses, toll roads and other services that individuals do not have to use. In Alabama, as is the case across the United States, fees for crimes have also been on the rise. In fact, the median fine for a felony there has doubled from $1,000 in 1995 to $2,000 in 2005 (Greenberg et al., 2016). Because the assumption is that individuals should not commit crimes in the first place, less attention has been given to Alabama's overall user fee revenue generation scheme. To raise funds for roads, schools or other public projects in Alabama, residents are not able to impose taxes on themselves, as is the case for the majority of the US states (Kasier-Shatzlein, 2022). They are left with relying upon State Legislature to pass laws, and or to initiate a constitutional amendment allowing them to pass such laws (Kasier-Shatzlein, 2022). Because most middle- to upper-class Americans can afford to pay the fee, or for an attorney, the excessive assessment of fines and fees for felonies typically results in a system where the poor are adversely impacted. One reason for this inequity stems from the financial impact of the Great Recession which left states and cities scrambling for money. In a study conducted by the Brennan Center for Justice and the National Center for State Courts, between 2010 and 2014, 48 states had increased their civil and criminal court fees (Shaer, 2019). According to a Governing.com report, "Jurisdictions relying more on fines to fund their budgets have often sustained decades of economic decline, leaving them with weak tax bases" (Maciag, 2019). Furthermore, the report found that states where fines and forfeitures amounted to more than 20% of general fund revenues, also had median household incomes of $39,594 (Maciag, 2019). According to Mitali Nagrecha, director of Harvard's National Criminal Justice Debt Initiative, "What we're seeing in these situations is that not only are the poor in the United States treated differently than people with means, but that the courts are actually aggravating and perpetuating poverty" (Shaer, 2019). Finally, other states where fines and related court revenues fund significant portions of budgets include, Arkansas, Georgia, Louisiana, Texas and Oklahoma, along with New York (Maciag, 2019). Joanna Weiss, co-director of the Fines and Fees Justice Center stated, "What we've seen in our research is that the mechanisms vary, depending on the region, they have one thing in common: They use the justice system to wring revenue out of the poorest Americans—the people who can afford it the least. Aside from taxes, criminal-justice debt is now a de facto way of funding a lot of American cities" (Shaer, 2019).

Conclusion

We began the chapter discussing the reasons why governments choose to tax residents of communities and the objectives of the various taxes. While most individuals do not enjoy the "idea" of being taxed, they do understand the rationale. Whether the objectives of taxation are to effectively redistribute wealth so that those who are on the lower end of the socioeconomic curve will have opportunities to attain a good education, find adequate jobs that will allow them to earn a decent income, or to have equal access to healthcare, the goals stem from the idea of fairness and equity. Additionally, aside from wealth redistribution, taxation provides necessary revenue flexibility for a jurisdiction to provide and deliver effective services. Tiebout (1956) famously asserted that individuals vote with their feet when choosing where to live because their decision is based, in large part, upon the quality of services that are delivered to them. As cities aim to grow economically, governments try to provide necessary services that will enhance the lives of current residents while also attracting new ones.

This chapter also covered the inequity of the Tax Cuts and Jobs Act (TCJA). While there are some positives of the legislation, like reducing tax avoidance by decreasing incentives for taxpayers to keep profits in overseas accounts, there are many more negatives associated with the TCJA. For example, the TCJA will contract federal revenues which we have already seen evidence of through changes in the AMT. In 2018, Gross Domestic Product (GDP) was only 2.5, which was lower than the Trump Administration predicted at the time (Gale, 2019). The TCJA raises deficits, and may make policymakers less likely to embark in discretionary programs to improve a distressed economy, ultimately presenting challenges to overcome recessions. Furthermore, and perhaps most important to note, TCJA is regressive because it makes the distribution of after-tax revenue more unequal further compounding the problem of inequity (Gale, 2019).

Addressing unfairness in tax legislation is essential to creating an equitable economy and society. Historically, wealthy individuals have always been more likely to receive tax breaks, worsening racial inequities, with this trend continuing today (Kitson, 2021). If equity through taxation is not addressed to change the manner in which lower-income individuals are unduly impacted by tax and revenue policies, we are likely to see a continued growth of income and wealth inequality along with overall inequity. Between 1989 and 2016, the income inequality gap in the United States doubled (Shaeffer, 2020). There are several other examples that show how economic inequity continues to be a pervasive issue in the United States, including middle-class income growing at a slower rate (49%) in comparison to income by those in the upper tier (63%) over the past 50 years. Also, the difference in median household incomes between White and Black Americans has grown from about $23,800 in 1970 to roughly $33,000 in 2018 (as measured in 2018 dollars) (Shaeffer, 2020). Furthermore, while some states do provide some income tax equity for their residents, the largest tax subsidies offered greatly benefit businesses that are profitable and households with higher incomes. Each of the above groups tends to have a smaller percentage of Blacks, Latinas and people of color.

In Chapter nine, we will discuss the racial wealth and income gap in more detail and how it has continued to be pervasive and grow over time.

References

Bartle, J. R., Kriz, K. A., & Morozov, B. (2011). Local government revenue structure: Trends and challenges. *Journal of Public Budgeting, Accounting & Financial Management*, *23*(2), 268–287.

Cooper, M., McClelland, J., Pearce, J., Prisinzano, R., Sullivan, J., Yagan, D., Zidar, O., & Zwick, E. (2016). Business in the United States: Who owns it and how much tax they pay. *Tax Policy and the Economy*, *30*(1), 91–128.

Davis, C., Guzman, M., & Scheider, J. (2021). *State income taxes and racial equity—Narrowing racial income and wealth gaps with state personal income taxes*. Institute on Taxation and Economic Policy (ITEP).

Dennis-Escoffi, S., & Fortin, K. (2005). *Taxation for decision makers*. Pearson-Prentice Hall.

Duff, D. G. (2004). Benefit taxes and user fees in theory and practice source. *The University of Toronto Law Journal*, *54*(4), 391–447.

Durante, A., Kallen, C., Li, H., McBride, W., Muresianu, A., York, E., & Watson, G. (2021). *House build back better act: Details & analysis of tax provisions in the budget reconciliation bill*. Tax Foundation. https://taxfoundation.org/build-back-better-plan-reconciliation-bill-tax/

Farley, R. (2017). Fact check: Trump claimed tax bill provides $3.2 trillion in tax cuts, but it's actually less than half that. *USA Today*. https://www.usatoday.com/story/news/politics/2017/12/22/fact-check-trump-claimed-tax-bill-provides-3-2-trillion-tax-cuts-but-its-actually-less-than-half/977318001/

Fensterwald, J. (2022). *California prop. 13's 'unjust legacy' detailed in critical study—Wider wealth gaps, unstable education funding, housing shortages 4 decades later*. https://edsource.org/2022/californias-prop-13s-unjust-legacy-detailed-in-critical-study/674412

Fudge, M. (2018). The inequity of user fees and the overreliance by communities to generate revenue. In H. Levine & K. Moreno (Eds.), *Positioning markets and governments in public management* (pp. 147–158). IGI Global Scientific Publishing. https://doi.org/10.4018/978-1-5225-4177-6.ch011

Gale, W. (2019). A fixable mistake: The tax cuts and jobs act. *Brookings Institute*. https://www.brookings.edu/articles/a-fixable-mistake-the-tax-cuts-and-jobs-act/

Greenberg, C., Meredith, M., & Morse, M. (2016). The growing and broad nature of legal financial obligations: Evidence from Alabama Court Records. *Connecticut Law Review*, *48*(4), 1079–1122.

Gruber, J. (2019). *Public finance and public policy* (6th ed.). Worth Publishers.

Guzman, M. (2020). *State taxation of capital gains: The folly of tax cuts & case for proactive reforms*. Institute on Taxation and Economic Policy (ITEP).

Hoene, C. (2004). Fiscal structure and the post-proposition 13 fiscal regime in California's cities. *Public Budgeting and Finance*, *24*(4), 51–72.

Institute on Taxation and Economic Policy. (2021, October). *Analysis is for tax year 2019*. Institute on Taxation and Economic Policy.

Jang, H. S., & Kwon, M. (2014). Enterprising government: The political and financial effects of fee-supported municipal services. *Public Administration Quarterly*, *38*(2, Summer), 128–162.

Kasier-Shatzlein, R. (2022). Alabama takes from the rich and gives to the poor. *New York Times*. https://www.nytimes.com/2022/07/27/opinion/alabama-fines-fees.html?searchResultPosition=2

Kenton, W., Boyle, M., & Velasquez, V. (2024). *Price level: What it means in economics and investing*. https://www.investopedia.com/terms/p/price_level.asp#:~:text=Economists%20widely%20believe%20that%20prices,demand%20for%20goods%20and%20services

Kitson, K. (2021). *Promoting racial equity through California's tax and revenue policies*. California Budget & Policy Center.

Lincoln Institute of Land Policy. (2015). *Cities increasing reliance on fees as other revenues fall*. Retrieved May 27, 2016, from http://atlincolnhouse.typepad.com/weblog/2015/05/

Maciag, M. (2019). Addicted to fines: A special report—Hundreds of small cities and towns throughout the country rely significantly on fines to fund their budgets. *Governing.com*.

Mazerov, M. (2023). *Tax-related migration is greatly exaggerated-a research preview*. Center on Budget and Policy Priorities. https://www.cbpp.org/blog/tax-related-migration-is-grossly-exaggerated-a-research-preview

National Constitution Center. (2023). https://constitutioncenter.org/interactive-constitution/amendment/amendment-xvi

Probascu, J. (2024). Alternative Minimum Tax (AMT) definition, how it works. *Investopedia*. https://www.investopedia.com/terms/a/alternativeminimumtax.asp

Propheter, G., Levine, H., & Fudge, M. (2017). An Exploration of the Great Recession's Impact on States’ Reliance on User Fees. *Public Finance and Management*, *17*(3), 259–282.

Rancano, V. (2018). *How proposition 13 transformed neighborhood public schools throughout California*. https://www.kqed.org/news/11701044/how-proposition-13-transformed-neighborhood-public-schools-throughout-california

Rohaly, J., Carasso, A., & Saleem, M. (2005). *The Urban-Brookings Tax Policy Center microsimulation model: Documentation and methodology for version 0304*. Urban-Brookings Tax Policy Center.

Ross, J. (2023). *Biden tax proposals would correct inequities created by Trump tax cuts and raise additional revenues*. Center for American Progress. https://www.americanprogress.org/article/biden-tax-proposals-would-correct-inequities-created-by-trump-tax-cuts-and-raise-additional-revenues/

Saxton, G. D., Hoene, C. W., & Erie, S. P. (2002). Fiscal constraints and the loss of home rule: The long-term impacts of California's post-proposition 13 fiscal regime. *The American Review of Public Administration*, *32*(4), 423–454. https://doi.org/10.1177/027507402237869. https://www.pewresearch.org/fact-tank/2020/02/07/6-facts-about-economic-inequality-in-the-u-s/

Shaeffer, K. (2020). *6 facts about income inequality in the U.S.* Pew Research Center.

Shaer, M. (2019). How cities make money by fining the poor. *New York Times*. https://www.nytimes.com/2019/01/08/magazine/cities-fine-poor-jail.html?searchResultPosition=7

Skelton, G. (1991). The times poll: 64% oppose raising taxes to cut deficit. *Los Angeles Times*. https://www.latimes.com/archives/la-xpm-1987-11-05-mn-18844-story.html

Stiglitz, J., & Rosengard, J. (2015). *The economics of the public sector* (4th ed.). W.W. Norton & Company.

Tankersley, J. (2023). Black Americans are much more likely to face tax audits, study finds. *New York Times*. https://www.nytimes.com/2023/01/31/us/politics/black-americans-irs-tax-audits.html

Tax Policy Center. (2024). *Tax policy center briefing book—Key elements of the U.S. taxing system*. https://www.taxpolicycenter.org/briefing-book/what-are-pass-through-businesses

Tiebout, C. M. (1956). A pure theory of local expenditures. *Journal of Political Economy*, *64*(5), 416–424.

Tucker, W. (2021). *More states making equity-focused tac choices*. Center on Budget and Policy Priorities. https://www.cbpp.org/blog/more-states-making-equity-focused-tax-choices

Urban-Brookings Tax Policy Center. (2023). "*Sources of flow-through business income by expanded cash income percentile, current law, 2022.*" Model Estimates, Table T23-0027. Urban-Brookings Tax Policy Center.

Wagner, R. (1991). *Tax norms, fiscal reality, and the democratic state: User charges and earmarked taxes in principle and practice*. Routledge.

Wiehe, M., Nieves, E., Greer, J. & Newville, D. (2018). Race, wealth & taxes: How the tax cuts and jobs act supercharges the racial wealth divide. Institute on Taxation and Economic Policy (ITEP).

Young, C. (2018). *The myth of millionaire tax flight—How place still matters for the rich*. Stanford University Press.

Young, C., Varner, C., Lurie, I., & Prisinzano, R. (2016). Millionaire migration and taxation of the elite: Evidence from administrative data. *American Sociological Review*, *81*(3), 421–446.

4

VOTER SUPPRESSION AND DISENFRANCHISEMENT

In 2020, the US Presidential Election when Joseph Biden beat Donald Trump, voter turnout reached historic numbers. In fact, data indicates that 66.8% of eligible voters casted ballots in the 2020 election. This figure was the largest percentage of eligible voter turnout since 1992 when 67.7% of eligible voters visited the polls (Frey, 2021). Moreover, the figures from 2020 represented a 5% increase from the 2016 Presidential Election. Instead of the increased voter turnout being celebrated and seen positively as increased civic engagement, the United States has been fraught with an unceasing number of restrictive voting laws proposed and passed. We have also witnessed evidence of organizations openly questioning the authenticity of registered voters in an effort to purge or decrease votes.

In 2023, James McWhorter, who is a veteran and an owner of a barbershop in Dekalb County, Georgia, had his voting status challenged. The challenge, brought by Gail Lee, asserted that McWhorter improperly registered to vote at a commercial address thus invalidating his voting status. McWhorter and Lee had never met and she did not know that he had lived in his barbershop in 2008 when he was registered to vote (Kaplan et al., 2023). According to a *CBS News* investigative report, over 80,000 challenges against Georgia voters have been filed, primarily from conservative activists. Karli Swift, chair of the election board in Dekalb County, Georgia says the people being targeted are "young voters, it's people of color, and it's people that are unhoused. Those are generally the types of people that end up in voter challenges" (Kaplan et al., 2023). Typically, those who are targeted do not have the resources to challenge these accusations and are unfortunately left to deal with the repercussions which result in the

DOI: 10.4324/9781032670850-5

inability to vote. Disenfranchising votes appears to be the goal of Lee and other conservative organizations. According to Bryan Sells, voting rights attorney, "Unless someone happens to know to call the LDF (National Association for the Advancement of Colored People-NAACP, Legal Defense Fund) or the ACLU (American Civil Liberty Union) or someone else and flags that for them, and we happen to have the resources to bring that litigation, nothing ever happens. There's so many things that I think slip through the cracks and have a real impact on Black representation" (Levine & Rao, 2020).

Instances of voter suppression, or purging votes, are often disguised as ways to ensure "our elections are fair" and do not begin, nor end with a small percentage of eligible voters in a few, random places. In 2013, Arizona legislators passed a law requiring everyone voting in statewide and local elections to show proof of citizenship prior to voting (Levine & Rao, 2020). In Texas, Alabama and Mississippi, voters are now required to show photo identification to vote, despite the fact that requiring photo IDs when voting has been found to disenfranchise marginalized people's ability to vote. More evidence of voter suppression occurred between 2012 and 2018, when there were 1,688 polling place closures in states previously covered by section five of the Voting Rights Act (Levine & Rao, 2020).

The Brennan Center (2023) found that 14 states enacted 17 restrictive voting laws including provisions making it more difficult for eligible voters to register and remain on voter rolls or vote. Also, between January 1 and December 7 of 2021, 19 states passed 34 laws that would restrict voting access and in 49 states, 440 bills were introduced that would also restrict voting access (Brennan Center, 2021).

Across the United States in states such as Georgia, Arkansas, Ohio, Indiana, Alabama and several others, new restrictive voting laws were introduced immediately after the 2020 Presidential Election. A great deal of misinformation has been spread regarding the details of these new laws and whom it will mostly impact. As a result of the misinformation, it may cause individuals who were otherwise interested in voting, not to do what is their right as a citizen. Important questions emerge as a result of the new legislation being passed across the country, such as, why have states suddenly begun to implement new restrictive voting laws? Who are the most likely beneficiaries of the new laws and who are the most adversely impacted? By implementing new restrictive voting laws, voter turnout ultimately decreases. New restrictive voting requirements thus have a direct impact on equity because large groups of individuals may not be able to effectively express their concerns and needs to elected officials. When this occurs, government *is not* acting on behalf or in the best interest of its residents.

According to the Brennan Center for Justice, many of the new laws decrease the amount of time an individual can apply to be sent a mail-in ballot, restrict assistance in returning a voter's mail ballot and reduce the locations and the hours available of polling places availability (Brennan Center). In a backlash to 2020's historic voter turnout and unprecedented vote-by-mail usage, state lawmakers have imposed a variety of significant restrictions on both mail voting and in-person voting.

In 2021, The Georgia House of Representatives passed House Bill (HB) 531 that would reduce the amount of time for absentee voting from 180 to 78 days, and no later than 11 days prior to an election. HB 531 would also prohibit officials from sending absentee ballot applications to voters who specifically requested them and would require absentee voters to include their driver's license number or other state ID number on their application form. Similarly, in Arkansas (HB 1112), Montana (SB 169) and Wyoming (HB 175), lawmakers have made it harder to vote in-person by passing legislation imposing stricter voter identification laws. Other states such as Alabama (HB 538), Arkansas (SB 643), Iowa (SF 413), Kentucky (HB 574) and Ohio (HB 2663) have passed legislation to shorten the length of time that individuals can apply for mail-in voting ballots. Similar to legislation in Georgia (SB 202), Iowa (SF 413) and Kansas (HB 2332), voters who do not request mail-in ballots will not receive them, or find it more difficult to obtain them.

Some states such as Florida (SB 90), Iowa (SF 413) and Indiana (SB 398) have passed legislation that limits the number, location or altogether availability of mail-in ballot drop boxes. Georgia's new legislation decreases the number of voter drop boxes by 75% in the four counties in metropolitan Atlanta from 94 to 23. As the number of mail-in ballot locations and polling places has significantly decreased, it has resulted in longer lines of people waiting to vote. In an effort to presumably discourage those individuals from voting even more, Georgia and Florida have banned people from receiving snacks or water while waiting in line to vote. Richard Hansen, University of California Irvine law professor expressed concern over the need of the new law: "Allowing at least one box per county helps in smaller counties with no drop boxes before, but the law also causes a drastic cutback in the number of boxes allowed in larger counties, for no good reason." (Robertson & Keily, 2021).

What, then, has been the impetus for the recent aggrandizement of restrictive voting laws? The reasons are numerous and include the information we consume from the news media along with that inaccurate and incomplete information seized upon by opportunistic politicians. Finally, there has been a long and dark history of voter suppression in the United States that continues to be pervasive, divisive and racist.

Reasons for increased restrictive voting laws

The news media

The public may be generally skeptical of the news media and the information they provide, but when the information is in agreement with what we may be thinking, then it is more likely that we will believe and support it. As pernicious as the effect trusted elected officials have on shaping public opinion, and as complicit as politicians have been in making baseless and false claims regarding election result impropriety, perhaps the most deleterious impact on influencing the public arises from the news media. In November 2020, Fox News host Tucker Carlson continued to voice the sentiments of Donald Trump supporters by stating the 2020 US Presidential Election was "rigged." Carlson stated, "The 2020 presidential election was not fair, and no honest person would claim that it was. The system was rigged against one candidate and in favor of another, and not in ways that were hidden from view" (Carlson, 2020). In 2022, Fox News led all news outlets in the number of prime-time viewers with 1.52 million individuals tuning in to the information they provided. This figure more than doubled the number of viewers who watched MSNBC (668,000) and nearly tripled CNN viewers (582,000) (Watson, 2022).

On what basis did Fox News and other outlets base their assertions of a rigged US Presidential Election? The baseless and false assertions made by Fox News, and former and now current, President Trump, were largely based upon them publicly stating Dominion Voting Systems, the company that provided the software used for many voting machines used around the United States, was switching votes for Trump to those for Joe Biden (McNamara, 2020). The software used by Dominion Voting Systems is used in 28 states, over 600 US municipalities, and internationally (Dominionvoting.com). Accusing the Dominion of purposefully switching votes is a serious charge and Trump, along with Fox News, were at the center of those allegations. Fox News, with the largest megaphone to communicate news in the United States, never stated the false, or baseless claims Trump made were inaccurate. It was not until Dominion Voting Systems filed a lawsuit against Fox News for defamation that we began to hear of the complicity of Fox News. The news organization ultimately settled its lawsuit with Dominion and was ordered to pay the software company $787,500,000 in a settlement agreement. Dominion CEO John Poulos said, "Fox has admitted to telling lies about Dominion that caused enormous damage to my company, our employees and the customers that we serve. Nothing can ever make up for that. Throughout this process, we have sought accountability. Truthful reporting in the media is essential to our democracy" (Folkenflik & Yang, 2023). Despite the settlement agreement by Fox News with Dominion, a large percentage of people continue to believe the election was "stolen." These beliefs lead to continued support of restrictive voting legislation across several US states.

Simply put, the impact that Fox News has on shaping public opinion is enormous. As we previously mentioned, our sensibilities are partly based upon our experiences along with the information we consume. If individuals believe the information they read, and what they see on television and listen to is accurate, it is likely to have an impact on their actions. As a result of the lies and misinformation reported by President Trump, his political sycophants and the largest news media company in the United States, a great deal of people believe voter fraud happens with regularity and are likely to act in ways make it more difficult to vote in the future.

Opportunistic politicians

A common message after the 2020 election was that there were significant examples of election fraud, impropriety, and cheating leading to a "rigged" election result. Making accusations of voter fraud in the United States carries deep, negative connotations, especially among Blacks, women, Latinas and people of color. When individuals make unfounded claims of voter fraud, it causes those who have been the recipients of voter suppression to cast a cynical eye towards the accuser because if they were really serious about conducting fair elections, they would have stronger opinions on the historical suppression of voting in America. After the 2020 US Presidential Election, numerous claims of impropriety and election fraud continued to emerge. US Representative from Georgia, Marjorie Taylor Greene, espoused several claims of voter fraud: "Without the widespread voter fraud, out-of-state voters, mail-in ballots from dead people, and 'discovery' of hidden ballots, we all know that President Trump wins our state in a landslide" (Funke, 2022). Former US Senator also from Georgia, David Perdue, went so far as to file a lawsuit claiming the election was a fraud. His suit alleged fraudulent or counterfeit ballots were counted in Fulton County, Georgia during the 2020 general election (Brumback, 2022). Unfortunately for Perdue and those who believed the lies espoused by many, a federal judge dismissed the suit in May 2022. US Senator from Wisconsin, Ron Johnson, while stopping short of saying the election was fraudulent did say, "large percentage of the population don't view this election as legitimate" (Glauber, 2021). After losing his bid for reelection and when lawmakers were considering the ramifications from the January 6, 2021 insurrection at the White House that was done to stop the US Congress from certifying the 2020 US Presidential Election, then former US

President Donald Trump asked, "Why is it that the Unselect Committee of totally partisan political hacks, whose judgment has long ago been made, (sic) not discussing the rigged Presidential Election of 2020?" Unfortunately, Trump has a history of claiming voter fraud when he loses elections, like he did after losing the Republican Iowa Caucus. After losing the Caucus in 2016, Trump claimed, "based on the fraud committed by Senator Ted Cruz during the Iowa Caucus, either a new election should take place or Cruz results nullified" (Hilderbrandt, 2020). And yet after winning the Republican nomination for president and running against Hillary Clinton in 2016, Donald Trump then tweeted, "*Of course there is large scale voter fraud happening on and before election day. Why do Republican leaders deny what is going on? So naive!*" (Roth, 2016).

An overwhelming majority of US residents want fair elections to take place because it is one way to freely express their views with the hopes that positive changes will occur for them and their families. While there has been no evidence of voter fraud that would have changed the results of the US 2020 Presidential Election, we do have evidence, however, of large percentages of women, Blacks, and other people of color voting in record numbers. As a result of how the election turned out and the high number of minorities who participated, numerous laws and legislation were passed to decrease the number of minorities from participating in future elections. As of June 2021, 17 states had enacted 28 new laws that have restricted the access of residents to cast votes. The multitude of states that have passed these laws are based upon the premise that the 2020 US Presidential Election contained millions of cases of voter fraud thus casting significant doubt on the outcome of the election.

Historical voter suppression

As we previously mentioned, the voting process remains the most effective and efficient manner in which the public can express their preferences regarding candidates and public policies. It is also true that suffrage is the most equitable manner that affords individuals the opportunity to have a "voice." This is true as long as that voice is allowed to be heard and is not suppressed. The United States has a long and dubious history of countless examples of voter suppression. In 1867, the former US President Andrew Johnson stated that Black Americans had "less capacity for government than any other race of people," and would "relapse into barbarism" if left to their own devices. Johnson believed that giving Blacks voting rights would result in "a tyranny such as this continent has never yet witnessed" (p. 30, EJI). In his first State of the Union address, Johnson would not use his executive powers to permit Blacks the ability to vote. Instead, he left that decision up to the individual states. US Representative from Pennsylvania, Thaddeus Stevens stated the obvious, "If we leave [freed Black people] to the legislation of their late masters, we had better left them in bondage" (p. 80, EJI). Despite President Johnson's veto, the Reconstruction Act of 1867 was passed which imposed military rule on southern states. It also required those states who sought readmission into the Union to ratify the 14th Amendment to the Constitution which granted citizenship and equal protection under the law to any person born in the United States (EJI, 2020). Despite the act, in various states across the United States, from Louisiana to Georgia, to Mississippi to Tennessee to South Carolina to Kentucky and elsewhere, White mobs attacked, lynched and killed Blacks who simply wished to express their policy and candidate preferences by voting (EJI, 2020). It was not until the 15th Amendment to the Constitution, in 1870, that prohibited the denial of the right to vote based on race, color or previous condition of servitude, and the 19th Amendment, nearly 50 years later in 1919, that permitted women the right to vote. Despite these constitutional amendments, many states still created voter suppression policies, such as poll taxes, and literacy and English language requirements that aimed to prevent Blacks, people of color, immigrants and low-income individuals from voting (Carnegie Corporation of NY, 2019, https://www.carnegie.org/our-work/article/voting-rights-timeline/). After years of voter suppression tactics, in ***1964***, the 24th Amendment to the Constitution was passed that outlawed the use of poll taxes in all states. The Voting Rights Act (VRA) of 1965, finally "banned the use of literacy tests, provided for federal oversight of voter registration in areas where less than 50% of the non-white population had registered to vote, and authorized the US attorney general to investigate the use of poll taxes in state and local elections" (https://www.history.com/topics/black-history/voting-rights-act#voting-rights-act-signed-into-law). Instrumental to the powerful effect of the VRA is Section 5 which requires jurisdictions that have had a history of racial discrimination to obtain approval from the US Department of Justice before voting rules, and or, procedures can be changed. Without Section 5 of the VRA, many jurisdictions, as we have seen, have simply changed voting rules. Another key component of the VRA is Section 2 which allows individuals, groups and civil rights organizations the ability to sue jurisdictions that have enacted laws, policies and procedures denying equal opportunities for voters to elect political candidates of their choosing. The VRA of 1965 did not eliminate voter suppression but it did pave the way to increase representation at the polls of Black voters. In Mississippi, for example, the percentage of Black voters increased from 6% in 1964, prior to the VRA, to 59% in 1969. Further, while discrimination against Blacks was more prevalent in the private sector and as public-sector employment opportunities began to increase with the growth of government, Blacks were able to take advantage of these opportunities and find jobs earning higher salaries than they would in the private sector (Aneja & Avenancio-Leon, 2020). As this was occurring, the improved economic plight of Black workers led to a spillover effect in the private sector whereby firms needed to increase salaries to remain competitive. According to Aneja and Avenancio-Leon (2020), "Faced with the higher wages paid by government agencies, private employers likely had to offer more competitive pay to attract workers" (p. 6). In the states where VRA legislation was implemented, there was an increased income of Blacks that did not decrease the income of Whites, and ultimately narrowed the racial wage gap between 1950 and 1980 (Aneja & Avenancio-Leon, 2020). In Figure 4.1, we see the impact that the Voting Rights Act had on public-sector employment between 1962 and 1983.

Despite the positive effects of the VRA, the Shelby v. Holder decision from 2013 has greatly undermined its overall effectiveness. In the case, Shelby County, Alabama successfully argued that preclearance exceeds Congress' powers to enforce the 14th and 15th Amendments to the US Constitution. The results of the Shelby v. Holder decision, unfortunately, are obvious. Between 2012 and 2020, the racial voter turnout gap has increased significantly in five of the six states that previously required preclearance (Morris et al., 2024). In fact, the White-Black voter turnout gap between 2012 and 2020 has grown from –1.0% to 8.2% in Alabama, –4.2% to 6.8% in Louisiana, –5.8% to 15.1% in South Carolina, 0.3% to 13.4% in Virginia and –2.9% to 6.3% in Georgia (Morris et al., 2024).

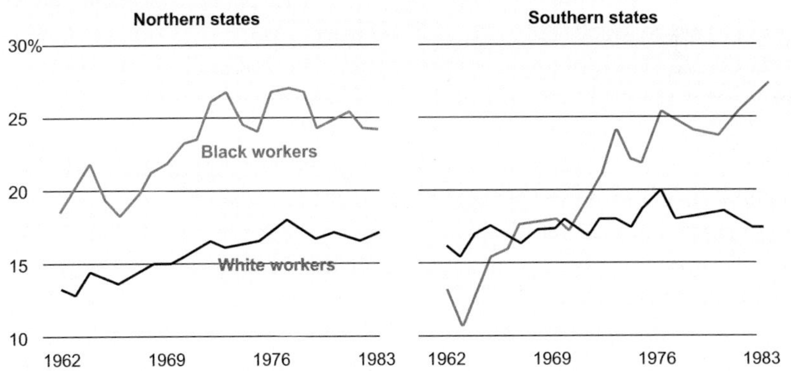

FIGURE 4.1 The Growth of Public-Sector Employment, by Race, 1962–1983.

Source: Adapted from Aneja and Avenancio-Leon (2020)

These figures indicate that the results of the Shelby Case have significantly decreased voter turnout among Black voters in these states.

As we previously mentioned, the 2020 US Presidential Election saw a significant increase in voter turnout compared with recent elections, and the results at the federal, state and local levels are uncomfortable for many people. While the perception to some may be that the election was plagued with fraud, thus propelling the passage of numerous laws, it is important to note that voter suppression is not a new phenomenon.

"What are the problems that can arise when government is not solely interested in maximizing the well-being of voters?", Gruber (2019) poses. His question leads to the obvious: Suppression. When attempts are made to suppress the votes of individuals, it is an attempt to **suppress** their voices, which as a result leads to ineffective governance while also sacrificing democracy. The relationship between stricter voter registration laws and voter participation has been clearly established in previous research (Burnham, 1965; Rusk, 1974). Studies consistently show that as voter registration laws become more strict, simultaneously making it more challenging to vote, individuals are less likely to vote. This issue mainly affects "fringe voters," or those less inclined to participate in the first place. Many individuals already believe that their vote does not matter and anything that makes it more challenging for them is a sufficient reason not to vote. Those whose goal is to demobilize their political opposition know that stricter voting laws will lead to a lower turnout which has the desired effect of allowing conservative interests and the Republican political party to maintain or re-establish political power. Dating back to the Reconstruction Period when Black men were first granted the right to vote, to 50 years later, in 1920, when women were given the right to vote, until modern times in 2008 when new voting legislation was passed, imposing stricter voting laws to quell the voices of a larger group of people is not new in America. According to Groarke (2016), the impetus for the new voter laws that emerged as a result of the 2008 US Presidential Election was not based upon the belief that the voting system was in need of repair because of fraud, but for the reason of political power. "There is a clear political calculus involved here: the groups that are less likely to be registered—low-income people, people of color, and young adults—are more likely to be Democrats. Democrats usually believe they will benefit from an expansion of the electorate, and Republicans usually expect they will not" (p. 574). Political parties similarly compete for voters who will support them, as they also compete to demobilize voters less likely to support them (Groarke, 2016). Based upon the complaints levied by several prominent politicians regarding the 2020 Presidential Election, it would appear as if there were surreptitious reasons leading to many of the newly introduced voting laws in several states. Decreasing the number of individuals who are likely to vote along with bringing chaos to the US election process seem to be paramount reasons for the new laws.

In a just society, there would be no need for the Voting Rights Act, nor would its upheaval be seen as severely problematic. But we acknowledge and realize that no society is completely just. What is perhaps more interesting is the extreme polarization of politics in the United States. When government works in the best interest of its residents then those who are elected are most likely to be individuals who possess fewer extreme views. With the two major US political parties consistently at odds with each other, compromising on issues often feels as if we are all playing an extreme version of a zero-sum game. In the next section, we examine the field of political economy and explore how median voter theorem applies less in contemporary American politics.

Political economy

The relationship between what government does for the residents it serves and what individuals' specific needs and wants are can best be understood by carefully examining the fields of politics and economics. Lindbloom (1959) states that the relationship between politics and economics is intertwined. Other noted economists such as Milton Friedman and John Kenneth Galbraith similarly express the view that there are no purely economic issues and that economics does not usefully exist apart from politics. The field of study that intertwines economics and politics is referred to as political economy. Gruber (2019) states that political economy is the theory of how the political process produces decisions that affect individuals and the economy. According to Weingast and Wittman (2008), "political economy is the methodology of economics applied to the analysis of political behavior and institutions" (p. 3). How do various methods of understanding the public's preferences impact the choices government makes for its residents? Clark (1998) says that the fields of politics and economics can be separated by three distinctive characteristics: the primary goal that is being pursued; the institutional arena in which that goal is being pursued; and the primary actor who chooses that goal. Table 4.1 shows the primary goals, institutional arena and primary actors within economics and politics.

As we can see from the chart earlier, the primary goal of economics is prosperity, while for politics it is justice in the arena of government. How do the two relate with each other and is there one that supersedes the other? Further, can we honestly say that in all times of US history justice was the primary goal of government? The answers to that question are likely to be different for women, men, Hispanics/Latines, Blacks, Asians,

TABLE 4.1 Primary Goals, Institutional Arena and Primary Actors Within Economics and Politics

	Economics	*Politics*
Primary Goal	Prosperity	Justice
Institutional Arena	Market	Government
Primary Actor	Individual	Community

Source: Chart based upon categorization by Clark (1998)

Native Americans and Indigenous. One can easily argue that justice, if equitably administered, is more valuable because it should lead to fairer outcomes in most situations. Conversely, are there moments when prosperity outweighs justice? It would seem that even in a situation where all of the residents of a community are prosperous that their prosperity is the result of a just system. Furthermore, individuals who live in a gated community, with many amenities, may all be viewed as prosperous yet there will be those who are *more prosperous* than others. The challenge in accepting the notion that prosperity is more valuable than justice assumes that all individuals have an acceptable level of prosperity, yet we know this does not exist in all communities. Thus, one of the government's roles is to ensure that a system of justice is fairly implemented that results in individuals being able to achieve the highest level of prosperity possible. Economics is less concerned with justice so long as prosperity is achieved. In this case, government is responsible for ensuring that both goals are achieved or, at least, close to being achieved. Clark (1998) states that the institutional arena of economics is based on the market or the private sector, while the politics institutional arena is government or the public sector. The goals of these two arenas are vastly different (profit for the market and effectiveness for government). Similarly, measuring the success or the achievement of goals among the two arenas is also very different. How do we know if success is achieved within each of these arenas? In the market, success is largely measured based upon profit, which because it is quantifiable is easily understood and achieved. Measuring success in politics is largely based upon factors or variables that we assume lead to a positive outcome. For example, we may ask how satisfied a person is in the community in which they live. Based upon their response, we then are informed to what extent they feel satisfied living there. To judge the level of satisfaction, we may define their level of satisfaction based upon some type of scale where five equals most satisfied, while one equals least satisfied. Finally, the primary actor in economics is the individual and in politics it is the community. Certainly, the opinions and perceptions of the community outweigh those of any one individual. We see evidence of the value of the community over the individual in democratic societies where choices and alternatives to those choices are afforded to residents. Taking all of this into account, government is in the unique position where it must be mindful of creating a prosperous community that is just, fair and equitable to all.

Public choice

A subset of political economy that gained prominence in the 1960s is Public Choice (Persson & Svensson, 1994; Alessina, 1987). Public choice relies upon models in assisting individuals to make rational choices that lead to decision-making in the public sector. Relying on the same principles, rational individual choice is used to explain the actions of consumers and firms, and public choice theorists apply those models to analyze political decision-making (Mueller, 2003; Clark, 1998). Thus, politics is seen as economic activity in the public sector as opposed to the private market of firms (Clark, 1998).

> Public choice theorists claim that voters, bureaucrats, and politicians behave in the same fashion as do private consumers and producers: they pursue their private interests, seeking maximum utility at minimum costs. Ultimately, the guiding principle of politicians is vote maximization since they must be reelected to maintain the benefits of public office.
>
> *(Clark, p. 50)*

Hyman (2014) defines public choice as decisions "made through political interaction of many people according to established rules" (p. 155). One of the central results of modern welfare economics is that in a competitive economy, the resulting resource allocations are efficient. How does government determine what is in the best interest of the residents it serves? We can attend public meetings, complete surveys or contact our elected officials directly, but the primary manner in which public choices or opinions are accumulated by government is through voting and elections. According to the 26th Amendment to the Constitution, US citizens are eligible to vote in elections, at all levels of government, once they reach the age of 18. It is during this time that individuals have the ability to support or deny support to candidates whom they would like to represent their respective interests.

During elections, individuals also have the ability to vote in favor or against specific policies, propositions and laws prior to them being enacted. In general terms, individuals tend to get a sense of utility out of voting, meaning that they envision it as meeting their civic responsibility to take part in the political process. Casting a vote can leave an individual feeling satisfied with themselves in "making a difference" among candidates and on issues of importance. For others, the benefits of voting are not viewed particularly highly and certainly not more than not voting at all. According to Census Bureau data, 18% of individuals did not vote in the 2020 Presidential Election because they were disinterested. Another 17% forgot to vote altogether and 15% did not like the choices of available candidates. Those who had an illness, disability, or were concerned about Covid-19 represented 17% of those who did not vote as well.

While voting is the main method by which public choices and opinions are garnered by government, there are challenges to the voting process. According to Stiglitz and Rosengard (2015) in deciding how to support proposed laws and legislation, congress and legislatures face two primary issues: How do they ascertain the views of their constituents, and how do they decide how much weight to give their views? Thus, because of the large amount of research and data that are available to politicians, coupled with the limited amount of time they have for analysis, special interest groups tend to be a primary source of information for them. In fact, the power and influence of special interest groups has grown significantly in recent years. Special interest groups can lower the cost of being informed whereby information is made readily available that supports their own views. Moreover, special interest groups support political candidates through political contributions and campaign donations. Ultimately, these factors can provide a demand-revealing mechanism for public goods. Taken together, information from the news media and the opportunistic nature of politicians to seize on that information, whether accurate, or not, results in individuals making choices that we are not sure that they would otherwise make if we were better informed. Further, the political polarization, which is a byproduct of that information, leads to a less effective government and governing process for all.

In the private sector, individuals can express their preferences towards private goods by deciding which ones to purchase, or not purchase, at a given time. In the public sector, there typically is not an option on which goods to purchase. To travel to and from work, one has to use public roads or transportation. If there is a fire at your home, short of attempting to extinguish it on your own, the local fire department needs to be called for assistance. In terms of elections, this leads to the Private Decision v Public Decision Dichotomy:

> Elections of public officials convey only limited information about voters' attitudes toward specific public goods; at best, they convey a general notion that voters prefer more or less government spending.
>
> *(Stiglitz & Rosengard, 2015, p. 231)*

Median voter theory

Unless individuals are faced with a choice of competing items, it is difficult for them to make choices. Oftentimes, choices are based upon giving up something to get something else. The Median-Voter Theory refers to an individual whose preferences are in the middle of all of the other voters. Half of the other voters prefer less and half of the voters prefer more than she or he does. The Median-Voter Theory assumes voters can place alternatives on one spectrum and that a majority-rule voting system will select the outcome most preferred by the median voter. In the public sector, this type of choice is narrow when it comes to identifying which candidate to vote for in an election. There are likely several issues that the candidate supports but every issue may not completely align with what the individual prefers. In addition, there may be issues that occur when encouraging individuals to state precisely what public goods they actually prefer. "If what they have to pay does not depend on their answer, then there is a tendency to ask for more of the good" (Stiglitz & Rosengard, 2015, p. 232). Thus, ascertaining the desired level of public goods of each individual becomes challenging. Moreover, while preferences are seen as a singular choice of a candidate or a specific policy (i.e., increasing a tax to fund dialysis treatment centers), government does not disaggregate individual preferences. Take, for example, the various factors that may influence individual preferences. Different individuals have different preferred levels of public expenditures. Their preferred level may depend on both individuals' income and the current tax system. Other things being equal, the rich typically prefer higher levels, and the cost of increased public expenditure may be higher for the rich. Further, as Downs (1957) established, political candidates are likely to align themselves, and their positions, in the "center" of policy issues in an effort to appeal to more voters. Currently, the "political fallout" is not as severe for candidates who espouse extreme, radical, and otherwise ridiculous views. Because of the toxic nature of American politics, individuals are more inclined to vote for one candidate over another because they actually support that candidate, and their views, as they are to oppose the other candidate from being elected. This level of extremism, while not new, has seemingly increased with no end in sight. The resultant effects lead to a system of political dysfunction (The US House of Representatives passed a pitiful 27 bills that became law in 2023), the prioritizing of draconian and conservative views (The repeal of Roe v Wade), and the marginalized are left with less, as we have demonstrated throughout this book.

Despite these issues, there is not a more effective nor efficient manner for the public to provide feedback to government on what it prefers. Most notably, voting has the potential to be the most equitable manner in which individuals can voice their opinion on candidates, policy proposals and propositions, as long as the voting process is conducted fairly where every eligible voter can equally cast their respective votes.

A popular trend in voting that has emerged in recent years in the United States is Ranked Choice Voting (RCV). Already utilized at various levels of government in other countries such as Australia, Ireland and New Zealand, RCV is gaining popularity in the United States as well. Several cities have begun using this form of voting at the local level to vote for mayors and councilmembers including New York City, East Hampton, MA, San Francisco, CA, Telluride, CO, Portland, ME and several other jurisdictions. Alaska and Maine will also utilize RCV for all state and federal general elections.

Broadly speaking, the ranked-choice voting process unfolds as follows for single-winner elections:

1. Voters rank the candidates for a given office by preference on their ballots.
2. If a candidate wins an outright majority of first-preference votes (i.e., 50% plus one), she or he will be declared the winner.
3. If, on the other hand, no candidates win an outright majority of first-preference votes, the candidate with the fewest first-preference votes is eliminated.
4. All first-preference votes for the failed candidate are eliminated, lifting the second-preference choices indicated on those ballots.
5. A new tally is conducted to determine whether any candidate has won an outright majority of the adjusted voters.
6. The process is repeated until a candidate wins a majority of votes cast.

Assume that there are four candidates for mayor in a hypothetical city. Table 4.2 presents the raw first-preference vote totals for each candidate.

In the above scenario, no candidate won an outright majority of first-preference votes. As a result, the candidate (Candidate D) with

TABLE 4.2 Raw First-Preference Vote Tallies in a Hypothetical Mayoral Race

Candidate	*First-Preference Votes*	*Percentage*
Candidate A	475	46.34%
Candidate B	300	29.27%
Candidate C	175	17.07%
Candidate D	75	7.32%

Source: Original creation

TABLE 4.3 Adjusted First-Preference Vote Tallies in a Hypothetical Mayoral Race

Candidate	*Adjusted First-Preference Votes*	*Percentage*
Candidate A	525	51.22%
Candidate B	325	31.71%
Candidate C	175	17.07%

Source: Original creation

the smallest number of first-preference votes is eliminated. The ballots that listed candidate D as the first preference are adjusted, raising their second-preference candidates. Assume that, of the 75 first-preference votes for Candidate D, 50 listed Candidate A as their second preference and 25 listed Candidate B. The adjusted vote totals would be as follows (see Table 4.3).

As a result of candidate D's votes being reallocated to candidates A & B, candidate A is now the winner of the election.

California voting propositions

At all levels of government, lower voter turnout not only impacts which candidates have a better chance of winning their respective elections, it also decreases the number of individuals who are likely to vote on legislation that appears on the ballot. In the state of California, 12 propositions appeared on the 2020 Presidential Election ballot. The propositions ranged from subjects covering housing to healthcare. While the majority of residents do not vote in national, state or local elections, even fewer vote on the various propositions listed on the ballot. Restricting votes also has the perilous outcome of decreasing the number of individuals who are likely to vote on topics such as Affirmative Action. The narrow margins of the results of the propositions show the extent to which voter suppression could potentially have on important issues. California Proposition 16, which aimed to repeal Proposition 209, sought to assess whether, or not, the government and public institutions could "discriminate against or grant preferential treatment to persons on the basis of race, sex, color, ethnicity, or national origin in public employment, public education, and public contracting." (https://ballotpedia.org/California_Proposition_16,_Repeal_Proposition_209_Affirmative_Action_Amendment_(2020)). A "yes" vote would repeal Proposition 209, which was originally passed in 1996. Proposition 209 was curiously named the Affirmative Action Initiative, and allowed government and public institutions the ability to develop and use Affirmative Action programs that afford preferences based upon ethnicity, race, national origin and sex in public employment, public education and public contracting. To many, the proposition appeared to "protect" the interest of minority groups but in reality it did the opposite. The independent and nonpartisan California Legislative Analyst stated the following regarding Proposition 209:

> *[T]he measure would eliminate a variety of public school (kindergarten through grade 12) and community college programs such as counseling, tutoring, student financial aid, and financial aid to selected school districts, where these programs are targeted based on race, sex, ethnicity or national origin.*
>
> [Opinion Letter to the Attorney General, *10/15/95]*

Since Proposition 209 has been in effect in California for over 20 years, the presumption may have been that the status quo is sufficient and there is no need to implement an unnecessary policy that provides opportunities to traditionally marginalized and discriminated groups. For many, policies that attempt to address historic and structural racism are viewed as "reverse racism," and adversely impact those who are not directly responsible for the plight of the marginalized and discriminated groups and people. According to Vincent Pan, executive director of Chinese for Affirmative Action, "Both in California and across the country, we're not witnessing a repudiation of Trumpism that we'd like to see. There's a lot of work to do to help enlist more folks who are championing the promotion of policies that really fix structural racism." (https://ballotpedia.org/California_Proposition_16,_Repeal_Proposition_209_Affirmative_Action_Amendment_(2020)). Then US Representative, and now mayor of Los Angeles, Karen Bass stated that prior to Proposition 209, efforts at advancing equity had made progress. The repeal of "Proposition 209, deceptively titled the California Civil Rights Initiative, passed by referendum in 1996 amidst an orchestrated campaign of dog-whistle politics attacking all attempts to level the playing field for women and people of color. But the Wall Street-backed authors of the initiative saw a threat to their economic stranglehold from an increasingly diverse and highly educated population in California; a population better situated to compete in jobs, education, government contracts and other areas of the state's economy." (https://ballotpedia.org/California_Proposition_16,_Repeal_Proposition_209_Affirmative_Action_Amendment_(2020)). Congresswoman Bass went on to say, "in passing Prop 209, those groups limited competition in their industries and benefited their own businesses by erecting new institutional barriers burdening the ability of California's women and people of color to achieve positions of economic and business leadership." (https://ballotpedia.org/California_Proposition_16,_Repeal_Proposition_209_Affirmative_Action_Amendment_(2020)). The proposition was roundly defeated by more than 10% (54.55% in favor and 44.45% against) of voters in a state that many consider "blue" and liberal. The results may have been somewhat surprising, but when we take a deeper look at this case, perhaps the results are simply in line with the way many Americans feel about the topic of Affirmative Action. The title of the proposition may have led to some confusion among voters. A "yes" vote meant that you were in favor of *eliminating* Proposition 209 and not in favor of Affirmative Action policies that took into consideration ethnicity, race, national origin and sex.

While Proposition 16 dealt with the issue of Affirmative Action in California, three of the 12 propositions on the 2020 ballot dealt specifically with taxation or government-issued bonds. Proposition 14 asked voters to determine if they supported issuing 5.5 billion dollars in general obligation (GO) bonds for the state's stem cell research center. The California Secretary of State (SOS) provides an assessment of the fiscal impact of each of the propositions that were related to public finance and in terms of Proposition 14, the SOS estimated that the cost to repay the bonds would be approximately $260 million annually for the next 30 years. (https://ballotpedia.org/California_Proposition_14,_Stem_Cell_Research_Institute_Bond_Initiative_(2020)). Proposition 14 narrowly passed with 51.09% in favor and 48.91% against providing $5.5 billion to continue funding the state's stem cell research institute.

Proposition 15 asked voters to assess the constitutional amendment to require commercial and industrial properties (except those zoned as commercial agriculture) to be taxed based upon their current market values instead of the original purchase price. (https://ballotpedia.org/California_Proposition_15,_Tax_on_Commercial_and_Industrial_Properties_for_Education_and_Local_Government_Funding_Initiative_(2020)). In terms of Proposition 15, the SOS stated that increased property taxes on commercial and industrial properties valued at $3 million or more would generate between $8 billion and $12.5 billion annually. Arguments against Proposition 15 centered around the impact it would have on maintaining and attracting new businesses to California. (https://ballotpedia.org/California_Proposition_15,_Tax_on_Commercial_and_Industrial_Properties_for_Education_and_Local_Government_Funding_Initiative_(2020)). The proposition was not passed by a margin of 51.97% against and 48.03% in favor.

One of the primary provisions of Proposition 19 asked voters to determine if they were in favor of allowing eligible homeowners to transfer their tax assessments anywhere in the state while allowing tax assessments to be transferred to a more expensive home with an upward adjustment. Proposition 19 would continue to allow homeowners, 55 or older, severely disabled, or whose homes were destroyed by wildfire or disaster, to transfer their primary home's tax base value anywhere in the state, including residences that are more expensive. It would not permit however a parent to transfer a property to their child, or a grandparent to transfer a property to their grandchild that would not be used as their primary residence. (https://ballotpedia.org/California_Proposition_19,_Property_Tax_Transfers,_Exemptions,_and_Revenue_for_Wildfire_Agencies_and_Counties_Amendment_(2020).

According to the California Secretary of State, the fiscal impact of Proposition 19:

> *"Local governments could gain tens of millions of dollars of property tax revenue per year. These gains could grow over time to a few hundred million dollars per year." "Schools could gain tens of millions of dollars of property tax revenue per year. These gains could grow over time to a few hundred million dollars per year." "Revenue from other taxes could increase by tens of millions of dollars per year for both the state and local governments. Most of this new state revenue would be spent on fire protection."*

(https://ballotpedia.org/California_Proposition_19,_Property_Tax_Transfers,_Exemptions,_and_Revenue_for_Wildfire_Agencies_and_Counties_Amendment_(2020)). Ultimately, the proposition was passed by a margin of 51.11% in favor to 48.89% against.

As a result of voting, Propositions 14 (stem cell research) and 19 (property tax transfers) were passed by a majority of the voters, while Propositions 15 (market value taxation) and 16 (affirmative action) were not. One could argue what the passage, and non-passage, of those propositions mean in terms of public policy, but when we introduce equity into the framework, then our understanding of their relative importance to residents in California becomes clearer.

While suffrage in California has not come under the scrutiny like it has in several other states, one could only imagine the results of their propositions if many were simply disenfranchised. Because overwhelming disenfranchisement is not seen as problematic in California, the results of the elections in the state are also viewed differently. When certain legislation is or is not passed, it is usually the blame of strong interest groups who can unduly sway public opinion and their votes. Again, the narrow margin of the results of the above propositions shows the impact that efforts to purge votes, the suppression of votes and misinformation can play in an election and with issues that can have a significant impact on the lives of individuals.

In other states, it is likely that the purging of votes may indeed have deleterious consequences preventing equity from being achieved. As the US continues to see increased laws, policies and scare tactics being implemented to make equity and diversity illegal, ensuring that voting remains fair and available to all eligible becomes critically important for democracy.

Conclusion

Whether we realize it or not, the fiscal policies implemented at all levels of government, have a direct impact on every one of us. While it is common for most individuals to think about voting primarily at the time of presidential elections, it is perhaps more important to consider the implications state and local government elections have on us. In fact, what occurs in the states we reside in and in our local communities has a greater impact on our everyday lives—especially from a fiscal perspective (Alt & Lowry, 1994). That is because what local and state government elected officials do and the laws that are passed by them, such as sales tax rate adjustments, new school construction, new and updated service fees, access to healthcare facilities such as dialysis treatment centers, affordable housing construction, transportation policy and many other issues, are things that we may benefit from or experience in our daily routines. Table 4.4 shows the elected officials who will influence the various fiscal policies that impact us (Itsuptous.org., n.d.).

It is believed by the majority of US residents that politicians are less likely, and sometimes, not likely at all to listen to the public's views. According to 2018 report by the Pew Research Center, 40% of respondents said that if

TABLE 4.4 A Voters Guide to Local Fiscal Issues: From the Ballot Box to the Bottom Line—How Your Vote Shapes Fiscal Policy

Level of Government	*Federal*	*State*	*Local*
Who you vote for that influences fiscal policy	President US Senator US Representative	Governor State Treasurer/ Controller/ Comptroller State Senator State Representative Assembly member	Mayor County Supervisor Commissioner City Council member Township board member

Source: Original creation

they contacted their US House of Representatives they would be less likely to assist them. Another 21% said that the representative would not be likely to help them at all. (https://www.pewresearch.org/politics/2018/04/26/6-quality-and-responsiveness-of-elected-officials/).

In the same report, 76% of those surveyed felt as if government is run by a few big interests and are really only out for themselves. (https://www.pewresearch.org/politics/2018/04/26/6-quality-and-responsiveness-of-elected-officials/) (Pew Chartiable Trust, n.d.).

This perception, whether true or not, has an impact on the extent to which individuals vote in elections. When the voting population shrinks through various policies and procedures, ultimately making it more challenging for people to vote, those whom are affected are more often than not Blacks, Latinas, people of color and women. As suffrage is sacrificed and democracy comes perilously close to becoming an autocracy, achieving fiscal policies that take into consideration equity simultaneously diminish. Taken together, with the recent restrictive voter registration laws, the percentage of people voting is likely to significantly shrink in the future.

References

Alessina, A. (1987). Macroeconomic policy in a two-party system as a repeated game. *The Quarterly Journal of Economics*, *102*(3), 651–678. https://doi.org/10.2307/1884222

Alt, J. E., & Lowry, R. C. (1994). Divided government, fiscal institutions, and budget deficits: Evidence from the states. *The American Political Science Review*, *88*(4), 811–828.

Aneja, A., & Avenancio-Leon, C. (2020). *Voting rights equal economic progress: The Voting Rights Act and US economic inequality*. The Washington Center for Equitable Growth. https://equitablegrowth.org/voting-rights-equal-economic-progress-the-voting-rights-act-and-u-s-economic-inequality/

The Brennan Center for Justice. (2021). *Voting laws roundup: December 2021*. https://www.brennancenter.org/our-work/research-reports/voting-laws-roundup-december-2021

The Brennan Center for Justice. (2023). *Voting laws roundup: 2023 in review*. https://www.brennancenter.org/our-work/research-reports/voting-laws-roundup-2023-review

Brumback, K. (2022). *Perdue suit pushing election fraud claims dismissed by judge*. https://www.sfgate.com/news/article/Perdue-suit-pushing-election-fraud-claims-17169284.php

Burnham, W. (1965). The changing shape of the American political universe. *American Political Science Review*, *59*(1), 7–28.

California Proposition 16, Repeal Proposition 209 Affirmative Action Amendment. (2020). https://ballotpedia.org/California_Proposition_16,_Repeal_Proposition_209_Affirmative_Action_Amendment_(2020)

Carlson, T. (2020). *Tucker Carlson: Yes, the election was rigged for Joe Biden. Here's how—how democrats, big tech and the mainstream media waged an unfair fight in 2020*. https://www.foxnews.com/opinion/tucker-carlson-2020-presidential-election-rigged-big-tech-mainstream-media

Carnegie Corporation of NY. (2019). https://www.carnegie.org/our-work/article/voting-rights-timeline/
Clark, B. (1998). *Political economy—A comparative approach* (2nd ed.). Greenwood Publishing Group.
Dominion.com. (2024). *Setting the record straight: Facts about dominion.* https://www.dominionvoting.com/setting-the-record-straight/
Downs, A. (1957). An economic theory of political action in a democracy. *Journal of Political Economy*, *65*(2), 135–150.
Equal Justice Initiative. (2020). *Reconstruction in America: Racial violence after the civil war, 1865–1876.* https://eji.org/report/reconstruction-in-america/
Folkenflik, D., & Yang, M. (2023). *Fox News settles blockbuster defamation lawsuit with dominion voting systems.* NPR. https://www.npr.org/2023/04/18/1170339114/fox-news-settles-blockbuster-defamation-lawsuit-with-dominion-voting-systems
Frey, W. (2021). *Turnout in 2020 election spiked among both Democratic and Republican voting groups, new census data shows.* Brookings. https://www.brookings.edu/articles/turnout-in-2020-spiked-among-both-democratic-and-republican-voting-groups-new-census-data-shows/
Funke, D. (2022). What rep. Marjorie Taylor Greene has said about election fraud, QAnon and other conspiracy theories. *Poynter.* https://www.poynter.org/fact-checking/2021/what-rep-marjorie-taylor-greene-has-said-about-election-fraud-qanon-and-other-conspiracy-theories/
Funke, D. (2022). Fact check: How we know the 2020 election results were legitimate, not 'rigged' as Donald Trump claims. *US Today.* https://www.usatoday.com/story/news/factcheck/2022/01/06/fact-check-donald-trump-2020-election-results/9115875002/
Glauber, B. (2021). U.S. Sen. Ron Johnson from Wisconsin to join 10 others from GOP in refusing to certify Electoral College results. *Milwaukee Journal Sentinel.* https://www.jsonline.com/story/news/politics/elections/2021/01/02/ron-johnson-oppose-certifying-joe-bidens-electoral-college-win/4113042001/
Groarke, M. (2016). The impact of voter fraud claims on voter registration reform legislation. *Political Science Quarterly*, *131*(3), 571–595.
Gruber, J. (2019). *Public finance and public policy* (6th ed.). Worth Publishers.
Hilderbrandt, E. (2020). When Donald Trump lost the Iowa caucus to Ted Cruz in 2016, "he immediately cried that Cruz cheated." *Poynter-Politifact.* https://www.politifact.com/factchecks/2020/nov/20/tweets/yes-donald-trump-claimed-fraud-after-2016-iowa-cau/
Hyman, D. (2014). *Public finance – A contemporary application of theory to policy* (11 ed.). Cengage.
Itsuptous.org. (n.d.). *Up to us—A voters guide to local fiscal issues: From the ballot box to the bottom line—How your vote shapes fiscal policy.* https://www.itsuptous.org/resource/voters-guide-local-fiscal-issues
Kaplan, M., Samu, S., & Garrett, M. (2023). Eligible voters are being swept up in conservative activists efforts to purge voter polls. *CBS News.* https://www.cbsnews.com/news/eligible-voters-swept-up-conservative-activists-purge-voter-rolls/
Levine, S., & Rao, A. (2020). In 2013 the Supreme Court gutted voting rights—How has it changed the US? *The Guardian.* https://www.theguardian.com/us-news/2020/jun/25/shelby-county-anniversary-voting-rights-act-consequences
Lindbloom, C. (1959). The science of muddling through. *Public Administration Review, 19*(2), 79–88.
McNamara. (2020). Trump spreads baseless claims about Dominion Voting Systems after losing election. *CBS News.*

Morris, K., Miller, P., & Grange, C. (2024). *Racial turnout gap grew in jurisdictions previously covered by the voting rights act*. https://www.brennancenter.org/our-work/research-reports/racial-turnout-gap-grew-jurisdictions-previously-covered-voting-rights
Mueller, D. (2003). *Public choice III*. Cambridge University Press.
Persson, M., & Svensson, L. E. (1994). *Monetary and fiscal policy: Politics* (Vol. 1). MIT Press.
Pew Charitable Trust. (n.d.). https://www.pewresearch.org/politics/2018/04/26/6-quality-and-responsiveness-of-elected-officials/
Robertson, L., & Keily, E. (2021). *Factchecking claims about the Georgia voting law*. https://www.factcheck.org/2021/04/factchecking-claims-about-the-georgia-voting-law/
Roth, Z. (2016). *Donald Trump's 'rigged election' claims raise historical alarms*. https://www.nbcnews.com/politics/2016-election/donald-trump-s-rigged-election-claims-raise-historical-alarms-n667831
Rusk, J. G. (1974). Comment: The American electoral universe: Speculation and evidence. *American Political Science Review, 68*(3), 1028–1049.
Stiglitz, J., & Rosengard, J. (2015). *The economics of the public sector* (4th ed.). W.W. Norton & Company.
Watson, A. (2022). *Leading cable news networks in the United States in April 2022, by number of primetime viewers*. https://www.statista.com/statistics/373814/cable-news-network-viewership-usa/
Weingast, B., & Wittman, D. (2008). The reach of political economy. In *The Oxford handbook of political economy*. Oxford Academic. doi:10.1093/oxfordhb/9780199548477.003.0001
Why does fiscal policy matter? (n.d.). https://www.itsuptous.org/fiscal-policy-2020-elections

5

HEALTHCARE

What is the importance of healthcare?

There are countless examples where we, as a society, are reminded of the value and importance of an individual's health and well-being. From commercials supporting the positive results from a "heart-healthy" diet, joining gyms and regularly exercising, to purchasing in-home equipment like a Peloton exercise bike, we are constantly inundated with options and opportunities to be healthier. There are also many applications one can use from their mobile phones to track the number of calories you have consumed, or to track the number of steps you have taken while walking, jogging or running. In general, we are continuously made aware of ways to improve our overall health. Our public schools include physical education classes that are required for students to complete so that they learn, at an early age, the importance of living and leading a healthy lifestyle. Additionally, most people are aware of the health dangers associated with smoking as states prohibit the sale of cigarettes to those under the age of 21.

With all of the information related to health available, prior to 2010, many people would even suggest that the United States could do yet more to address the healthcare system. Because education is casually related to income, earning a college and advanced degrees leads to better jobs and ultimately a higher salary. Unfortunately, as we continue to express in this book, not everyone is able to increase their respective salary as much as they would like. Healthcare is costly and since health insurance is closely tied to an individual's employment, many U.S. residents had not been able to effectively take care of their own health or that of their loved ones

DOI: 10.4324/9781032670850-6

because they simply did not earn enough money to do so. In 2010, under former President Barrack Obama, the United States passed the Affordable Care Act (ACA), or Obamacare as it is commonly referred to, which among other things, made it significantly easier for individuals to obtain healthcare. Other goals of ACA were to expand the number of people who relied upon Medicaid for health insurance, including those whose incomes were 138% below the federal poverty limit (FPL). Another goal was to support innovative medical care delivery methods designed to lower the overall costs of healthcare (healthcare.gov). While ACA has faced a considerable amount of pushback politically and in the court system, it has increased the number of individuals who have healthcare. Moreover, one of the greatest benefits of the ACA is the elimination of denial of coverage for those with prior medical conditions (Dalen et al., 2015). As of April 2022, the US Department of Health and Human Services (DHHS) reported that total enrollment for Medicaid expansion, Marketplace coverage, and the Basic Health Program in participating states had reached a record high with more than 35 million people enrolled.

After the first year of its implementation, over 10 million residents now had health insurance (Dalen et al., 2015). Also, the percentage of individuals who did not have health insurance decreased from 18% in 2013 to 13.4% in 2014 (Dalen et al., 2015). In 2020, the Center for Budget and Policy Priorities reported that ACA expansion of Medicaid had improved access to healthcare. Specifically, the report found that there were "more low-income adults with a personal physician, getting check-ups and other preventative care, and getting regular care for chronic conditions; increases in the number of people getting medication-assisted treatment for opioid-use disorders, and; greater access to mental health care" (CBPP, 2020). Among states that had expanded Medicaid, there was a 55% decrease in hospital uncompensated care cost along with an 18% decline in states that had not expanded Medicaid (CBPP, 2020). Uncompensated costs for hospitals are higher among community hospitals that tend to serve lower-income populations. A reduction in uncompensated costs for these hospitals will result in them being able to continue to serve lower-income and traditionally disadvantaged without the likelihood of it closing. While the number of individuals who had insurance increased in all states, states where Medicaid was expanded also witnessed significantly larger decreases in the percentage of individuals uninsured.

In 2013, 35% of non-elderly adults in expansion states, with incomes below 200% of the poverty line, were uninsured. That number decreased to just 17% in 2018. In non-expansion states, 43% of non-elderly adults whose income was 200% below the poverty line were uninsured, while by

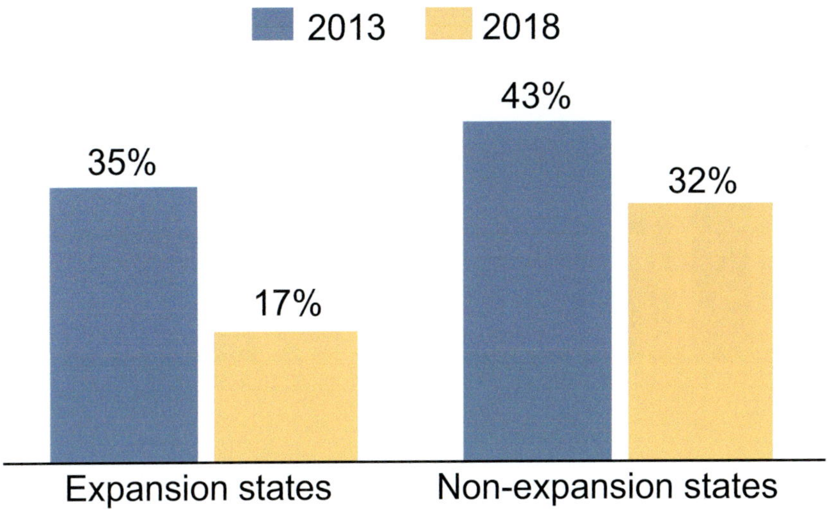

FIGURE 5.1 Expansion States Saw Large Drop in Uninsured Rates. Uninsured Rate Among Non-Elderly Adults With Incomes Below 200% of Poverty Line

Source: Adapted from CBPP (Center on Budget and Policy Priorities, CBPP.org) analysis of Census Bureau data

Note: States can expand their Medicaid program to low-income adults under the Affordable Care Act. Expansion took effect in 2014

2018 that figure had decreased to 32%. Overall, it has become obvious that the ACA had addressed the goals it sought to achieve.

The Covid-19 pandemic obviously adversely impacted the financial well-being of individuals, in particular those who were already considered "low-income." In a study conducted by the US Federal Reserve to examine the financial health of consumers and communities, with particular emphasis being placed on financially vulnerable populations, their results indicated mixed results (Federal Reserve System, 2020). In *Consumer and Community Context*, the percentage of individuals who stated that they were "doing at least okay financially" was around 70% for all surveyed, but only 51% for those who had lost their jobs, or had their hours of work reduced (Federal Reserve System, 2024).

As a result of job loss, and or, decreased wages, healthcare outcomes for Blacks, Hispanics/Latines, Asians and other minorities deteriorated during the pandemic. While the ACA would not serve as a panacea for the health outcomes during and immediately after the pandemic, it is difficult to imagine how much worse the conditions of the most vulnerable would

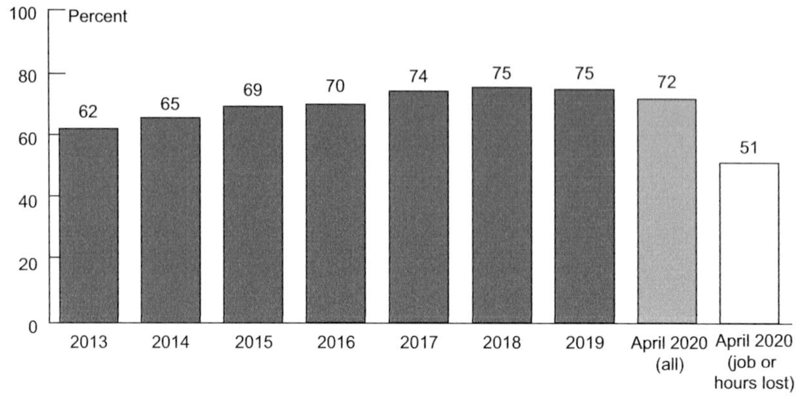

FIGURE 5.2 Percent Doing At Least Okay Financially

Source: Adapted from https://www.federalreserve.gov/consumerscommunities/shed.htm

Note: All respondents, n = 12,173 in 2019; 1,030 in April 2020. For the number of respondents in earlier years, see https://www.federalreserve.gov/consumerscommunities/shed.htm

have been absent of it. On average, there has been a $1,140 reduction in the amount of medical debt for individuals who live in ACA Medicaid Expanded states, along with a reduction in evictions among low-income individuals (CBPP, 2020). Reducing medical-related costs has been a benefit individually but also to the economy. As a result of increased financial security, individuals are gaining better access to credit, thus lowering interest rates on homes, automobiles and other loans (CBPP, 2020).

ACA has also decreased racial and ethnic disparities in states that expanded Medicaid compared with states who did not. Figure 5.3 shows reductions in coverage and access to care for Hispanic/Latine, Black and White residents between 2013 and 2018. In both sets of states, health disparities decreased significantly. Also, the share of Hispanic/Latine, Black and White adults avoiding medical care due to cost declined between 2013 and 2018.

Opposition to the affordable care act

The Affordable Care Act became legislation in the United States in 2010, but it did not do so without a great deal of opposition from a variety of sources. Despite the positive outcomes associated with ACA, many Americans ardently opposed its implementation and utilization. There was a perception that government was too large and overreaching, thus making individuals question any government action to be intrusive. Certainly,

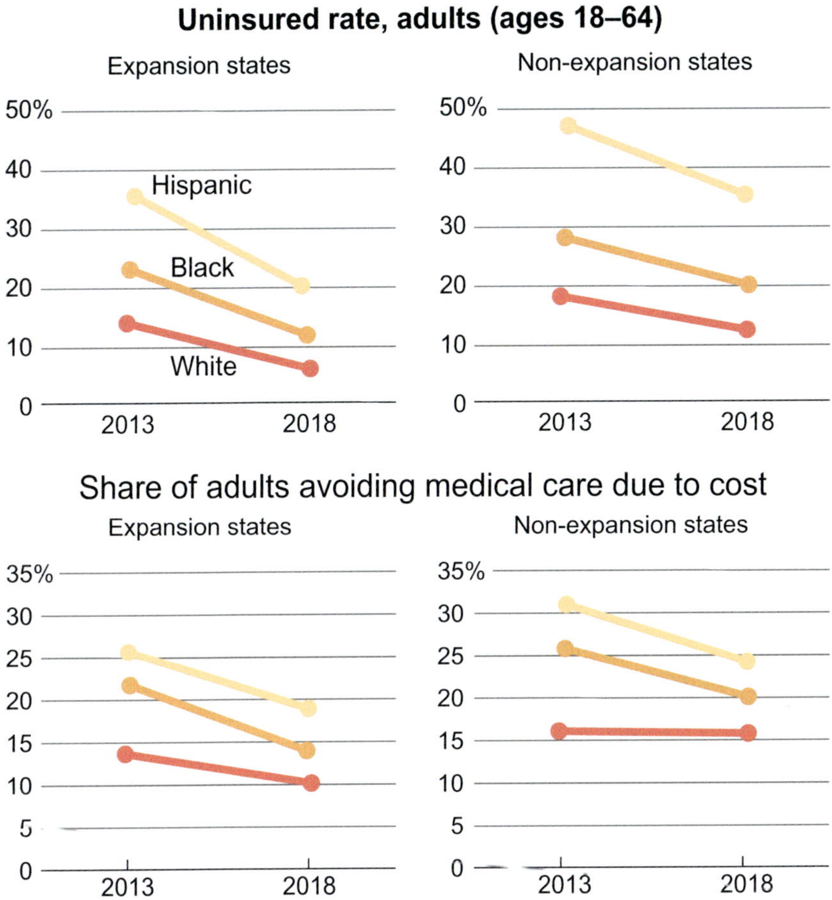

FIGURE 5.3 Medicaid Expansion Reduced Racial and Ethnic Disparities in Both Coverage and Access to Care

Source: Census 2013 and 2018 American Community Surveys (uninsured rate), and Commonwealth Fund (share avoiding care). Adapted from Center on Budget and Policy Priorities (CBPP.org)

Note: ACA = Affordable Care Act. Black and White racial categories exclude those identifying as Hispanic; Hispanic can include any race

there are examples where government indeed is too intrusive such as the overturning of Roe v. Wade in 2022, or the ineffectiveness of the unfunded mandate "No Child Left Behind," but arguing against healthcare does not seem to be the best example. Further, it appears as if many who oppose ACA would benefit from the provisions in the legislation and are simply arguing against their own best interests. Opposition to ACA becomes even

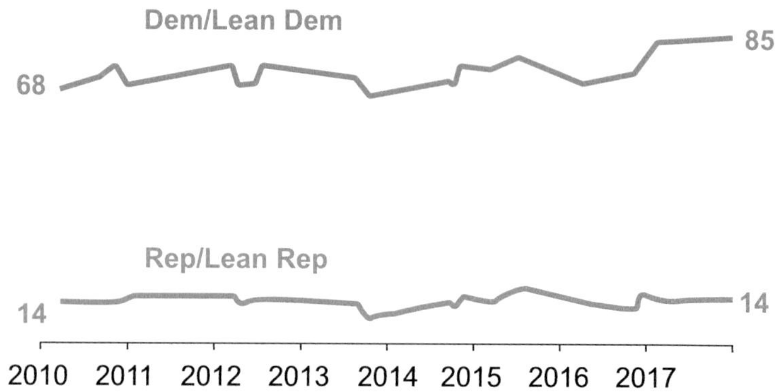

FIGURE 5.4 Views of 2010 Healthcare Law Remain Highly Partisan % Who Approve of Healthcare Law Passed by Barack Obama and Congress in 2010.

Source: Adapted from PEW Research Center, Survey of US adults conducted during November 29–December 4, 2017

more perplexing and contradictory because Medicare, administered by the US federal government and in place since 1965, earns high approval ratings by the majority of Americans (Dalen et al., 2015). The answer to this conundrum lies somewhere between the facts that overall, Republicans are less supportive of government's role in healthcare than Democrats and that Republican candidates have largely run for office on the idea of overturning ACA. According to the Pew Research Center, political party affiliation plays a large role in whether, or not, an individual is supportive, or not, of the ACA.

In the 2012 and 2014 elections, many of the advertisements shown on TV negatively depicted ACA as something that will reduce Medicare advantage benefits for seniors, is an overstep by government, and is too costly. Furthermore, many of the attack ads refer to the Affordable Care Act as "Obamacare" so that negative feelings an individual may have had towards the president transcended into also negative feelings towards legislation he supported and ultimately signed. In fact, at the time, over 60% of Americans stated that what they had learned about the ACA came from television advertisements (Dalen et al., 2015). Interestingly, opposition by politicians to ACA was all done without any significant alternative healthcare legislation being provided or introduced.

Leading up to the 2014 elections, Kantar Media reported that opponents of ACA had spent over $450 million on negative advertisements that significantly outpaced positive ads (Yaraghi, 2014). Nevertheless, the millions of dollars spent on negative TV advertisements against ACA may have had the opposite effect. A Brookings Institution report indicated that after

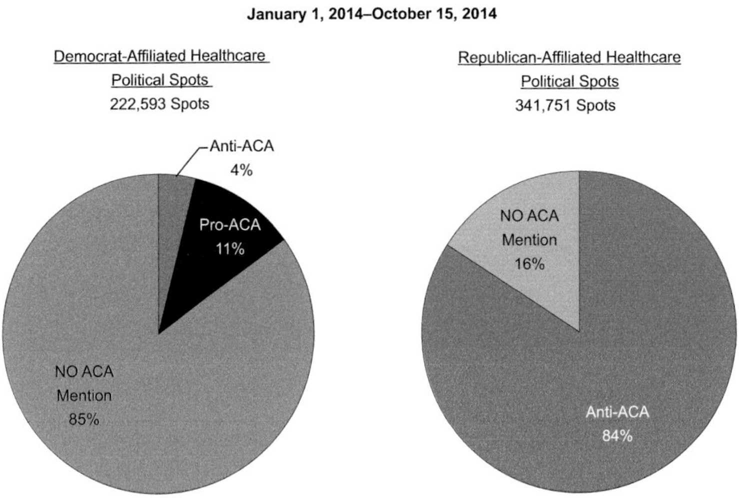

FIGURE 5.5 Republican Healthcare Ads Largely Anti-ACA, While Democrats Rarely Mention the Law.

Source: Adapted from Kaiser Family Foundation (KFF) analysis of data from Kantar Media's Campaign Media Analysis Group (January 1, 2014–October 15, 2014)

controlling for "low per capita income population and average insurance premiums that there was a positive association between the anti-ACA spending and ACA enrollment" (Yaraghi, 2014). This may have been the result of so much negative information and energy being pointed towards ACA that otherwise uninformed or uninterested residents may have actually learned some of the benefits ACA could actually bring to them. Moreover, according to a Pew Research Center report (Fingerhut, 2017), when we examine the opinion of ACA based upon gender, race, age, education and income, we see stark differences in individual's opinions.

The results of their study show that 56% of those surveyed approved of the ACA. When we look more closely at the numbers, women, Blacks, Hispanics/Latines, younger individuals, and lower-income individuals were significantly more likely to approve of ACA by more than 60%. In fact, the only groups that were near even in their views of ACA were Whites and those between the ages of 50 and 64.

Social determinants of health

When one begins to closely examine an individual's relative health in comparison to others, we learn not only that health is predicated on diet, exercise and heredity but that there are numerous other factors at play. For example, if a study were conducted that examined the likelihood that

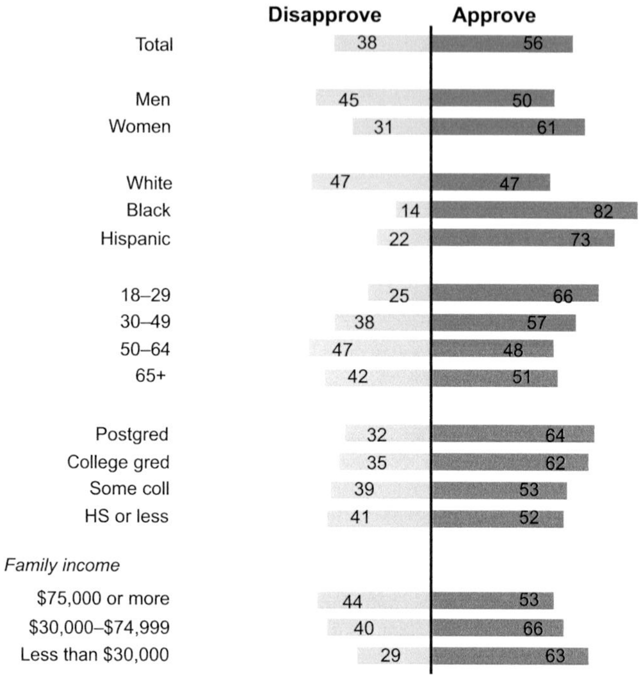

FIGURE 5.6 Race, Age and Gender Divisions in Views of Affordable Care Act % Who support the Healthcare Law Passed by Barack Obama and Congress in 2010.

Source: Adapted from Fingerhut (2017), PEW Research Center, Survey of US adults conducted during November 29–December 4, 2017

Note: Don't know responses not shown

individuals would develop hypertension (high blood pressure) but they were the same age, lived in cities that had similar per capita incomes, had similar incomes and years of education themselves, and exercised three times per week, then we would be able to narrow down a more precise reason for their ailment. Developing hypertension, in this case, may be the result of their family's health history. It could also be because of their body mass index (BMI) or the amount of alcohol they consume. We know that individuals live in all types of socioeconomic environments with various degrees of incomes, education, and access to healthy supermarkets and parks to exercise at, thus impacting whether, or not, developing hypertension is likely. The socioeconomic factors within various environments are referred to as **social determinants** and are directly related to an individual's health. Essentially, the social determinants of health are the external environmental factors that impact an individual's degree of health. Freeman (2015) states that the social determinants of health refer to the availability of the opportunity to be healthy. "This means having an income sufficient to ensure adequate housing and food, to have heat in the winter, to have neighborhoods that are safe enough to be active in without risking your life" (Freeman, 2015, p. 43). According to the World Health Organization (WHO), the social determinants of health are "the non-medical factors that influence health outcomes. They are the conditions in which people are born, grow, work and live, and the wider set of forces and systems shaping the conditions of daily life. These forces and systems include economic policies and systems, development agendas, social norms, social policies and political systems" (retrieved from https://www.who.int/health-topics/social-determinants-of-health#tab=tab_1, June 2023). As one can imagine, there are many factors that likely impact and influence health outcomes. The WHO identifies ten such factors that include income and social protection, education, unemployment and job insecurity, working life conditions, food insecurity, housing, early childhood development, social inclusion and nondiscrimination, structural conflict, and access to affordable health services of decent quality. Acknowledging the environmental factors that impact health highlights the importance of decreasing and ultimately eliminating the barriers that can ensure individuals lead lives where positive healthy outcomes are a reality. According to Ndugga and Artiga (2023), health outcomes are driven by a wide range of factors, and while the extent to which each factor is challenging to measure, research indicates that health behaviors along with social and economic factors are key drivers of health outcomes and that human behaviors are shaped by these social and economic factors. Figure 5.7 (Ndugga & Artiga, 2023) shows health disparities that are influenced by social and economic inequities such as economic stability, neighborhood and physical environment, education, food, community and the healthcare system. Each of these inequities can adversely impact an individual's mortality, morbidity, life expectancy, health status and the amount they spend on healthcare.

Spending and health outcome data

Most people reasonably assume that since the United States spends more money on healthcare that it would also yield the best results and outcomes for individuals. This is similar to the concept that we discussed earlier where the more years of education an individual has, the more likely that they will have higher incomes. In terms of healthcare spending, it would

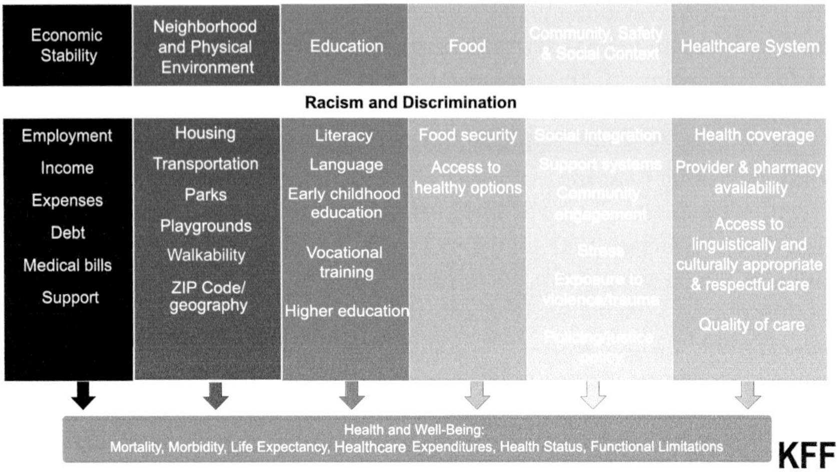

FIGURE 5.7 Health Disparities Are Driven by Social and Economic Inequities.

Source: Adapted from KFF

seem as if this analogy would make sense, yet in the United States, it actually does not. Of the 17 wealthiest countries in the world, the United States ranks 14th in mortality from communicable disease, 16th in mortality from noncommunicable disease, 16th in life expectancy at birth for females and 17th for males, and last in the probability of survival to age 50 (Freeman, 2015). Figure 5.8 shows the relationship between the amount of money spent on healthcare by OECD countries and life expectancy. The United States clearly spends the most on healthcare at approximately $8,000 per capita annually, yet we rank last among the OECD countries in life expectancy. In fact, life expectancy in the United States only exceeds a small number of OECD countries who each spend less than $2,000 per capita annually (Freeman, 2015).

One is forced to ask, how has the US healthcare system gotten so poorly managed and administered leading to such poor outcomes? According to Bataldan's Law, "every system is perfectly designed to get the results that it gets" (Batalden & Buchanan, 1989). The healthcare system in the United States has been built to increase profits and revenues in favor of saving lives and providing better health outcomes for individuals. Freeman (2015) says that the healthcare system was not necessarily designed in a particular way, but that "it grew, and it grew in response to forces that are not about justice, not about equity, and not always or even mostly about health for our entire population" (Freeman, 2015, p. 9).

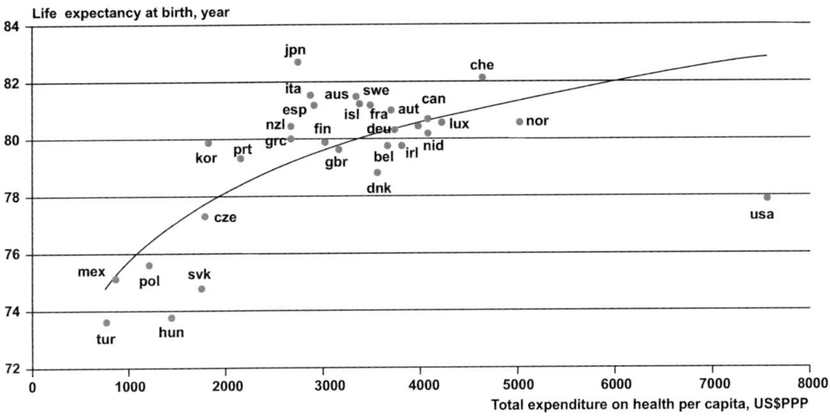

FIGURE 5.8 There Are Large Differences in Life Expectancy and Healthcare Spending Across OECD Countries. 2010 or Latest Year Available

Source: Adapted from OECD Health Data 2010

According to the Centers for Disease Control and Prevention (CDC), health equity is

> the state in which everyone has a fair and just opportunity to attain their highest level of health. Achieving this requires ongoing societal efforts to: Address historical and contemporary injustices; Overcome economic, social and other obstacles to health and health care; and eliminate preventable health disparities.
>
> *(Office of Disease Prevention and Health Promotion, 2021; Braveman et al., 2017)*

The CDC's definition of health equity is similar to the definition of justice espoused by theorist John Rawls where he states:

> All social primary goods—liberty and opportunity, income and wealth, and the bases of self-respect—are to be distributed equally unless an unequal distribution of any or all of these goods is to the advantage of the least favored.

The part of Rawls' definition that most closely resembles how we describe equity is *unless an unequal distribution of any or all of these goods is to the advantage of the least favored.* Equity does not aim to distribute goods and opportunities equally among recipients. Eliminating inequity in healthcare seeks to help those who are most disadvantaged, and who live lives adversely impacted by not being able to attain proper healthcare. Essentially, a key component of equity in healthcare seeks to help those who have been forgotten and neglected.

In the United States, Black, Hispanic/Latine, and Indigenous people were 2.5 times more likely than Whites to be hospitalized as a result of contracting Covid-19, and 17 times more likely to die from it (Cui et al., 2023).

Prenatal care and pregnancy

Another health outcome that shows enormous disparities and inequities is prenatal care and pregnancies. Disturbingly, the United States has the highest infant mortality rate among high-income countries. What makes these numbers and rates most astounding is that the United States spends more money on healthcare than all of the OECD nations.

According to Gunja et al. (2023), the United States spends far more per person and as a share of Gross Domestic Product (GDP) than other "high-income" nations. Between 1980 and 2021, the United States spent 17.8% of GDP on health, while during the same time period, the U.K. spent 11.9% of GDP on health, Switzerland 11.8% and Sweden 11.4%. In comparison, the average percent of GDP spent on health by OECD countries was 9.6% during the same time period. In a country like the United States where many expect to have the best of everything, it remains a mystery as to why healthcare, in general, and prenatal care specifically, yields such poor outcomes. It is estimated that over 700 women die from maternal causes and 40,000–50,000 suffer from maternal morbidities annually (Valerio et al., 2023). Figure 5.9 shows the maternal mortality rate of 13 OECD countries in 2020. While the OECD average is 9.8, the rate in the United States is more than double and stands at 23.8.

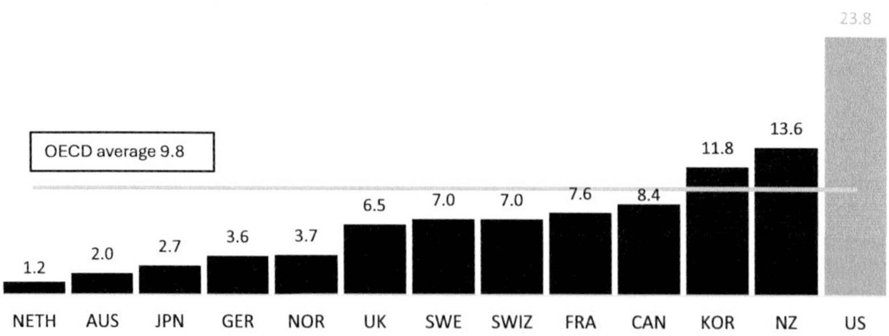

FIGURE 5.9 Maternal Mortality, Deaths per 100,000 Live Births.

Source: Gunja et al. (2022)

What is more confounding is the maternal morbidity rates of non-White women in the United States. Morbidity is a measure that tracks illness or disease among a population or sample. Black women are two to three times more likely than non-Hispanic/Latine White women to experience severe maternal morbidity (Valerio et al., 2023). When we examine US maternal mortality, which measures deaths among a population or sample, we notice that Black women, and most other women of color, have higher pregnancy-related mortality rates than White women. According to the CDC's Pregnancy-Related Mortality Ratio (PRMR) (pregnancy-related deaths per 100,000 live births) between 2011 and 2015, the national PRMR was 17.2 per 100,000 live births. At the same time, Black women had a PRMR of 42.8 and Native American/Alaska Native women's rate was 32.5. Each of these figures was significantly higher than White women's PRMR which was 13.0. During the same time period, Asian/Pacific Islander PRMR was 14.2 and Hispanic/Latine women's ratio was 11.4. Petersen et al. (2019). Overall, Black women are two to three times more likely to experience maternal death than non-Hispanic/Latine White women. While we acknowledge that race is a social construct, and that there are no genetic or biological reasons to suggest that Black women, in general, have more problems with pregnancies than White women, it does beg the question, "Why do the outcomes for Black and White women differ so greatly?"

These are questions that there are few answers for. Unfortunately, for many Black women and their families, maternal morbidity and mortality are much more commonplace and tolerated than they ever should be. In 2023, Tori Bowie died from complications related to childbirth. She was 32 years old and eight months pregnant at the time. What makes this case different from the countless other Black women who have died from complications related to childbirth is the fact that Tori Bowie was a world champion sprinter and three-time Olympic medalist (Da Silva, 2023). According to the Orange County, Florida Medical Examiner's Office, Bowie showed evidence that she was in labor at the time of her death (Da Silva, 2023). Tori Bowie's autopsy indicated that eclampsia and respiratory distress likely caused her death. Research has also found that eclampsia (and preeclampsia) can potentially lead to hypertension and other cardiovascular issues well after women have given birth. "Preeclampsia is associated with a 4-fold increase in future incident heart failure and a 2-fold increased risk in coronary heart disease, stroke, and death because of coronary heart or cardiovascular disease" (Wu et al., 2017, p. 1). According to the Mayo Clinic, eclampsia can occur without any previous signs or symptoms of preeclampsia, such as seizures, severe headaches, vision problems or mental confusion (*Preeclampsia*, retrieved from https://

www.mayoclinic.org/diseases-conditions/preeclampsia/symptoms-causes/syc-20355745 on August 2023).

Some have espoused the view that Black women are "valued" less by their respective doctors and healthcare providers, thus leading to a decreased lack of attention during this critical and potentially life-threatening point in their (and their unborn child's) lives. After repeated visits to the hospital, being diagnosed with "false labor" and told to return home, Brooke Smith delivered a stillbirth baby girl in 2014 (Eldeib, 2022). Brooke Smith would later go on to say, "But if you're a Black woman, you get dismissed because it's like, 'What are you complaining about now?'" (Eldeib, 2022). Black women are twice as likely, than White women, to have a stillbirth and in South Carolina, Tennessee and Kansas, that number increases to three times. Moreover, in 2020, the stillbirth rate for White women in the United States was 4.7, while the rate for Black women was more than double at 10.7 (Eldeib, 2022).

Another health inequity issue is the ability of women to find providers in close proximity to their homes when they reside in rural communities. According to Hassanein (2022), approximately 2 million women, who are of "childbearing" ages, live more than 25 miles from labor and delivery units. Moreover, hospitals and obstetric wards are already scarce in rural areas, and they are continuously shut down (Hassanein, 2022). Valerio et al. (2023) found that the level of healthcare afforded differed depending on what U.S. county women resided in. According to their study, vulnerabilities in reproductive healthcare and general healthcare were highest in southern states (Valerio et al., 2023). Figure 5.10 shows the maternal

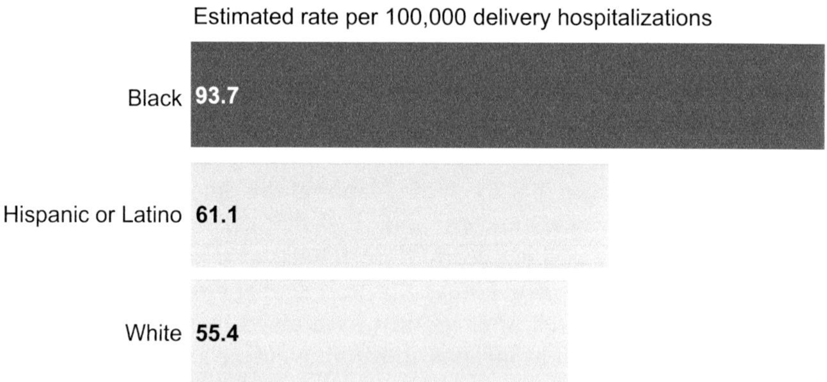

FIGURE 5.10 National Estimated Rates of Severe Maternal Morbidity in Rural Areas by Race and Ethnicity, 2016–2018. Estimated Rate per 100,000 Delivery Hospitalizations

Source: Adapted from GAO analysis of Agency for Healthcare Research and quality's Healthcare Cost and Utilization Project National Inpatient Sample data

morbidity rate in rural areas for Black, Latine/Hispanic and White women between 2016 and 2018. The rate for White women during this time stood at 55.4 per 100,000 delivery hospitalizations, while the rate for Latine/Hispanic women was 61.1 and for Black women it was 93.7.

Infant mortality inequity

The rate of infant mortality in the United States is just as grim as other vital health statistics and again, data from the U.S. is among the worst of all OECD countries. In 2020, of the 13 OECD nations examined by Gunja et al. (2023), the infant mortality rate in the United States was 5.4. This number was higher than all other comparator countries, and higher than Germany and Japan combined.

Following the same sad pattern, Black infants are two to two-and-a-half times more likely to die within their first year than White infants are (Florido, 2014). Again, the social determinants of health and healthcare

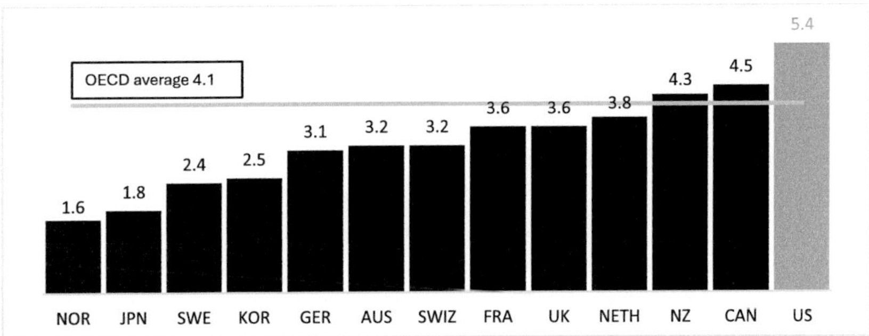

FIGURE 5.11 Infant Mortality, Deaths per 1,000 Live Births.

Source: Gunja et al. (2022)

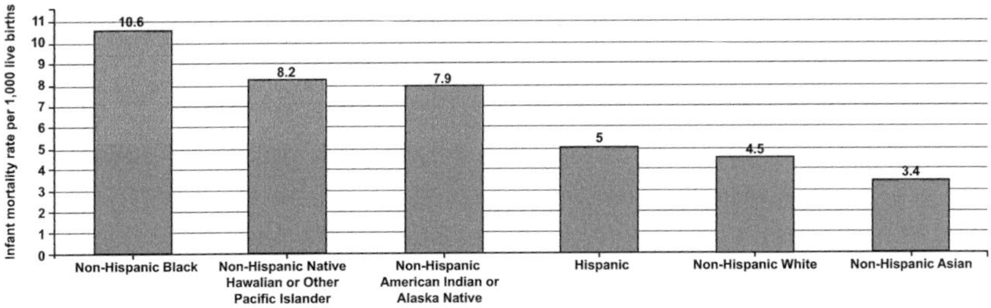

FIGURE 5.12 Infant Mortality Rates by Race and Ethnicity, 2019.

Source: Adapted from Centers for Disease Control and Prevention, 2019

play a role in these inequitable outcomes, but not to the degree one would expect.

Organizational changes that can close racial gaps in healthcare outcomes

There is a great deal of work that must be done to ensure that everyone receives proper healthcare, feels valued and is respected by their healthcare professionals. If this can be achieved, it will ultimately lead to a decrease in inequities. It must be remembered that individuals are entrusting doctors, nurses, and those who work in hospitals with their lives and the lives of their loved ones. Unfortunately, the Covid-19 pandemic exacerbated the inequities in healthcare that have existed for a long time. A great deal of work must be done for improvements to be made in healthcare delivery and no singular solution will fix this problem. Cui et al. (2023) suggest a three-pronged approach to address healthcare inequities in the United States that include making equity a nonnegotiable object in every aspect of the process. "Aligning on a clear definition of health equity goals—including how they are measured—is a critical first step in this approach" (Cui et al., 2023, p. 2). The second part of their suggested approach is to embrace new ways of working, which includes empowering change from the top, adapting governance and decision-making, and creating a collaborative and interdisciplinary working model. The final prong in their approach is simply to "walk the talk." So many times we see examples of stated efforts being made by organizations to address diversity, equity, inclusion and accessibility, but oftentimes it does not lead to improvements, nor sustained success. Attaining health equity success requires a long-term approach and a strong commitment from all parties and not the ready, aim, study more approach that commonly plagues organizations when it comes to improving equity. Attainable goals should be set that result in data collection and analysis. "Data can be a powerful tool for organizations to use to establish a robust, fact base, to create transparency around equity outcomes, and to myth-bust perceived roadblocks or misinformation" (Cui et al., 2023, p. 4).

A structural change that can decrease healthcare inequity is for hospitals to begin assessing their own financial conditions. While there are many examples of methods relied upon to assess fiscal conditions at the local and state levels of government, there is scant evidence of fiscal assessment occurring for hospitals in the United States. Slowly, the fiscal performance of hospitals, in particular those that primarily serve disadvantaged populations, has increasingly begun to gain more attention. An important element in determining a jurisdiction's fiscal condition is a consideration of its overall level of fiscal sustainability. Crosby and Robbins (2013) define fiscal sustainability as the ability of a jurisdiction to pay its bills today, tomorrow and beyond. Fiscal sustainability as it relates to hospitals that serve disadvantaged populations needs to pay yet even closer attention to their respective "bottom lines." While governments' purpose is not to earn significant profits, they do aim to be profitable so that they can effectively and efficiently deliver more and better services to the public. Profitability ratios help public-sector organizations assess the extent to which they are profitable and, most importantly, fiscally healthy. A common profitability ratio is the *total margin* which compares the excess of revenues over expenses with total revenues. Additionally, hospitals and healthcare providers should be keenly aware of issues surrounding their long-term solvency such as *days of cash on hand*. The days of cash on hand ratio is calculated by dividing cash, and cash equivalents, by the daily operating expenses that require payment. The days of cash on hand compares cash and marketable securities with daily operating expenses (Finkler et al., 2016). This ratio assesses the length of time a hospital would be able to meet its typical expenses by using just the cash, along with near cash assets, on hand. Days of cash on hand is an important assessment tool because it tells us if future cash inflows were eliminated how long the hospital could meet its cash outflows with just the resources it has on hand. For organizations and hospitals that serve the neediest of populations, assessing days of cash on hand is essential for patients and the hospital's own survival.

Conclusion

The value of healthcare cannot be overstated, but *effective* healthcare administration is even more critical. We have discussed the importance of healthcare in this chapter and have carefully outlined the significant role the Affordable Care Act has played in improving health outcomes for millions of Americans since its adoption. Despite hostility and resistance to the ACA, we are a much healthier country because of it, but there still is a great deal of work that must be done-especially in the areas of prenatal care. While a great deal of recent attention has been made of the overall inefficiency of government, no area is more ripe for an efficiency improvement than is healthcare. The U.S. spends a great deal more money on healthcare, but the results simply do not match. In fact, one would be challenged to better understand how we could be so inept at inadequately ensuring better health for Americans. In addition to the inefficiency of our healthcare system, inequity is prevalent in all areas of illness and disease. What then are next steps? Clearly, strategies need to be made by government and nonprofit organizations, along with firms to eliminate inequity in healthcare. One area where these three sectors can help decrease inequity in healthcare is in housing. In developed countries, like the United States, housing policies, administration and development originate from a variety of sources. Organizations and groups such as the Federal Housing Administration (FHA) and Housing and Urban Development (HUD), nonprofit organizations such as Habitat-for-Humanity and Mercy Housing and firms such as Citigroup can have a meaningful impact on reducing such inequities. In 2011, the British Medical Association (BMA) published a report Social Determinants of Health: What Can Doctors Do? A key area of the report discussed ways to address "cold housing," and how the temperature in homes is related to an individual's health. Among other things, the BMA report found that countries that had more energy-efficient housing had lower excess winter deaths (EWD's); EWD's are three times higher during the coldest time of year as opposed to the warmest time of year; 40% of EWD's are the result of cardiovascular disease and 33% from respiratory disease. The report pointed out that investing in energy-efficient housing can not only reduce health and housing inequities but it could also help stimulate the economy.

In order to address all of these concerns, a collective effort must occur that includes overhauling legislation, similar to what ACA did. This time, however, the healthcare policy must take into consideration how spending will lead to improved, equitable results for all Americans, but particularly for the poor and traditionally marginalized.

References

Batalden, P. B., & Buchanan, E. D. (1989). Industrial models of quality improvement. In N. Goldfield & D. Nash (Eds.), *Providing quality care: The challenge to clinicians*. American College of Physicians.

Board of Governors of the Federal Reserve System – Consumer & Community Context (2024). https://www.federalreserve.gov/publications/consumer-community-context.htm

Braveman, P., Arkin, E., Orleans, T., Proctor, D., & Plough, A. (2017). *What is health equity? And what difference does a definition make?* Robert Wood Johnson Foundation.

Center on Budget and Policy Priorities (CBPP). (2020). *Chart book: The far-reaching benefits of the affordable care Act's Medicaid expansion*. https://www.cbpp.org/

research/health/chart-book-the-far-reaching-benefits-of-the-affordable-care-acts-medicaid-expansion

Crosby, A., & Robbins, D. (2013). Mission impossible: Monitoring municipal fiscal sustainability and stress in Michigan. *Journal of Public Budgeting, Accounting and Financial Management*, *25*, 522–555.

Cui, A., Feehan, E., Julien, J. P., & Nagarajan, N. (2023). *Reimagining public health programs to deliver equitable impact*. McKinsey & Company.

Dalen, J. E., Waterbrook, K., & Alpert, J. S. (2015). Why do so many Americans oppose the Affordable Care Act? *American Journal of Medicine*, *128*(8), 807–810.

Da Silva, C. (2023). Olympic sprinter Tori Bowie died from childbirth complications, autopsy finds. *NBC News*. https://www.nbcnews.com/news/us-news/olympic-sprinter-tori-bowie-died-childbirth-complications-autopsy-rcna88995

Eldeib, D. (2022). She says doctors ignored her concerns about her pregnancy. For many Black women, it's a familiar story. *Propublica*. https://www.propublica.org/article/stillbirths-pregnancy-mothers-parents-racial-disparities

Fingerhut, H. (2017). *Support for 2010 health care law reaches new high*. Pew Research Center.

Finkler, S., Calabrese, T., & Smith, D. (2016). *Financial management for public, health, and not-for-profit organizations*. CQ Press.

Florido, A. (2014). Why do black infants die so much more often than white infants? *NPR—Morning Edition*. https://www.kpcc.org/news/2014/03/03/42483/why-do-black-infants-die-so-much-more-often-than-w/

Freeman, J. (2015). *Health, medicine and justice—Designing a fair and equitable healthcare system*. Copernicus Healthcare.

Gunja, M. Z., Gumas, E. D., & Williams, R. D. II. (2023). U.S. health care from a global perspective, 2022: Accelerating spending, worsening outcomes. *Issue Brief (Commonwealth Fund)*. https://doi.org/10.26099/8ejy-yc74

Hassanein, N. (2022). In rural America, maternal health care is vanishing. These moms are most at risk. *USA Today*. https://www.usatoday.com/in-depth/news/health/2022/08/11/maternal-health-care-disparities-people-of-color-rural-america/10086706002/

Ndugga, N., & Artiga, S. (2023). *Disparities in health and health care: 5 key questions and answers*. https://www.kff.org/racial-equity-and-health-policy/issue-brief/disparities-in-health-and-health-care-5-key-question-and-answers/

Office of Disease Prevention and Health Promotion. (2021). *Healthy people 2020: Disparities*. U.S. Department of Health and Human Services. https://www.healthypeople.gov/2020/about/foundation-health-measures/Disparities

Petersen, E., Davis, N., Goodman, D., Cox, S., Mayes, N., Johnston, E., Syverson, C., Seed, K., Shapiro-Mendoza, C., Callaghan, W., & Barfield, W. (2019). Vital signs: Pregnancy-related deaths, United States 2011–2015, and strategies for prevention, 13 states, 2013–2017. *U.S. Department of Health and Human Services/Centers for Disease Control and Prevention*, *68*(18).

US Department of Health and Human Services. (2022). *New reports show record 35 million people enrolled in coverage related to the Affordable Care Act, with Historic 21 million people enrolled in Medicaid expansion coverage*. https://www.hhs.gov/about/news/2022/04/29/new-reports-show-record-35-million-people-enrolled-in-coverage-related-to-the-affordable-care-act.html

Valerio, V. C., Downey, J., Sgaier, S. K., Callaghan, W. M., Hammer, B., & Smittenaar, P. (2023). Black-White disparities in maternal vulnerability and adverse pregnancy outcomes: An ecological population study in the United States, 2014–2018. *The Lancet Regional Health - Americas*, *20*, 100456.

Virchow, R. C. (2006). Report on the typhus epidemic in Upper Silesia. 1848. *American Journal of Public Health*, *96*(12), 2102–2105. https://doi.org/10.2105/ajph.96.12.2102

Wu, P., Haththotuwa, R., Kwok, C. S., Babu, A., Kotronias, R. A., Rushton, C., Zaman, A., Fryer, A., Kadam, U., Chew-Graham, C., & Mamas, M. A. (2017). Preeclampsia and future cardiovascular health—A systematic review and meta-analysis. *Circulation*, *10*(2). https://doi.org/10.1161/CIRCOUTCOMES.116.003497

Yaraghi, N. (2014). Have the anti-Obamacare ads backfired? *Brookings*. https://www.brookings.edu/articles/have-the-anti-obamacare-ads-backfired/

6

HOUSING

In 2021, Nathan Connolly and Shani Mott placed their Homeland, Maryland house on the market for sale. When their home was appraised for $472,000, they felt as if it was lower than other similar homes on the market. While they did not want to assume that the low valuation was solely because the appraiser was White and they were Black, they decided to conduct an experiment. The couple removed all pictures of themselves in the home and anything that would indicate that a Black family lived there. When the home was reappraised, without any racially identifying pictures, their home was appraised for $750,000, nearly $300,000 more than the original appraisal.

In 2020, Marin City, California couple Paul and Tenisha Austin sought to have their home appraised in an effort to refinance the mortgage. They had bought their home in 2016 for $550,000. In the four years they lived there, their home underwent significant renovations which included expanding the total square footage by 270 feet. They also refinished floors along with upgrading appliances and fixtures. When their home was appraised, they too felt as if the $995,000 appraisal amount was below market value. The Austins conducted a similar experiment as Connolly and Mott by removing photos of themselves along with all African-American artwork. Additionally, they asked a White friend to greet the appraiser along with placing photos of her family in their home. The result of the Austins experiment was similar to that of Connolly and Mott which saw the reappraisal price soar to a whopping $1,482,500, which was nearly $500,000 more than the original appraisal. If these examples were outliers, or events that occurred with irregularity, it would be simple to disregard them as such.

DOI: 10.4324/9781032670850-7

Unfortunately, these are not outliers, nor irregular and in fact, examples like these occur with much more frequency than most people are aware of.

The "experiment" that both homeowners conducted is considered "whitewashing," where Blacks and people of color remove pictures, images, artwork and other items in their home that would lead someone else, in this case an appraiser, to believe that a White individual or family lived there. According to Paige Glotzer, the John W. and Jeanne M. Rowe Chair in the department of History of American Politics, Institutions, and Political Economy at University of Wisconsin-Madison, and author of *How the Suburbs Were Segregated: Developers and the Business of Exclusionary Housing—1890–1960,* "If you whitewash your house, you're going in with historical awareness of what is it that your average kind of White appraiser would want to see" (Davis et al., 2022). What Glotzer is describing is the concept of implicit bias. Implicit bias are associations between concepts that are activated automatically and it is an internal process. It is one type of bias that may occur unintentionally (Forscher & Devine, 2017). Devine (1989) states that implicit bias is developed early in one's life from continuously being exposed to stereotypical information, thus it can be assumed to be learned behavior. Implicit biases become so well-rehearsed, from being exposed to stereotypical information of a particular group that they are triggered or stimulated unintentionally. Once the biases are stimulated, it is theorized that they "affect behavior in situations where people lack motivation, awareness, or the ability to think about their responses" (Forscher & Devine, 2017, p. 1). While this may be the case in some of the devaluations of home appraisals for Blacks and people of color, it does not completely dismiss the strong evidence of racist policies and actions that have made housing in the United States so inequitable.

Valuation gap by race

Mortgage leader Freddie Mac examined whether, or not, a gap in the appraised value and the contracted price of homes in various property tracks across the United States existed among Whites, Hispanics/Latines and Blacks. Freddie Mac was chartered by Congress in 1970 to support the US housing finance system and to help ensure a reliable and affordable supply of mortgage funds across the country. Rather than lending directly to borrowers, Freddie Mac operates in the US secondary mortgage market, buying loans that meet their standards from approved lenders (About Freddie Mac, retrieved, September 2023 from https://www.freddiemac.com/about). Property tracks were classified based upon the minority share of the population from the 2010 Census data. The threshold to define a minority track was 50%, whether that be Black or Hispanic/Latine. If the total minority population was less than 50%, the track was classified as White. They additionally classified Black and Hispanic/Latine tracks as:

[50%–80%] if the Black (or Latino) share is≥ 50% and < 80%
[80%–100%] if the Black (or Latino) share is ≥ 80%

The results of their study indicated that 7.4% of appraisals for White homes were less than the contracted price. In comparison, appraisals for Black homes were 12.5% below the contracted price and for Hispanic/Latine homes appraisals versus the contracted price grew to 15.4% (Freddie Mac, 2021). Table 6.1 shows the devaluation of homes based upon the racial composition of communities between 2015 and 2021.

Devaluation refers to "the percent discount in median home values between neighborhoods with 50% Black population and neighborhoods with no Black residents, after accounting for structural characteristics of homes and neighborhood amenities" (Perry et al., 2018). Structural characteristics of homes are the year the home was built, total square feet and the number of rooms and bedrooms. The quality of public education, access to employment and commute times, walkability and accessibility to retail are included in the definition of neighborhood amenities (Perry et al., 2018). Taken collectively, structural characteristics and neighborhood amenities are the only variables, or factors, that should be considered when appraising the value of a home.

Figure 6.1 depicts mean home appraisals in White neighborhoods and those in communities of color. Howell and Korver-Glenn (2021) found that the "neighborhood racial inequity in home appraisals was twice as large in 2015 as it was in 1980" (p. 1062).

TABLE 6.1 Appraisal Gaps in White, Latiné and Black Communities 2015–2021

Property Tract	*Count*	*% Lower Than Contract Price*	*Gap v. White*
Overall	12,752,779	8.3%	–
White	10,632,616	7.4%	–
Latino/a/é [50%–100%]	**553,470**	**15.4%**	**8.0**
Latino/a/é [50%–80%]	443,218	15.0%	7.7%
Latino/a/é [80%–100%]	110,252	16.7%	9.4%
Black [50%–100%]	**373,747**	**12.5%**	**5.2%**
Black [50%–80%]	245,428	12.1%	4.8%
Black [80%–100%]	128,319	13.3%	5.9%

Source: Appraisals for the purchase of single-family or one-unit homes January 1, 2015–December 31, 2021 (Adapted from Freddie Mac, 2021)

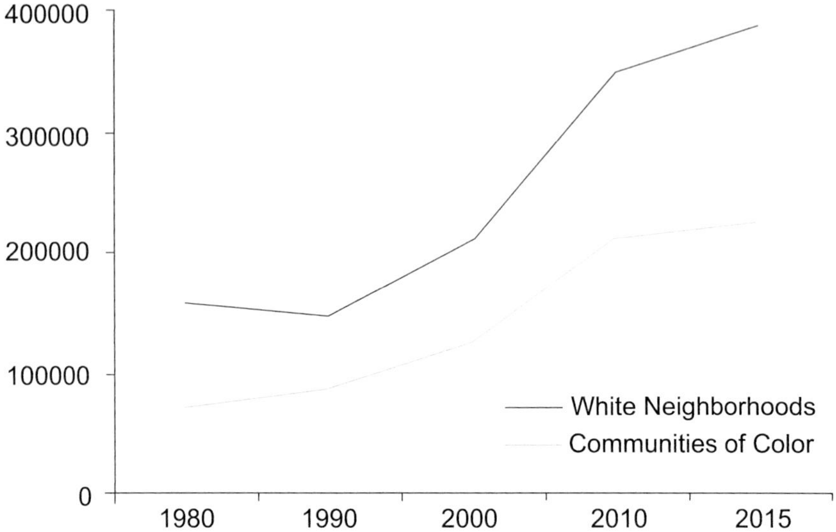

FIGURE 6.1 Mean Home Appraisals for White Neighborhoods and Communities of Color—1980–2015.

Source: Adapted from Howell and Korver-Glenn (2021)

What do lower valuations of Black homes mean from a financial standpoint? Rothwell and Perry (2022) estimate that this amounts to a deficit of $48,000 per home and $156 billion cumulatively in Black neighborhoods. Inequities in home appraisals not only affect the current value of the home and potential resale, and or, refinancing opportunities but they impede home wealth accumulation. Howell and Korver-Glenn (2021) found that in 1980 a home located in a 100% Black or Hispanic/Latine community would be valued at $94,000 (real dollars), but the same house in a community with 0% Black or Hispanic/Latine population would be worth $145,000 as shown in Figure 6.2. By 2015, the same homes would be valued at $125,000 in a 100% Black or Hispanic/Latine community, but valued at $370,000 in a community absent of Black and Hispanic/Latine residents. In other words, homes in White communities were worth $245,000 more than comparable homes in communities of color (Howell & Korver-Glenn, 2021), thus demonstrating the widening of housing inequities between the years 1980 and 2015.

Examining the devaluation of homes in communities where the majority of residents are Black continues to highlight housing inequities and disparities. The Brookings Institution created an interactive map that shows the median home value, the estimated median home value in the absence

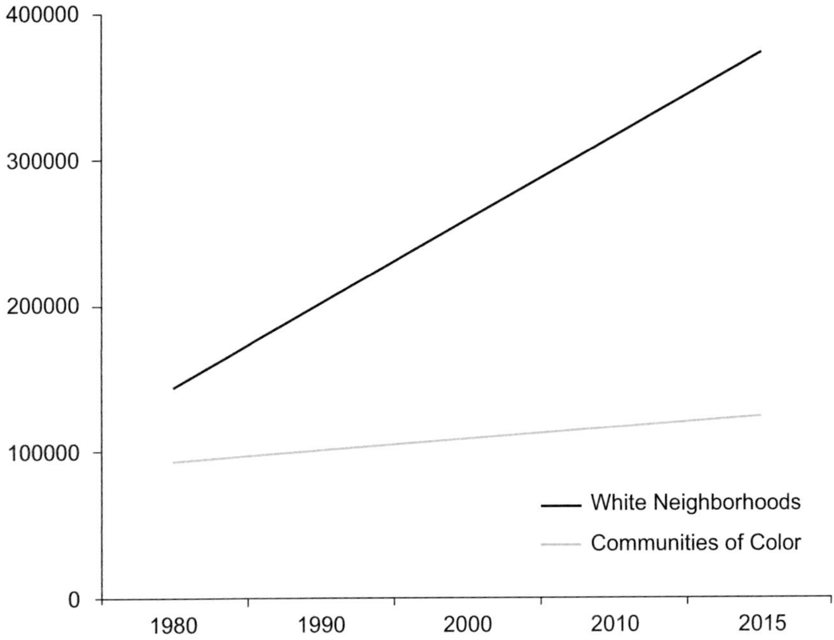

FIGURE 6.2 Predicted Average Appraised Values for Comparable Homes in Comparable Neighborhoods in an Average Metropolitan Area—1980 and 2015.

Source: Adapted from Howell and Korver-Glenn (2021)

of devaluation and the percentage that homes in Black communities were devalued. The interactive map also shows the percentage of the population that is Black in those cities as well. Figure 6.3 shows eight US cities from Brookings interactive map.

Narragon et al. (2021) found that even beyond structural characteristics and neighborhood amenities, the race and ethnicity of individuals do in fact explain appraisal gaps. For example, when appraisals were conducted for White and Black homes by the same appraiser, and where the homes had similar structural characteristics and neighborhood amenities, the valuation of White homes was higher than those of Black homes 85% of the time and 74% of the time when comparing White and Latine home appraisals (Narragon et al., 2021). The lack of wealth that is not accumulated based upon these estimations is enormous because it also means that less resources are available to make substantive changes in these communities. Such changes could improve schools, hospitals, roads, infrastructure and economic development opportunities that would make the communities more desirable places to live.

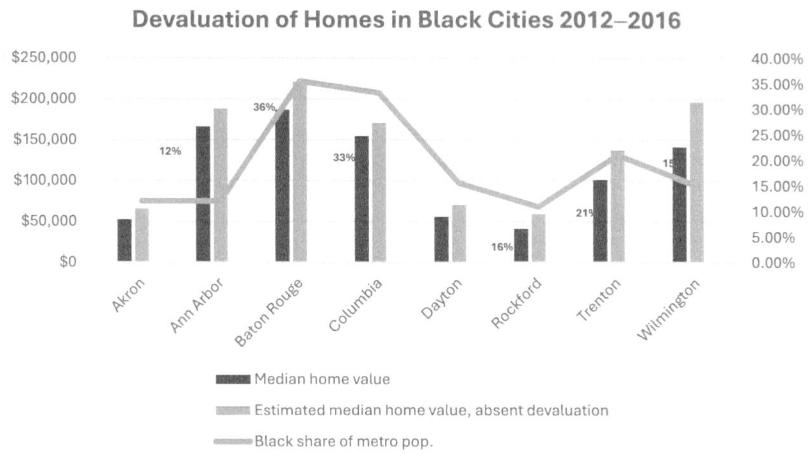

FIGURE 6.3 Devaluation of Homes in Black Cities 2012–2016.

Source: Adapted from Perry et al. (2018)

Home values are strongly correlated with neighborhood racial composition, and inequalities are influenced by historical segregation, socioeconomic factors, real estate demand and contemporary appraising practices. Inequality in home characteristics between White and Black neighborhoods explained 39% of racial inequality in home appraisals in 1980, but only explained 18% of racial inequality in home appraisals in 2015 (Howell & Korver-Glenn, 2021). In terms of socioeconomic inequality, in 1980, housing characteristics and neighborhood socioeconomic status explained over 80% of the racial inequities but in 2015 these two variables only explained 36% of racial inequality in home appraisals, thus 64% were due to something else. Real estate demand was also found not to be an accurate predictor of home appraisal discrepancies. As the Black and Hispanic/Latine population increases, so too do inequities between White home appraisals and those of Black and Hispanic/Latine communities. When we examine homes with the same value but compare those with communities with a decreasing percentage of Black and Hispanic/Latine residents and those with increasing Black and Hispanic/Latine population, the communities with a decreasing percentage of Black and Hispanic/Latine residents saw their appraisal value increase by $73,000 (Howell & Korver-Glenn, 2021). The homes in the communities where the Black and Hispanic/Latine percentage of residents increased saw their home appraisal value decrease by $22,000 (nearly a $100,000 difference). "This suggests that the sales comparison approach—the most used method for contemporary residential appraisals—perpetuates inequities through maintaining historical hierarchies and current racialized definitions of comparability" (Howell & Korver-Glenn, 2021, p. 1067). Two questions emerge: what are the causes of housing inequity in the United States and why have those inequities been so persistent over time? "Even after holding housing and neighborhood socioeconomic status constant, these real dollar differences are substantial. Moreover, they have significant implications for ongoing racial wealth gaps, intergenerational mobility, residential stability, educational achievement, and employment opportunities" (Howell & Korver-Glenn, 2021, p. 1063). Further, depriving Black's, Latinas and other people of color equal opportunities to enter into the housing (and real estate) market, like White families, severely depresses the ability to build equity and generational wealth.

Instead of decreasing, data consistently shows that inequity is not only pervasive but getting worse. Despite proclamations touting the advances the United States has made in terms of racial equality, housing continues to be plagued by a history of racist policies and practices. Instead of evidence demonstrating the gap in housing equity decreasing between Whites, Blacks, Hispanics/Latines and people of color, in the area of home appraisals, those gaps are widening (Howell & Korver-Glenn).

To understand housing inequity more fully, it is critical to gain a better understanding of the history of housing policies and practices in the United States.

History of racist housing policies

Wallace Stegner, Pulitzer Prize winner and known as the "dean of Western writers," started the Creative Writing Program and Writing Fellowships at Stanford in 1964 (Wallace Stegner biography retrieved from https://wallacestegner.org/bio.html). This prestigious fellowship offers accepted applicants $50,000 per year, for two years, with the aim "of providing young, talented writers the guidance, encouragement, and funding to further their writing knowledge and craft" (History of the Stanford Creative Writing Program: https://creativewriting.stanford.edu/about/history-stanford-creative-writing-program). As he was beginning his job as a professor at Stanford University, Stegner joined a cooperative known as the Peninsula Housing Association of Palo Alto. Housing was difficult to come by then and the cooperative primarily consisted of middle and working-class families in Palo Alto who sought available housing in the area. Because the majority of resources spent during World War II were used for military use, the US government forbade resident housing construction unless it was designated for the defense industry (Rothstein, 2017). The cooperative included 150 families, of which 3 were Black. While the cooperative purchased 260 acres of land near Stanford University with the idea of building 400 homes, along with recreational and commercial facilities, the Federal Housing Association (FHA) would not insure loans for homes that included members who were Black. Since banks would not guarantee loans nor finance construction without government approval, the cooperative was never able to secure homes as they had sought. This is another example of a US government organization, the FHA, that would not insure mortgages for Black residents. What other options would one have if they were Black and wanted to finance the purchase of a home? Short of paying the full asking price, there was nothing else that could be done, thus the FHA absolutely contributed to housing inequity in the United States and its complicit fingerprints helped to architect the racially segregated communities we see across the country today. Unfortunately for many, including Stegner and the cooperative, the FHA had been relying on racist policies for many years and would continue doing so for years to come.

As the United States was experiencing the worst economic downturn in its history, the calls for government intervention grew louder and louder. Because of unprecedented unemployment during the Great Depression, individuals were facing extreme difficulties making mortgage payments and paying their sales contract obligations (Harriss, 1951). The issues related to the Depression ultimately led to tax delinquencies, mortgage defaults and home foreclosures (Harriss, 1951). Thus, in response to these issues, and President Franklin Delano Roosevelt insisted to "protect the small homeowner from foreclosure, and relieve him of part of the burden of excessive interest and principal payments incurred during the period of higher values and higher earning power" (Harriss, 1951, p. 9), led to the creation of the Home Ownership Loan Corporation (HOLC). The HOLC and the creation of the Federal Housing Administration (FHA) in 1934 represented New Deal era programs that aimed to assist current homeowners and future buyers (https://www.hud.gov/program_offices/housing/fhahistory). In stark contrast to the mortgage industry at the time, the HOLC and the FHA introduced innovative loan programs that made fully amortized loans available over a 25-year period (Crossney & Bartelt, 2005). "This replaced the previous private and locally-based system in which mortgages were usually made only for five to ten years, at the end of which a 'balloon' payment, covering the entirety of the principal, was due" (Mitchell & Franco, 2018, p. 6). To assist appraisers in determining the approximate value of homes, the HOLC classified neighborhoods in different colors based upon four criteria: the best, or the top-ranking neighborhoods, were color-coded green and consisted primarily of wealthy White neighborhoods. Second in ranking were neighborhoods that we considered

"Still desirable" and were colored blue. Blue neighborhoods primarily consisted of middle-class White families. The third category colored yellow was referred to as "Definitely Declining," and consisted of racially mixed neighborhoods. The fourth category of neighborhoods was termed "Hazardous" and was colored red. These areas included impoverished Black and Brown residents (Howell & Korver-Glenn, 2021). Figures 6.4–6.8 are examples of HOLC maps for the cities of Atlanta, GA (1938), Los Angeles, CA (1939), Brooklyn, NY (1938), Pittsburgh, PA (1940) and Chicago, IL. (1940). As you can see, the pervasive nature of the HOLCs racist and inequitable scheme crossed many US cities. While these are only a small selection of maps that show redlining, this practice undoubtedly occurred

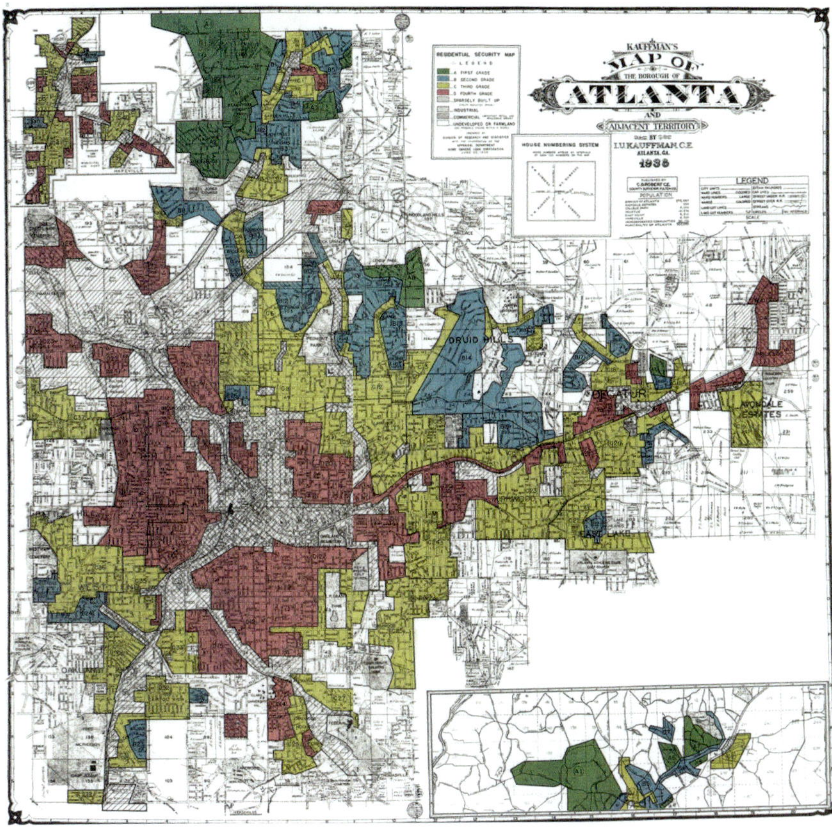

FIGURE 6.4 Home Ownership Loan Corporation Redlining Map, Atlanta, GA 1938.

Source: Nelson, R. K., Winling, L., et al. (2023). *Mapping Inequality: Redlining in New Deal America*. Digital Scholarship Lab. https://dsl.richmond.edu/panorama/redlining

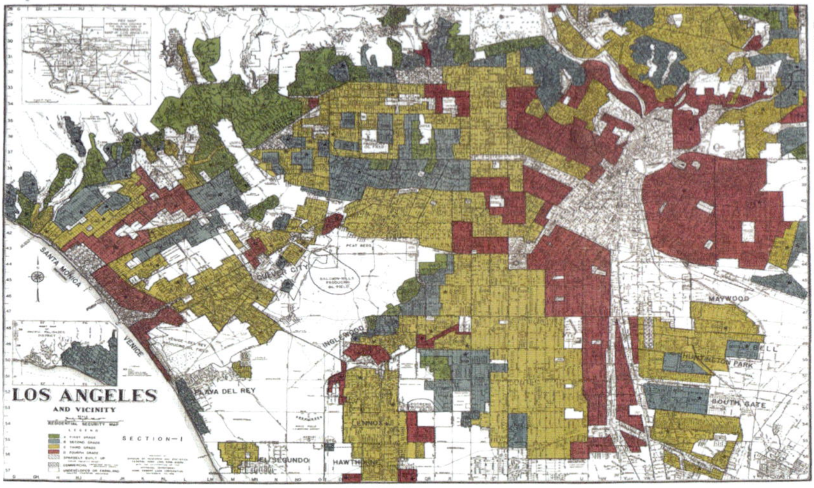

FIGURE 6.5 Home Ownership Loan Corporation Redlining Map, Los Angeles, CA 1939.

Source: Nelson, R. K., Winling, L., et al. (2023). *Mapping Inequality: Redlining in New Deal America*. Digital Scholarship Lab. https://dsl.richmond.edu/panorama/redlining

for the majority of cities in the United States. On the city of Los Angeles map, it states that it was produced by *The Division of Research and Statistics—Federal Home Loan Bank Board With the Cooperation of the Appraisal Department Home Loan Owners Corporation*. You will notice the four colored areas: green (best), blue (still desirable), yellow (declining) and red (hazardous).

Using these maps as guidelines for cities across the United States, homes in White neighborhoods were consistently appraised at higher values and worth significantly more than homes in the other categories, but worse yet, homes in Black and Brown neighborhoods that were colored red were viewed as poor investments and ultimately denied federally insured mortgages (Howell & Korver-Glenn, 2021). Thus began the policy and practice of "Redlining" areas on maps to identify where Blacks and other minorities lived.

In addition to the racially color-coded maps created by the HOLC, appraisers were also required to record the percentages of "Negro," and "foreign-born" residents in Area Description forms (Kimble, 2007). The FHA Underwriting Manual instructed lenders to make racially deterministic assessments of neighborhoods:

Areas surrounding a location are investigated to determine whether incompatible racial and social groups are present, for the purpose of

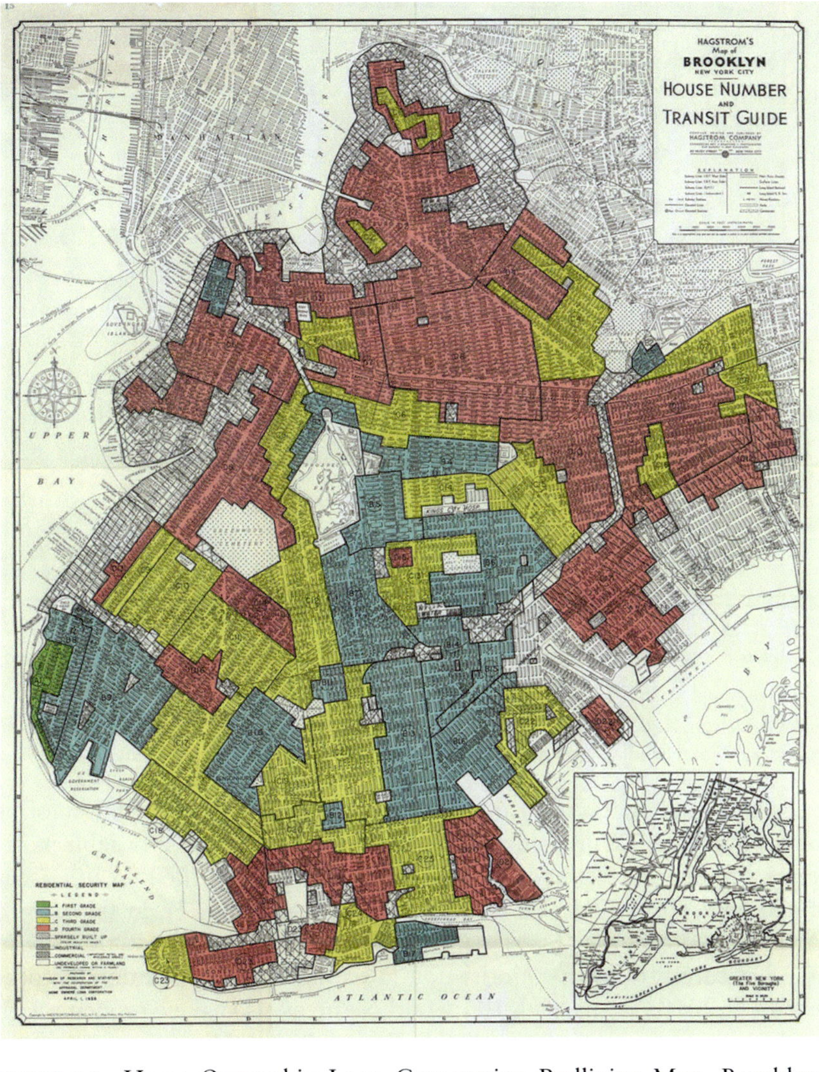

FIGURE 6.6 Home Ownership Loan Corporation Redlining Map, Brooklyn, NY 1938.

Source: Nelson, R. K., Winling, L., et al. (2023). *Mapping Inequality: Redlining in New Deal America*. Digital Scholarship Lab. https://dsl.richmond.edu/panorama/redlining

making a prediction regarding the probability of the location being invaded by such groups. If a neighborhood is to retain stability, it is necessary that properties shall continue to be occupied by the same social and racial classes. A change in social and racial occupancy generally contributes to instability and a decline in values (FHA 1938, sec. 937).

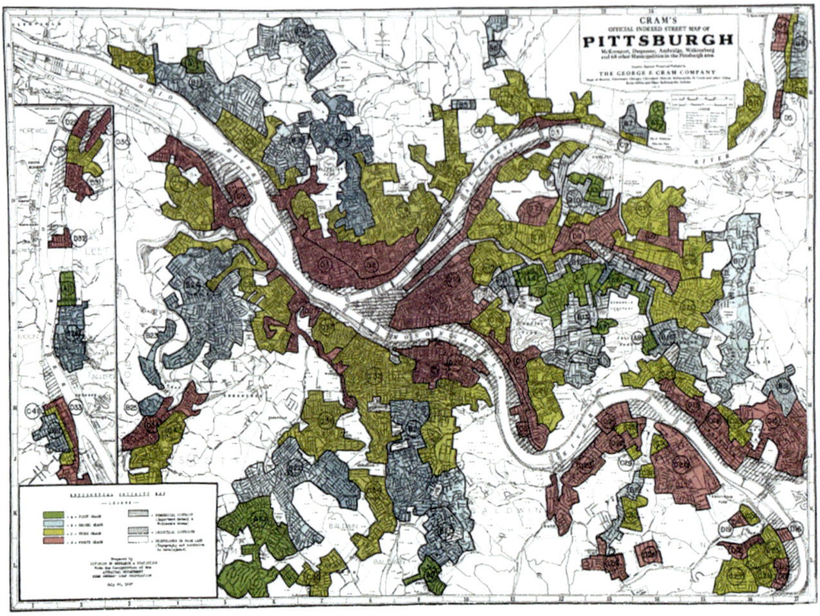

FIGURE 6.7 Home Ownership Loan Corporation Redlining Map, Pittsburgh, PA 1940.

Source: Nelson, R. K., Winling, L., et al. (2023). *Mapping Inequality: Redlining in New Deal America.* Digital Scholarship Lab. https://dsl.richmond.edu/panorama/redlining

As a result, "appraisals using HOLC's maps and Area Description forms not only ensured White individuals had access to the more affordable mortgages but enabled home value appreciation, escalating their wealth accumulation" (Howell & Korver-Glenn, 2021, pp. 1051–52). In the case of Atlanta, 100% of the area classified as "best" according to HOLC criteria in 1938 currently has a majority non-Hispanic/Latine population, according to the 2010 Census, with 100% of those areas also having residents with middle-to-upper incomes (Mitchell & Franco, 2018). Moreover, 81% of the areas in the city classified as "hazardous" in 1938 had "majority-minority" populations and 71% had low-middle incomes (Mitchell & Franco, 2018). If the data shown in the city of Atlanta is reflective of the rest of the United States, then it appears as if the HOLC's racially motivated method of identifying housing areas continues to have pernicious effects. Decades after the creation of the HOLC redlining scheme, inequitable outcomes for generations of residents based upon a racist policy endures well after segregation was deemed illegal.

As historian Kenneth Jackson astutely asserts, "No agency of the United States Government has had a more pervasive and powerful impact on the

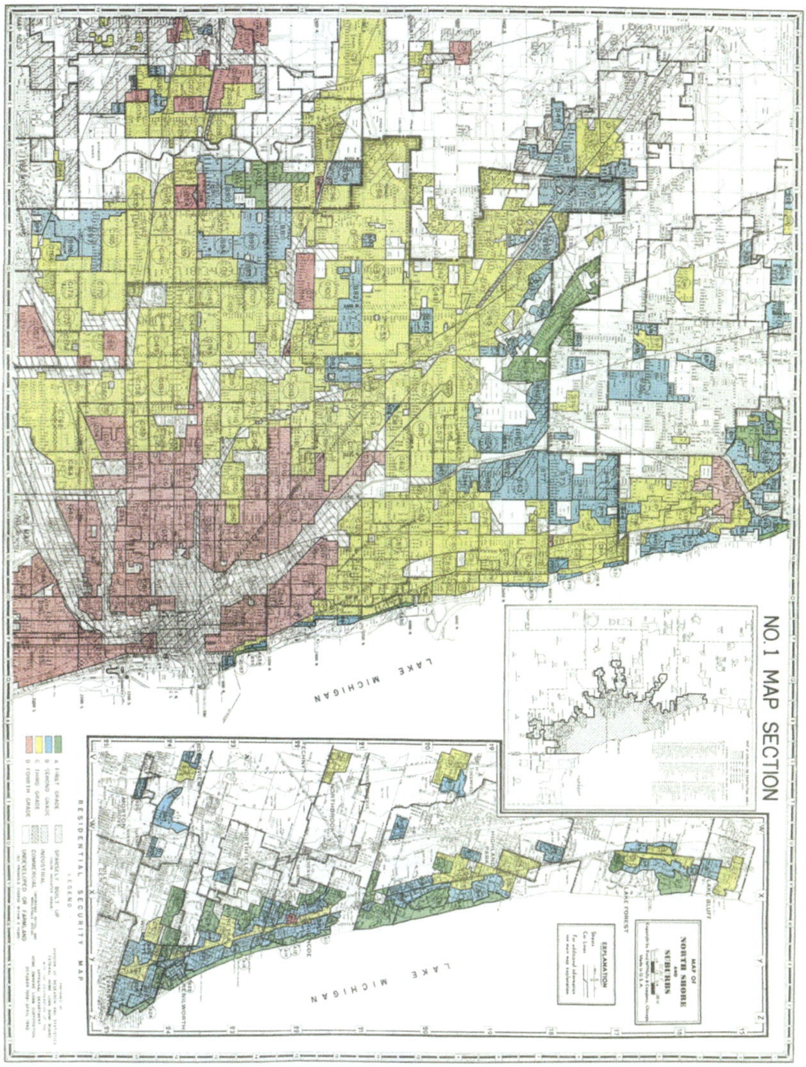

FIGURE 6.8 Home Ownership Loan Corporation Redlining Map, Chicago, IL 1940.

Source: Nelson, R. K., Winling, L., et al. (2023). *Mapping Inequality: Redlining in New Deal America*. Digital Scholarship Lab. https://dsl.richmond.edu/panorama/redlining

American people over the past half-century than the Federal Housing Administration" (Jackson, 1985, p. 203). In 1937, the FHA published an article in their *Insured Mortgage Portfolio* periodical that was written by an FHA state director titled, "City Growth and Population Patterns." In the article describing the area of Harlem in New York City, the author wrote, "When the first Negroes made their appearance in the area, it was inhabited by Whites, predominantly of German stock. When the Negroes began to invade the area, the Whites withdrew until the Negroes were in complete control" (Magee, 1937, p. 6). Using the term "invade, " shows the true sentiment of FHA officials and transcended down to appraisers, lenders and others creating an increased level of fear, racism and antipathy of Blacks and other minorities which helped shape the communities and cities socioeconomically across the U.S. (National Association of Real Estate Boards, 1924). Kimble (2007) articulates how FHA policies, practices and beliefs certainly helped to permeate the conscious and subconscious feelings of Whites towards Blacks at the time. "The use here, and throughout FHA literature, of the militarized language of 'invasion,' 'infiltration,' and 'control' cast African-Americans in the role of enemy combatants, which helped justify the federal government's draconian response to African-Americans' employment-driven migration into urban areas" (p. 408).

In a survey of members of the Society for American City and Regional Planning History (SACREPH), which is comprised of urban historians, social scientists, planning faculty, and working planners and architects, Fishman (2000) found that FHA regulation, the Housing Act of 1949, racial segregation and job discrimination in cities and suburbs, were among the top 10 influences on the American metropolis over the past 50 years. In terms of the FHA, Fishman writes,

> the FHA refused to insure mortgages on older houses in typical urban neighborhoods. This meant that a white home buyer who wished to stay in his old neighborhood had to seek old-style conventional mortgages with high rates and short terms. The same purchaser who opted for a new suburban house could get an FHA-insured mortgage with lower interest rates, longer terms, a lower down payment, and a lower monthly payment. By contrast, all African-American house-holds were excluded from FHA-subsidized suburbs, which meant that they were denied the benefit of better schools, rapid appreciation in home prices, and access to the booming suburban economy.
>
> *(p. 202)*

In Figure 6.9, we see the percentages of Black and White families who own homes based upon their respective incomes. In every income bracket

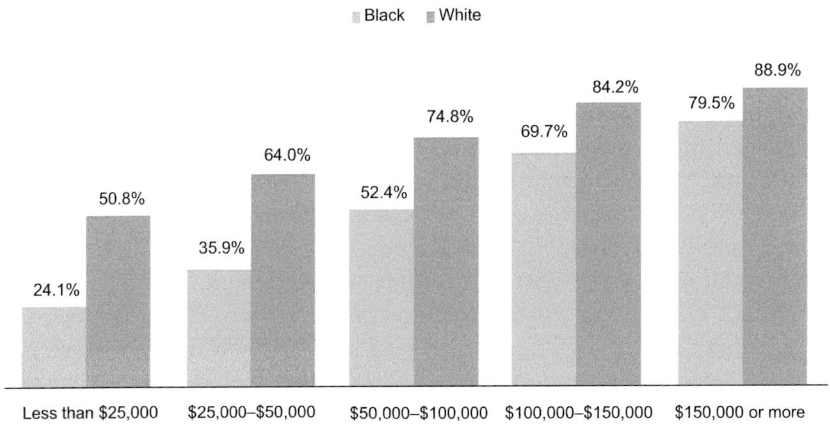

FIGURE 6.9 Homeownership Rate by Household Income, 2017.

Source: Adapted from 2017 American Community Survey—Urban Institute

examined, the percentage of homeownership rate is higher for Whites than it is for Blacks. In fact, not until incomes above $100,000 are compared do the rates come closer. White families who earn between $25,000 and $50,000 own homes 28% more than Black families with the same incomes.

It is reasonable to conclude that the FHA's policies had a significant influence on the social, educational and economic development, or lack thereof, for Blacks, Hispanics/Latines, Asians, Native Americans, Indigenous and other racial minorities in America.

Unequal protection under the law

In 1917, in what Blacks must have believed to have been a critical step towards equality, the US Supreme Court ruled in *Buchanan v. Warley* (n.d.) that discrimination to sell or rent property based upon the buyer's race was unconstitutional. While the decision overturned the Kentucky Court of Appeals ruling that permitted racial zoning ordinances in determining whom property owners could sell their homes to (Rothstein, 2017; Kimble, 2007; Grossman & Wells, 1988, Oyez, N.D.), enforcement of the Buchanan case was anything but a certainty. Refusal by realtors, and others, to have homes sold to Blacks continued as if was still legal to do so. One must pose the question, in what ways was the ruling going to be enforced, and by whom? It is dubious to believe that local governments or lenders would do anything to make their cities and communities more diverse. Many cities from Atlanta, to Birmingham, to Indianapolis, to Kansas City, to Norfolk, to Richmond, to West Palm Beach and many others in between simply ignored it and carried on with their own racist housing policies (Rothstein, 2017). How then were individuals and families able to overcome the poor conditions of their environments without government intervention and assistance? The answer to this question was addressed, in part, through federal legislation. The unintended consequences of the legislation, however, would continue to have lasting effects.

In 1938, the Standards Act was passed which established a minimum wage, outlawed child labor and created a regular and normal work week by mandating the payment of overtime wages (Dixon, 2021; Anderson, 1989). In addition to instituting fair and improved labor practices, the FLSA also adopted racist policies that excluded industries such as agriculture, farmworkers and domestic workers that included large numbers of Blacks (Dixon, 2021; Anderson, 1989; Rothstein, 2017). At the time, chairman of the National Committee on Rural and Social Planning, Gardner Jackson stated that including agricultural workers in the FLSA would not have been supported. "It has been deemed politically certain that their inclusion would have spelled the death of the legislation in Congress" (Dixon, 2021).

The Housing Act of 1949 (over 30 years past Buchanan v Warley) was an idea with good intentions, but ultimately it reinforced and rapidly accelerated racial housing segregation in the United States (Lang & Sohmer, 2000). At the time, President Harry S. Truman proposed a housing effort that would provide housing for veterans returning from World War II. Conservative Republicans supported the Lanham Act, which provided temporary housing to those whose work was related to the war, primarily because these homes would be either demolished or assumed by the local governments after the war ended (Rothstein, 2017). The Housing Act of 1949 would not gain congressional support unless residential integration of housing was omitted from the legislation. As Rothstein (2017) points out, "The Senate and House rejected the proposed integration amendments, and the 1949 Housing Act was adopted, permitting local authorities to continue to design separate public housing projects for Blacks and Whites or to segregate Blacks and Whites within projects" (p. 31). The general counsel of the Housing and Home Finance Agency was a man named Berchmans Fitzpatrick. Despite the "separate but equal" policy now becoming illegal as of 1954, Fitzpatrick ignored the Supreme Court's ruling stating their decision (*Brown v. Board of Education*) did not apply to housing (Rothstein, 2017).

In 1948, the US Supreme Court heard a case brought by Louis Kraemer, of St. Louis, against a Black couple, J.D. and Ethel Shelley. The Shelleys had purchased a home from a Black individual, who had bought the same home using the fictitious name Josephine Fitzgerald (Grossman & Wells,

1988; Oyez, N.D.). Once residents realized that a Black family had purchased the home, they created the Marcus Avenue Improvement Association and brought a suit against the Shelleys (Grossman & Wells, 1988). Changing the housing landscape in the United States was going to be a herculean task because of years and years of racist policies being put into practice and codified into law. Prior to the Shelley case, the general stance of the courts had been that they would not become involved in a transaction between two private parties and that racially restrictive language in deeds was permissible and legal. Chief Justice Vinson said at the time, "Whether the equal protection clause of the Fourteenth Amendment inhibits judicial enforcement by state courts of restrictive covenants based on race or color is a question which this Court has not heretofore been called upon to consider" (Grossman & Wells, 1988, p. 336). In terms of public policy, the FHA's Underwriting Manual of 1947 stated, "Protective covenants are essential to the sound development of proposed residential areas since they regulate the use of the land and provide a basis for the development of harmonious, attractive neighborhoods suitable and desirable to the upper groups forming the potential market" (Abrams, 1955, pp. 123–124). Also, according to Article 34 of the 1924 Code of Ethics by the National Association of Real Estate Boards, "A realtor should never be instrumental in introducing into a neighborhood a character of property or occupancy, members of any race or nationality, or any individuals whose presence will clearly be detrimental to the property values in that neighborhood." The ability to allow Whites, Blacks, Asians, Hispanics/Latines and other minorities to live in the same communities was not permitted by FHA policies and practices. These policies and practices thus permeated the consciousness of many people believing that different racial and ethnic groups did not want to live together, while in fact, they could not do so even if they wanted to. Not all Whites were supportive of racially restrictive covenants or FHA practices. Clearly unsatisfied with the state of housing in the United States, US Attorney General Tom Clarke and Solicitor General Phillip Pearlman wrote an amicus curiae brief on behalf of the United States to the Supreme Court noting the compunctious behavior of the FHA and other governmental agencies, at the time: "The fact that racial restrictive covenants are being enforced by instrumentalities of government has become a source of serious embarrassment to agencies of the Federal Government in the performance of many essential functions, including the programs relating to housing and home finance" (Clark & Perlman, 1975, p. 236). Ultimately, the question before the Supreme Court in the Shelley case was, whether, or not, the enforcement of a racially restrictive covenant violated the Equal Protection Clause of the 14th Amendment. At that time, and in particular with the *Shelley v. Kraemer* (n.d.) case, racial covenants were ruled to have legal standing because they were agreements between two individuals, private parties, and not based upon state actors or officials. Relying upon judicial precedent (Buchanan v Warley) and the 14th amendment to the US Constitution, the Court stated that racially restrictive covenants were not merely agreements between two private individuals and ruled in favor of Shelley, thus, striking down the legality of racially restrictive covenants in mortgage/housing deeds. Chief Justice Vinson delivered the opinion of the court: "We hold that in granting judicial enforcement of the restrictive agreements, in these cases, the States have denied petitioners the equal protection of the laws and that, therefore, the action of the state courts cannot stand" (Grossman & Wells, 1988, p. 338).

It would not be until the 1960s when civil rights legislation, along with the FHA recognizing complicity in their involvement in creating the segregated state of US housing, began to redress some of the racist and inequitable policies that permitted the country to become so segregated (Kimble, 2007). Yet, despite FHA acknowledgments of past racist policies and practices, racially driven legislation, and brazen disregard of the US Supreme Court rulings, neighborhoods and cities continued to remain segregated and inequitable through the present time.

As previously stated, federal legislation, Supreme Court rulings and assertions from the FHA were not sufficient antidotes to remedy the history of segregated housing and its aftermath in the United States. Prior to legislation in 1949, and even after, many cities and neighborhoods enacted legally enforceable language in property deeds, also known as racial covenants, that not only forbid the sale of property to non-Whites, it also did not allow a property to be rented by non-Whites. In Hennepin, Minnesota, for example, one such deed stated, "that the said land or buildings thereon shall never be rented, leased or sold transferred or conveyed to, nor shall the same be occupied by any negro or colored person or person of negro blood" (Sood et al., 2021, p. 38).

Exacerbating residential segregation was the construction of exclusively all-White communities across the United States. In Long Island, New York a new housing development was built between 1947 and 1951. Initially named Island Trees, the community changed its name to Levittown because of the builders, Levitt and sons (Sheidlower, 2020). Levittown, once fully developed, would comprise over 17,000 homes built for veterans returning from World War II. Each home would be approximately $8,000, but with no down payments required, FHA financing and the GI Bill, costs would be reduced by $400 (Sheidlower, 2020; Rothstein, 2017). In addition to the low costs, the homes would include modern kitchens and a television set. The one caveat with purchasing a home in Levittown was that they could only be sold to Whites.

Levittown, New York

As Rothstein notes (2017), housing developments, like Levittown, were built on the speculation that once they were finished, buyers would follow. Levitt and Sons never would have been able to build housing developments like Levittown absent assistance from the FHA and the Veterans Administration (VA). "But during the World War II years and after, the government had congressional authority to guarantee bank loans to mass-production builders like Levitt for nearly the full cost of their proposed subdivisions. By 1948, most housing nationwide was being constructed with this government financing" (Rothstein, p. 71). While Levitt and Sons would mass build other Whites-only communities in New Jersey and Bucks County, Pennsylvania, similar racially restrictive communities were simultaneously being used in communities to keep Blacks. And others from building wealth. Oak Forest (Houston, Texas), Prairie Village (Kansas City, Missouri), West Lake, located in Daly City (south of San Francisco), Lakewood and Westchester (south of Los Angeles) and Panorama City (San Fernando Valley, California), were all Whites-only communities financed by the FHA between 1946 and 1953 (Rothstein, 2017).

Another highly recognized and controversial figure, around that time, who had an impact on housing in the United States was Robert Moses. Moses was an enormously powerful political figure, who also worked in New York and had a great impact on the city, beginning around 1924. While Moses did not build housing tracts that forbade Blacks, Hispanics/Latines and other minorities from purchasing in certain neighborhoods, his infrastructure projects often provided physical barriers thereby segregating or demolishing the communities of these groups. During the course of his career, Moses was influential in changing the landscape of New York into a city of mass transit overseeing the following governmental organizations: Commissioner, New York City Planning Commission—1946–1960; President, Jones Beach Parkway Authority—1933–1963; Chairman, Triborough Bridge and Tunnel Authority—1934–1981; Commissioner, New York City Department of Parks—1934–1960; President, Long Island State Parks Commission—1924–1963; Chairman, New York State Council of Parks—1924–1963; and Secretary of State, New York State—1927–1928 (NYPAP, 2023). Moses had an enormous impact on the development of New York City and he is largely known for principally being responsible for major infrastructure projects including the Verrazano Narrows Bridge, the Triborough Bridge, the Queens Midtown Tunnel, the Whitestone Bridge in the Bronx, the West Side Highway and several others. While many credit Moses as being a visionary who saw the future potential of New York City, it would be his influential leadership in two projects that also led to him being remembered as an arrogant, uncompromising, uncompassionate and otherwise merciless power-hungry individual who accelerated racial and class divisions in the city (Ploschnitzki, 2017).

In 1921, the south shore of Long Island was just a "barren, deserted, windswept sand spit" until Moses' vision transformed it into a much sought-after destination for vacationers, city-dwellers and tourists (Caro, 1975, p. 8). By 1929, over 350,000 visited the beach during its first month of operation (NYC Parks; https://www.nycgovparks.org/about/history/timeline/robert-moses-modern-parks).

In fact, over 3 million people visited Jones Beach during the ten-year period of the 1930s (Maroney, 2013). As more and more residents began visiting the beach in which he constructed, it appears as if Moses simultaneously built barriers to prevent many from getting to Jones Beach. Holding multiple gubernatorial positions, including president of the Jones Beach State Park Authority, he vetoed the proposed development of a Long Island Railroad branch spur to the beach to prevent Blacks and low-income residents from going (NYPAP, 2023; Caro, 1975). In the *Power Broker—Robert Moses and the Fall of New York*, Caro (1975) says that the overpasses on the Southern State Parkway leading to Jones Beach were purposefully built lower than normal to prevent buses travelling from the city with Black and Hispanic/Latine to ably reach the shore. Others (Campanella, 2017) counter Caro's claim that bridges on the Southern State Parkway were purposefully built with low overpasses because other infrastructure projects built during that period of time also were constructed with lower bridge overpasses. Many people still hold the position of Caro and contend the lower built overpasses simply prevented minorities from moving to those locations, like Westchester, NY, as well. Although there may be some who do not think Moses' intentions were completely motivated by race in this case, countervailing evidence has not been presented regarding chartered buses carrying Blacks finding it extremely difficult to obtain parking permits at Jones Beach. Nor have there been sufficient affirmations refuting claims of Moses shunting Blacks, and other minorities, from using White beach areas, hiring a minimal number of Black lifeguards and discouraging Blacks from visiting "White" beach areas. Another thing that is not refuted about Moses is his failure to modernize Riverside Park in the 20-block section (125th Street—145th Street) of Harlem, New York, which is heavily populated by Black's, Latinas and other minorities (Caro, 1975).

Perhaps the greatest example of apathy towards minorities that Moses exhibited was the construction of the Cross Bronx Expressway.

Well before the time that the Express was completed, the area now known as the South Bronx was already heavily segregated and the residents experienced substandard housing conditions including, no heat,

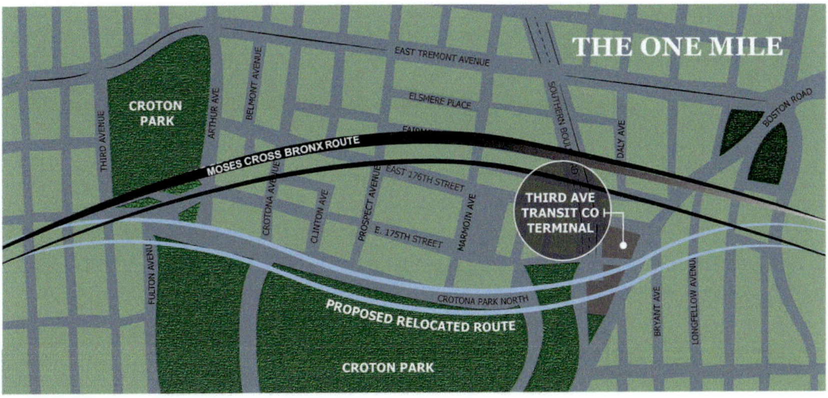

FIGURE 6.10 Robert Moses Cross Bronx Expressway Route and Proposed Route.

Source: Adapted from Caro (1975, p. 864)

hot water or toilet facilities (Gonzalez, 2004). What the construction of the Cross Bronx Expressway did however was create a physical barrier between the north and south sections of the Bronx that demolished 54 apartment houses and displaced over 1,500 residents, most of whom were low-income Jewish immigrants, Blacks and Hispanics/Latines (Gonzalez, 2004; Caro, 1975). Moses' callousness in building the Cross Bronx Expressway was particularly malicious as an alternative route could have been constructed by *only* displacing six small dilapidated homes (Caro, 1975). Figure 6.10 is an area map that shows the actual route of the Cross Bronx Expressway along with a proposed relocation route that would not have displaced the 1,500 plus residents.

It is likely that Moses and other city officials viewed this area of the Bronx as useless, thus reinforcing their belief that the construction of the Cross Bronx Expressway would not be significantly opposed. Other studies (Ploschnitzki, 2017; Jonnes, 2002) suggest that there were other, more unscrupulous reasons for Moses' decision. As Caro points out in *The Power Broker*: "It is a fact that the Third Avenue Transit Company secretly told Moses it was very anxious not to have the terminal condemned, for its location was strategic for buses" (Caro, 1975, p. 878). In other words, an area of a city that housed poor immigrants, Blacks and Hispanics/Latines was razed because of their lives were viewed less valuable and could be compromised for political gain. Figure 6.11 shows the pictures of the Fulton Avenue & 175th Street location in the Bronx before and after the creation of the Cross Bronx Expressway.

FIGURE 6.11 Fulton Avenue & 175th Street Before and After Cross Bronx Expressway Construction.

Source: Adapted from Susaneck (2024)

Figure 6.12 is a picture of one of the areas of the Bronx that was demolished in order to build the Cross Bronx Expressway.

Urban renewal was not only occurring in New York City but all across the United States. "By 1957, $133,000,000 of public monies had been expended on urban renewal in all the cities of the United States with the exception of New York; $267,000,000 had been spent in New York" (Caro, 1975, p. 12). For many, Moses and the model of razing primarily poor neighborhoods simply served as the model for urban renewal and infrastructure design in the United States. The country would witness countless examples of "urban renewal" occurring at the expense of people's lives who simply did not matter as much as others.

Conclusion

In 1938, a Los Angeles newspaper proclaimed that Americans "who have been protesting Hitler's despicable plan to herd German Jews into ghettos will be surprised to learn that their own government has been busily

FIGURE 6.12 Cross Bronx Expressway Under Construction.

Source: Adapted from Lehman College Library-CUNY (1957)

planning ghettos for American Negroes by the Federal Housing Agency. The American plan lacks the forthright and brutal frankness of Hitler's plan, but in the long run it is calculated to be as effective" (Hirsch, 2000, p. 158). This "plan" that has been in effect for nearly 200 years has dramatically reshaped residential housing in the United States. What is more evident is that absent policies by the FHA and other governmental organizations, it is likely that communities and cities would not be as segregated as they currently are. Carey Williams, California Commissioner of Immigration and Housing, stated that "the federal government had in effect been planting the seeds of Jim Crow practices throughout the region under the guise of respecting local values" (Rothstein, 2017, p. 37).

For well over 150 years, the United States government, along with private entities, have embraced racist housing policies fostering actions, beliefs and attitudes that have perpetuated segregated communities across the country. Many people believe that communities have been segregated simply because Blacks, Whites, Hispanics/Latines, Asians, Native Americans and Indigenous people preferred to live in close proximity to one another. While this may be true in some cases, it is not an absolute truth. It is more likely that racist policies led to certain beliefs that individuals have towards different groups of people. It is difficult to tear down a structure that has such deep roots in a relatively short period of time. We have shown current examples, such as inequitable home valuations by race, that continue to exacerbate the racist history sewn so deep into the American fabric. Individual perceptions and group thinking have led to these racist views that continue to permeate throughout our society which undoubtedly will take enormous efforts to change.

References

About Freddie Mac. (n.d.). Retrieved September 2023, from https://www.freddiemac.com/about

Abrams, C. (1955). The segregation threat in housing. *Commentary*, *7*(2), 122–131.

Anderson, P. (1989). The Agricultural Employee Exemption from the Fair Labor Standards Act of 1938, 12 HAMLINE L. REV. 649, 655 (1988–1989), citing "Bills to Provide for the Establishment of Fair Labor Standards in Employments In and Affecting Interstate Commerce and Other Purposes", Joint Hearings on S. 2475 and H.R. 7200 Before the Senate Comm. on Education and Labor and the House Comm. on Labor, 75th Cong., 1st Sess. at 1196 (1937).

Buchanan v. Warley. (n.d.). *Oyez*. Retrieved October 10, 2023, from https://www.oyez.org/cases/1900-1940/245us60

Campanella, T. (2017). Robert moses and his racist parkway, explained. *Bloomberg—City Lab Perspective*. https://www.bloomberg.com/news/articles/2017-07-09/robert-moses-and-his-racist-parkway-explained

Caro, R. (1975). *The power broker—Robert Moses and the fall of New York*. Random House.

Clark, T., & Perlman, P. (1975). Brief for the United States as Amicus Curiae. In P. Kurland & G. Casper (Eds.), *Landmark briefs and arguments of the Supreme Court of the United States: Constitutional Law* (Vol. 46). University Publications of America. (Originally submitted to the Supreme Court in December 1947)

Crossney, K. B., & Bartelt, D. W. (2005). The legacy of the home owners' loan corporation. *Housing Policy Debate*, *16*(3–4), 547–574.

Davis, L., Ross, K., & Ghebremedhin, S. (2022). *Couple's home value rose nearly $300K after it was shown by white colleague*. https://abcnews.go.com/US/couples-lawsuit-alleges-appraisal-firm-undervalued-home-based/story?id=88700992

Devine, P. G. (1989). Stereotypes and prejudice: Their automatic and controlled components. *Journal of Personality and Social Psychology*, *56*, 5–18.

Dixon, R. (2021). From excluded to essential: Tracing the racist exclusion of farmworkers, domestic workers, and tipped workers from the Fair Labor Standards Act. Hearing before the U.S. House of Representatives Education and Labor Committee, Workforce Protections Subcommittee. *National Employment Law Project*.

Fair Labor Standards Act. Act of June 25, 1938. Pub. L. 75–718, 52 Stat 1060, June 25, 1938, p. 1060.
Federal Housing Administration. (1938). *Underwriting manual: Underwriting and valuation procedure under title II of the National Housing Act*. USGPO [Record Group 287].
Fishman, R. (2000). The American metropolis at century's end: Past and future influences. *Housing Policy Debate*, *11*(1), 199–213.
Forscher, P. S., & Devine, P. G. (2017). *Knowledge-based interventions are more likely to reduce legal disparities than are implicit bias interventions*. Psychological Science Faculty Publications and Presentations. https://scholarworks.uark.edu/psycpub/5
Freddie Mac—Research Note. (2021). *Racial and ethnic valuation gaps in home purchase appraisals*. https://www.freddiemac.com/research/insight/20210920-home-appraisals
Gonzalez, E. D. (2004). *The Bronx*. Columbia University Press.
Grossman, J., & Wells, R. (1988). *Constitutional law and judicial policy making* (3rd ed.). Pitman Publishing, Inc.
Harriss, L. (1951). *Background of home ownership loan corporation legislation*. National Bureau of Economic Research.
Hirsch, A. (2000). "Containment" on the homefront: Race and federal housing policy from the New Deal to the Cold War. *Journal of Urban History*, *26*(2), 158–189.
History of the Stanford Creative Writing Program. (n.d.). https://creativewriting.stanford.edu/about/history-stanford-creative-writing-program
Howell, J., & Korver-Glenn, E. (2021). The increasing effect of neighborhood racial composition on housing values, 1980–2015. *Social Problems*, *68*, 1051–1071.
Jackson, K. (1985). *Crabgrass frontier: The suburbanization of the United States*. Oxford University Press.
Jonnes, J. (2002). *South Bronx rising: The rise, fall, and resurrection of an American City*. Fordham University Press.
Kimble, J. (2007). Insuring inequality: The role of the Federal Housing Administration in the urban ghettoization of African Americans. *Law & Social Inquiry*, *32*(2, Spring), 399–434.
Lang, R. E., & Sohmer, R. (2000). Legacy of the Housing Act of 1949: The past, present, and future of federal housing and urban policy. *Housing Policy Debate*, *11*(2), 291–298. https://doi.org/10.1080/10511482.2000.9521369
Lehman College Library, CUNY. (1957). *Cross Bronx expressway under construction*. https://dcmny.org/do/54806e77-e9c7-4e76-a3d4-5d7f9511d4d7
Magee, J. (1937). City growth and population patterns. *Insured Mortgage Portfolio*, 2(3), 5–6, 22 [Record Group 287].
Maroney, E. (2013). *Jones Beach State Park, historic structures and cultural landscape report*. New York State Office of Parks, Recreation & Historic Preservation.
Mitchell, B., & Franco, J. (2018). *HOLC "redlining" maps: The persistent structure of segregation and economic inequality*. National Community Reinvestment Coalition. https://ncrc.org/holc/
Narragon, M., Wiley, D., McManus, D., Li, V., Li, K., Wu, X., & Karamon, K. (2021). *Racial and ethnic valuation gaps in home purchase appraisals*. Freddie Mac Economic and Housing Research Note.
National Association of Real Estate Boards. (1924). *Code of ethics*. 17th Annual Convention.

Nelson, R. K., Winling, L., Marciano, R., Connolly, N., et al. (2017). *Mapping inequality: Redlining in new deal America*. https://dsl.richmond.edu/panorama/redlining

New York Preservation Archive Project (NYPAP). (2023). *About Robert Moses*. https://www.nypap.org/preservation-history/robert-moses/

Perry, A., Rothwell, J., & Harshbarger, D. (2018). *The devaluation of assets in Black neighborhoods*. Metropolitan Policy Program at Brookings.

Ploschnitzki, P. (2017). Robert Moses, the construction of the Cross-Bronx expressway and its impact on the Bronx.

Rothstein, R. (2017). *The color of law: A forgotten history of how our government segregated America*. W. W. Norton & Co.

Rothwell, J., & Perry, A. (2022). *How racial bias in appraisals affects the devaluation of homes in majority-Black neighborhoods*. Brookings. https://www.brookings.edu/articles/how-racial-bias-in-appraisals-affects-the-devaluation-of-homes-in-majority-black-neighborhoods/

Sheidlower, N. (2020). The controversial history of Levittown, America's first suburb. *Untapped New York*. https://untappedcities.com/2020/07/31/the-controversial-history-of-levittown-americas-first-suburb/

Shelley v. Kraemer. (n.d.). *Oyez*. Retrieved October 13, 2023, from https://www.oyez.org/cases/1940-1955/334us1

Sood, A., Speagle, W., & Ehrman-Solberg, K. (2021). *Long shadow of racial discrimination: Evidence from housing racial covenants*. Social Science Research Network (SSRN).

Susaneck, A. P. (2024). Segregation by design. *TU Delft Centre for the Just City*. https://www.segregationbydesign.com/

Wallace Stegner Biography. (n.d.). https://wallacestegner.org/bio.html

7

EDUCATION

Providing equal opportunities for education has been a consistent and long fight in the United States for numerous years. The lack of a "good" education impacts individuals in not only learning and increasing their respective knowledge base, but relatedly it also has a perverse impact income and employment opportunities later in life. The results of a poor education are only exacerbated when we consider the lack of financial freedom and mobility that occurs as well. In just over 40 years, the US Supreme Court has ruled on cases in support of Affirmative Action and also against it. This relatively short period of time has presumably led to massive changes in how society views equal and equitable educational opportunities for all students. More recently, the US Supreme Court has also ruled on how the federal government may proceed in attempting to assist students who have taken out loans to pay for their higher education. Affirmative Action and student loan debt are inextricably related to educational equity in the United States.

Affirmative Action

In 2023, the US Supreme Court reversed a lower court's decision in the *Students for Fair Admissions, Inc. v. President & Fellows of Harvard* and *Students for Fair Admissions, Inc. v. University of North Carolina* cases, ending the use of Affirmative Action in college admissions. Dissenting, Justice Sotomayor said of the decision, "The Court subverts the constitutional guarantee of equal protection by further entrenching racial inequality in education, the very foundation of our democratic government

DOI: 10.4324/9781032670850-8

and pluralistic society" (Totenberg, N., retrieved from https://www.npr.org/2023/06/29/1181138066/affirmative-action-supreme-court-decision). Also dissenting, Justice Ketanji Brown Jackson, the court's first Black female justice, said, "With let-them-eat-cake obliviousness, today, the majority pulls the ripcord and announces 'colorblindness for all' by legal fiat. But deeming race irrelevant in law does not make it so in life" (Totenberg, N., retrieved from https://www.npr.org/2023/06/29/1181138066/affirmative-action-supreme-court-decision).

The case was brought before the Supreme Court by Edward Blum who has long advocated against Affirmative Action in higher education and the 1965 Voting Rights Act. He also plans to fight against the makeup of corporate boards that are, in part, primarily comprised of minority members and also argue against the existence of minority scholarship and fellowship programs (Totenberg, 2023).

The rulings may be viewed as another step backward for those who support diversity, equity, inclusion and accessibility in higher education. While there have been notable gains in this area of higher education, it is important that we remember why Affirmative Action was implemented in the first place. The fight for equality, justice, fair treatment and equal protection of the law had been going on long before the ratification of the 14th Amendment in 1868. It was not until 1954 when the US Supreme Court ruled that it was unconstitutional to separate schools and educational facilities based upon race in the Brown v. Topeka Board of Education case. The case was consolidated among several separate plaintiffs from the states of Kansas, South Carolina, Virginia and Delaware. In each of the states, the plaintiffs claimed that their equal protection of the law under the 14th Amendment to the US Constitution was violated. The plaintiffs contended that segregated public schools were not 'equal' and could not be made 'equal,' and that hence they deprived individuals of the equal protection of laws (Grossman & Wells, 1988). The case struck down the 'separate but equal' law that had previously existed and ruled upon in the Plessy v Ferguson case of 1896. Although the ruling in the Plessy case affirmed segregation along racial lines, in the opinions dissent, Justice Harlan wrote, "What can more certainly arouse race hate, what can more certainly create and perpetuate a feeling of distrust between these races, than state enactments, which in fact, proceed on the ground that colored citizens are so inferior and degraded that they cannot be allowed to sit in public coaches occupied by white citizens?" (Grossman & Wells, 1988, p. 297). So we have a US Supreme Court justice questioning the logic behind the court's ruling in the Plessy case because it further separated Whites and Blacks according to racial lines. It also did not attenuate the differences in quality of education, resources and outcomes that had long been in place in the United States. Yet, despite the outcome of the Brown case, racism and racist behavior did not decrease as a result of the Supreme Court's ruling in 1954. On the contrary, the hostile reactions by many southern Whites actually exacerbated racial tensions (Grossman & Wells, 1988).

One of the first references to Affirmative Action occurred when President John F. Kennedy stated that government contractors needed to take "affirmative action to ensure that applicants are employed, and that employees are treated during employment, without regard to their race, creed, color, or national origin" (retrieved on November 13, 2023, from https://www.oeod.uci.edu/policies/aa_history.php). Unfortunately, there were many who countered the beliefs of Kennedy who supported the continuation of segregation in society. "The third-party presidential candidacy in 1968 and 1972 of Governor George Wallace of Alabama which epitomized the 'White backlash' to growing Black demands for equal treatment; the urban ghetto riots of the 1960's; and the 'southern strategy' of candidate and then President Richard Nixon marked this racial polarization" (Grossman & Wells, 1988, p. 288). This is the very same Governor Wallace who stood in front of an Alabama school forbidding Black children from entering and who stated, "segregation now, segregation tomorrow, and segregation forever."

History is the great equalizer when it comes to debunking myths, and providing facts that counter claims absent of truth and evidence. While Governor Wallace, Richard Nixon and other White racists supported segregation, some assume that segregated schools and communities have occurred by happenstance. De facto segregation is a term popularized during the 1960s to describe segregation, whether in schools, housing or elsewhere, as occurring naturally or from personal preferences. It is contended that De facto segregation is the result of groups of individuals and organizations using private practices to separate themselves from other groups in society based upon their own personal preferences. Notably, de facto segregation occurs absent law or government policies (Rothstein, 2017). Rothstein (2017) states that we often tell ourselves that the unintentional results of de facto segregation are what largely cause and lead to income, education, wealth and health gaps between Whites and all others. "African Americans haven't generally gotten the education that would enable them to earn sufficient incomes to live in White suburbs, and as a result, many remain concentrated in urban neighborhoods. Besides, many believe that Black families simply prefer to live with one another" (vii, Rothstein, 2017). Whereas some people prefer to live in communities with members of their own race, we have learned, however, that segregation in the United States did not occur without government law, policy or intervention. In fact, as we stated in Chapter 6

TABLE 7.1 Revenues per Pupil From State Sources

PUPIL AMOUNTS PER LOCATION	1950	1964	% INCREASE
Baltimore			
City	$71	$171	140.8%
Suburb	$90	$199	121.1%
Birmingham City			
City	$90	$201	123.3%
Suburb	$54	$150	177.7%
Boston City			
City	$19	$52	173.7%
Suburb	$30	$75	150.0%
Buffalo City			
City	$135	$284	110.4%
Suburb	$165	$270	63.6%
Chattanooga City			
City	$62	$136	119.4%
Suburb	$141	$152	7.8%
Chicago City			
City	$42	$154	266.6%
Suburb	$32	$110	243.8%
Cincinnati City			
City	$51	$91	78.4%
Suburb	$78	$91	16.7%
Cleveland City			
City	$50	$88	76.0%
Suburb	$39	$88	125.6%
Detroit City			
City	$135	$189	40.0%
Suburb	$149	$240	61.1%
New Orleans City			
City	$152	$239	57.2%
Suburb	$117	$259	121.4%
St. Louis City			
City	$70	$131	87.1%
Suburb	$61	$143	134.4%
San Francisco City			
City	$122	$163	33.6%
Suburb	$160	$261	63.1%

Source: Adapted from the US Commission on Civil Rights, "Racial Isolation in the Public Schools"

governmental policies and laws were exactly what caused segregation and its resultant effects. One such notable effect is the amount of revenue received by the US cities and the suburbs surrounding those cities. In Table 7.1, the Kerner Commission found the amount of revenue received per pupil was significantly higher when comparing students from the "city", mostly Black and students of color, and those who attended schools in the "suburbs," primarily White, between 1950 and 1964.

In the majority of examples, per pupil revenue remained higher in suburban areas as compared to the cities. During this time period, an increasing number of White families were moving from urban areas to suburban communities where the educational outcomes were believed to be superior. The migration of White families to the suburbs and out of the city, commonly referred to as "white flight," left those who remained to contend with learning in an educationally poorer environment. It also led to an increased gap in educational performance and outcomes among Whites, Blacks and Hispanic/Latine students (Gibson, 2010; Jayapal, 1987). White flight occurred in the United States, in part as a result of school desegregation (Gibson, 2010). Concurrently, funding for urban schools began to decline while funding for suburban schools began to rise. A large source of funding for public education stems from property tax revenue. In a study examining the impact of white flight in Rust-Belt states, Gibson (2010) found that the percentage of property taxes allocated to the school districts fell from 70.5% of total revenues to 36.1% of total revenues between 1960 and 2000. He goes on to state, "Based on the findings in this study, this disparity is related to the population changes attributed to White flight, meaning that more property tax revenue was being generated to educate the students in the mostly White school districts due to the increasing local wealth within those communities. Conversely, less money was being generated to educate the students in the mostly Black school districts, due to the decreasing wealth among the residents in the cities that the school districts served" (p. 93). In one of the largest school districts in the country, the Los Angeles Unified School District (LAUSD) experience of "white flight" was particularly acute. In 1966, there were 396,654 White students in LAUSD, but by 1980 that number had declined to 127,281—a 68% decrease in 14 years (Schneider, 2008).

Some contend that the overall impact the Affirmative Action ruling will not affect higher education admissions. According to a Brookings Institution report, the effect of the *Students for Fair Admissions, Inc. v. President & Fellows of Harvard* and *Students for Fair Admissions, Inc. v. University of North Carolina* cases may not be as significant as previously thought. That is, Affirmative Action was primarily used at a small number of very selective colleges, in the first place. Second, the use of Affirmative Action in college admissions at public universities is banned in Arizona, California, Idaho, Nebraska, Oklahoma, Michigan, Florida, New Hampshire and Washington (Reber et al., 2023). Further, 70% of undergraduate students, including those who are Black, Hispanic/Latine, Native American, Indigenous, Asian and other, attend two-year and four-year, less exclusive institutions (Reber et al., 2023). Whereas the implications of the Supreme Court's decision on students from traditionally marginalized populations are unclear, it is likely to decrease the number of students at the most selective of universities and colleges (Reber et al., 2023; Blume & Long, 2014). Blume and Long (2014) found that students of color will be 23% less likely to be admitted to a highly selective university or college as a result of banning Affirmative Action. This figure becomes even more pernicious when we examine states such as Arizona, Idaho, Nevada and New Mexico that have fewer higher selective universities and colleges. Those students are more likely to apply to more competitive universities and colleges in California where their chances of acceptance become lower (Blume & Long, 2014). It is also critical to note that Affirmative Action has only been in place since 1965 (50+ years) when President Johnson signed Executive Order 11246, prohibiting employment discrimination based upon race, color, religion and national origin by organizations that received federal contracts and subcontracts (Czachor, 2023; University of California Irvine, Office of Equal Opportunity and Diversity, n.d.; National Archives, Office of Federal Register, n.d.). Also, the Supreme Court affirmed the right of colleges and universities to use race as a basis to consider in admissions in 2003 in the Grutter v Bollinger case (Czachor, 2023). In that case, Justice O'Connor wrote, "in the context of its individualized inquiry into the possible diversity contributions of all applicants, the Law School's race-conscious admissions program does not unduly harm nonminority applicants" (Czachor, 2023). Thus, the use of Affirmative Action in education had only been in place for approximately 58 years, affirmed by the Supreme Court around 20 years ago, and now it is expected that that was a sufficient amount of time to eradicate all of the racist policies and treatment of non-White people leading to the educational inequities that exist today. It is extremely unlikely that centuries of racist policies and practices could be erased in less than 60 years and that we now have an equitable educational system in the United States. It is more likely that we have seen an increased emphasis on "pushing back" against equity efforts and that society is expected to forget what has transpired during the course of history of the United States.

Decreasing the number of Black and brown students from the most selective universities is critical as these institutions offer high returns on student investments because their graduates are overrepresented in the areas of business, media and government. Further, "eight of the nine justices who ruled on the Harvard and UNC cases graduated from law school at Harvard or Yale, one-third of former President Biden's initial cabinet was Harvard-educated, and graduates of elite colleges are more likely to have very high earnings or work at a prestigious firm as adults" (Reber et al., 2023). According to the Center for American Progress (CAP), there are five reasons to use Affirmative Action in college admissions:

1) Students of color remain underrepresented on college campuses
2) Prioritizing diversity benefits students of all races
3) Affirmative Action in education promotes diversity in ways a focus on income alone cannot
4) Affirmative Action helps colleges take steps towards greater equity in admissions
5) Affirmative Action helps promote social mobility.

(Maxwell & Garcia, 2019)

Opponents of Affirmative Action often state that Black and Hispanic/Latine students are likely to struggle if they are "unfairly" admitted to a university or college that they would not have been accepted into without Affirmative Action. On the contrary, Harper (2023) found that Black students who attended Harvard and Princeton graduated at a higher rate than the overall student body. Black students who attended Yale graduated at the same rate (98%) as the rest of the student body as well (Harper, 2023). A similar study conducted in 2013 found that Black student graduation rates at Wellesley, Bryn Mawr and Mount Holyoke colleges were higher than the graduation rates for White students (Harper, 2023).

Columbia University President, Lee Bollinger, who has been a proponent of Affirmative Action in higher education for over 30 years, said of the Supreme Court's ruling, "It feels like the country has been on a course of choosing between a continuation of the great era of civil rights, and another view of 'We've done this long enough, and we need a whole new approach.' It's now the second choice" (Totenberg, 2023). Unfortunately, it appears as if Bollinger is correct.

Underrepresentation and income inequality

Now that Affirmative Action has been eliminated as a consideration in higher education admissions, it is likely that there will be fewer Black, Hispanic/Latine and other minorities attending universities and colleges, especially attending more selective institutions (Czachor, 2023; Peele & Willis, 2020). Since voters in California outlawed the use of race as a basis for college admissions in 1996, the share of Black, Hispanic/Latine and Indigenous students has fallen. "Enrollment data from 1996 through 2018 reveals that voter rejection of affirmative action hurt the enrollment of Black, Latina and Native American students in California's public universities" (Peele & Willis, https://edsource.org/2020/dropping-affirmative-action-had-huge-impact-

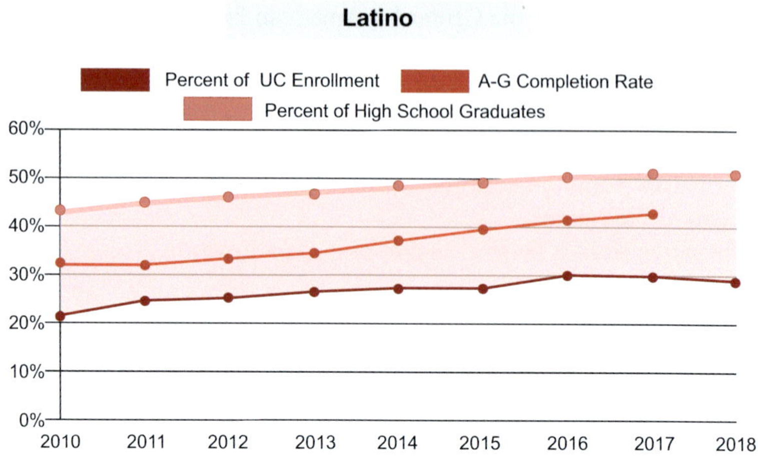

FIGURE 7.1 Percent of Hispanics/Latines Graduating From California High Schools in Comparison to the Percent of Hispanics/Latines Enrolling at a University of California Institution—2010–2018.

Source: Adapted from Xie (2020)

on-californias-public-universities/642437). In 2018, the percentage of Hispanic/Latine students graduating from high school was 52%, while the percentage of Hispanic/Latine students who enrolled at University of California (UCs) schools was only 29% (Peele & Willis, 2020). There are ten University of California colleges, including the University of California Los Angeles (UCLA), UC Berkeley and UC San Diego, and they are ranked higher than their California State University counterparts.

Examining data among other groups of students shows a similar pattern of underrepresentation at the University of California schools. Take, for example, Black students. In 2018, the percentage of Black students graduating high school in California amounted to 5.67%, while the percentage that enrolled as freshmen at a UC was just 4.74%.

Only for Indigenous, or Native American students was the share of high school graduates and freshmen enrolling at UC the same at 0.55%. In this case, however, you can see that the percentage of Indigenous/Native American students graduating from high school is extremely low.

Conversely, Asian students were overrepresented in terms of freshmen enrollment at a UC. In 2018, the percent of Asian students graduating from high school in California was slightly less than 14% (13.91), yet the percentage that enrolled as freshmen at a UC was 41%.

Finally, White students were slightly underrepresented in 2018. Whereas the share of White students graduating from a California high school in 2018 was 25%, they enrolled as freshmen at a UC at a share of 22%.

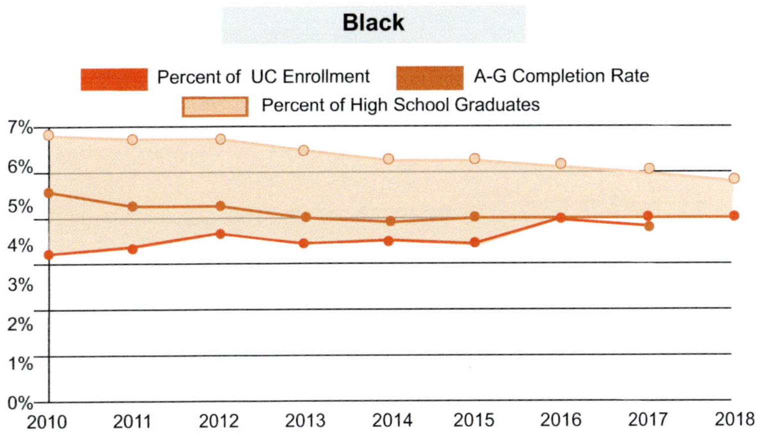

FIGURE 7.2 Percent of Blacks Graduating From California High Schools in Comparison to the Percent of Blacks Enrolling at a University of California Institution—2010–2018.

Source: Adapted from Xie (2020)

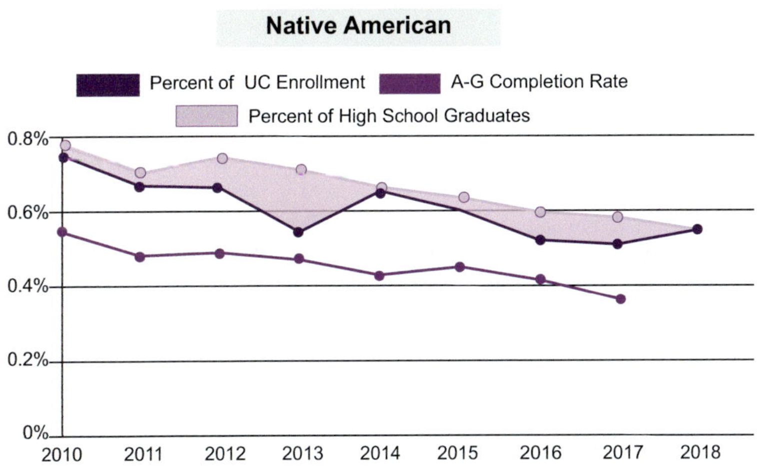

FIGURE 7.3 Percent of Indigenous/Native Americans Graduating From California High Schools in Comparison to the Percent of Indigenous/Native Americans Enrolling at a University of California Institution—2010–2018.

Source: Adapted from Xie (2020)

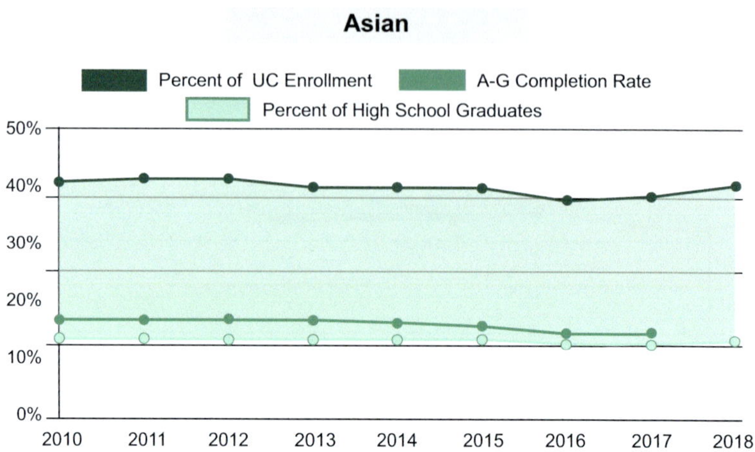

FIGURE 7.4 Percent of Asians Graduating From California High Schools in Comparison to the Percent of Asians Enrolling at a University of California Institution—2010–2018.

Source: Adapted from Xie (2020)

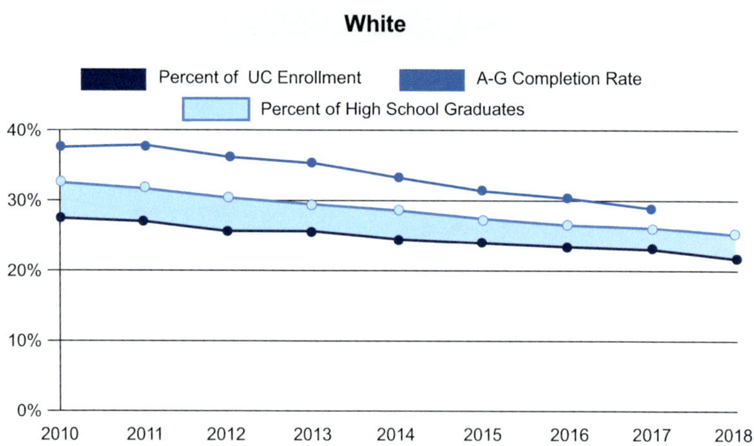

FIGURE 7.5 Percent of Whites Graduating From California High Schools in Comparison to the Percent of Whites Enrolling at a University of California Institution—2010–2018.

Source: Adapted from Xie (2020)

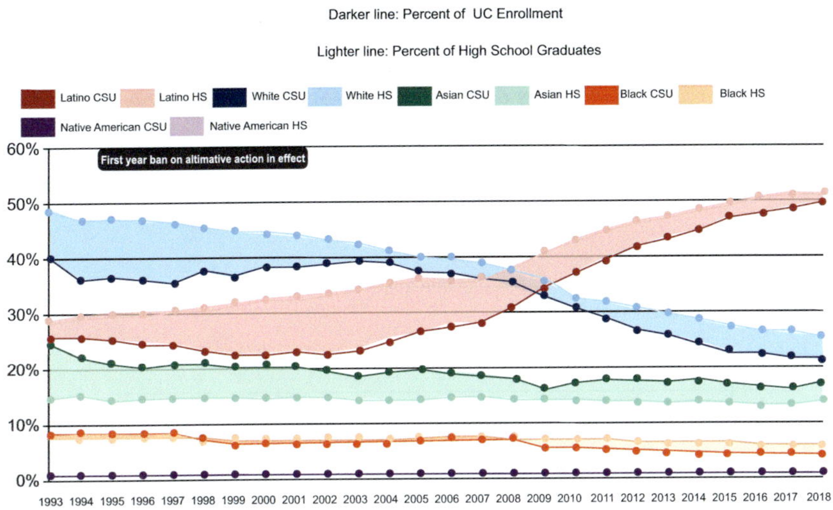

FIGURE 7.6 Freshmen Enrollment Compared to Percentage of High School Graduates.

Source: Adapted from Xie (2020)

The patterns of underrepresentation and overrepresentation that exist at the UCs are nearly identical at the California State Universities (CSUs), as shown in the following.

In addition to banning the use of Affirmative Action in higher education, the percentage of non-White faculty from California public colleges is also critically low and underrepresented based on the demographic characteristics of the state. The percentage of Hispanic/Latine tenured faculty at the UCs is 7%, 10% at the CSUs and 15% at community colleges. This is the case even though California's population is over 40% Hispanic/Latine (Census.gov). Moreover, 21 of the 23 CSUs are Hispanic-Serving Institutions (HSIs), where HSIs are defined as having, at least, 25% of the undergraduate, full-time enrollment being Hispanic/Latine and, at least, half of the institution's degree-seeking students being low income (California State University External Relations, 2021).

In California, the ban on Affirmative Action in higher education has had the desired effect for many that believe Blacks and people of color have not, or no longer are impacted based upon their race or ethnicity towards achieving any desired educational, employment or home ownership goals. The implications of these beliefs will result in a continuance to the White-male dominant position and in a much less diverse and less equitable society.

TABLE 7.2 Racial and Ethnic Composition of California Public Colleges—2016–2017 *Tenured Faculty*

	University of California	*California State University*	*California Community Colleges*
AANHPI	16%	18%	10%
White	70%	62%	61%
Hispanic/Latine	7%	10%	15%
Black	3%	4%	6%

Source: Adapted from Gordon (2018)

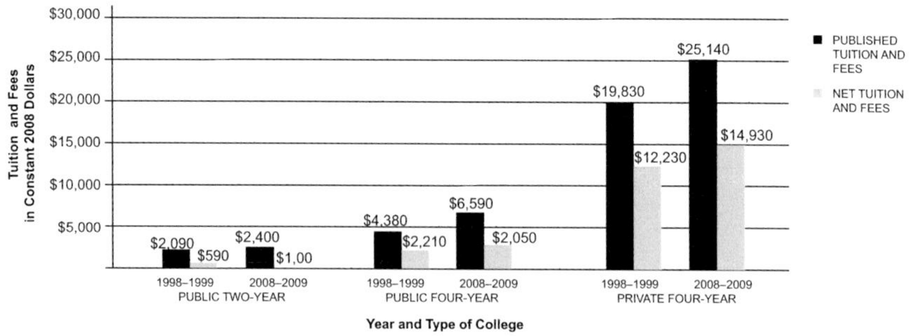

FIGURE 7.7 Net Tuition and Fees for Various Types of Colleges, 1998–1999 and 2008–2009.

Source: Adapted from Baum and Ma (2008, p. 11)

Another ramification from the Supreme Court's ruling is the impact it will have on wealth accumulation. Students who do indeed attend college now are much more likely to incur student debt through loans that they take out because of the dramatic increases in tuition. Tuition and fees at public two-year colleges increased by nearly 13% from 1999 to 2009. At public four-year colleges, tuition and fees increased by 34% and at private four-year colleges, the increase was 21%.

The reasons why this is an education equity issue are multifold. First, individuals who attain more years of education are more likely to earn higher incomes. In 2006, for example, individuals who had earned a professional or graduate degree earned more than three times the amount that individuals earned who had just a high school diploma. Furthermore, those individuals with graduate degrees earned approximately 20% more than individuals with a bachelors degree (Haskins, 2008).

This well-known fact positively encourages individuals to finish high school and college. Additionally, completing a postsecondary degree

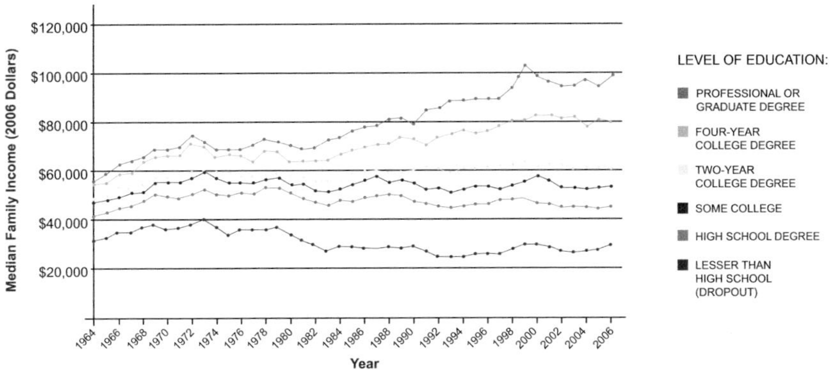

FIGURE 7.8 Median Family Income of Adults Aged 30–39 With Various Levels of Educational Attainment, 1964–2006.

Source: Adapted from Brookings tabulations of data from the Annual Social and Economic Supplement to the CPS, 1964–2006

becomes more valuable economically, especially if it is viewed as an important driver of income for an individual's particular field of work. Thus, paying for education is seen as an investment one makes in themselves for the potential to earn a higher income in life. While this is a positive perspective, it does not come absent of economic considerations based upon additional factors, including graduating in the first place, and the actual amount of income individuals will earn once they graduate. These factors need to be considered in relation to the amount of student debt one is willing to take on.

The six-year graduation rate for White students in 2010 was 64%, which was 4% higher than the average. At the same time, the graduation rate was 54% for Hispanic students, 51% for Pacific Islander students, 40% for Black students and 39% for Indigenous students. Asian students had the highest graduation rate during this period which stood at 74%.

If we drill down further and examine graduation rates, by race and types of institutions students attended, we see that public four-year and private nonprofit institutions have the highest graduation rates for all races (IPEDS, 2019). The average graduation rate at private for-profit institutions was the lowest at 26% which was 33% below public four-year institutions and 40% below private four-year institutions (IPEDS, 2019). While the graduation rate for all students at for-profit four-year institutions was lower than other institutions, it was particularly low for Blacks and Hispanic/Latine students; 30% for Hispanic/Latine students and just 18% for Black students.

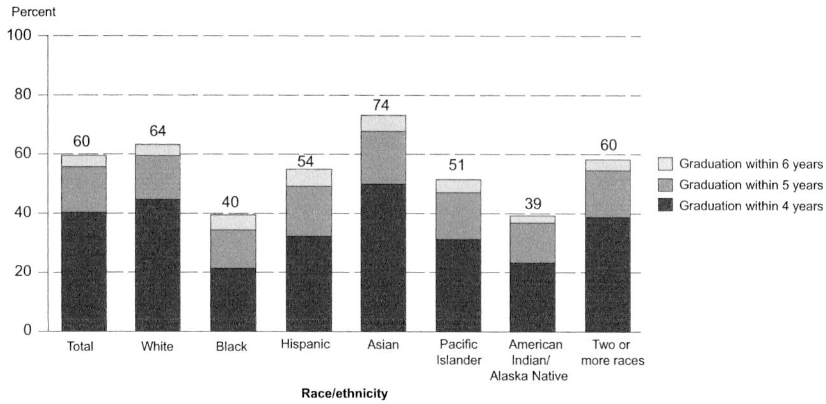

FIGURE 7.9 Graduation Rates at Four-Year Institutions, by Race and Ethnicity—2010.

Source: Adapted from US Department of Education, National Center for Education Statistics, Integrated Postsecondary Education Data System (IPEDS), Winter 2016–17, Graduation Rates component

Note: Data are for Four-year degree-granting postsecondary institutions participating in Title IV federal financial aid programs

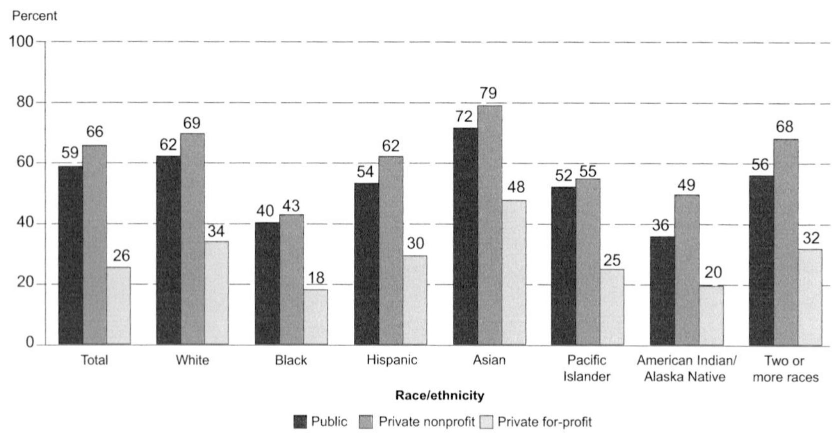

FIGURE 7.10 Graduation Rates at Four-Year Institutions, by Race, Ethnicity and Institution Type—2010. Integrated Postsecondary Education Data Systems (IPEDS)

Source: Adapted from US Department of Education, National Center for Education Statistics, Integrated Postsecondary Education Data System (IPEDS), Winter 2016–17, Graduation Rates component

What makes this matter even more troubling is the number of Black and Hispanic/Latine students who attend these institutions. According to Libassi (2018), Black and Hispanic students are more likely than White students to earn their certifications and degrees from for-profit schools and less likely to earn them from public four-year institutions. Between 2013 and 2015, the percentage of White students who attended public four-year institutions was 39%, while for Hispanics/Latines it was 30% and just 27% for Black students (IPEDS, 2018). Conversely, during the same time period, 28% of Black students attended for-profit four-year institutions, while 25% of Hispanic/Latine students and only 11% of White students. Compounding these figures is that public four-year institutions award twice as many credentials and degrees than their for-profit peers. Further, for-profit institutions are more likely to spend less per student, have lower

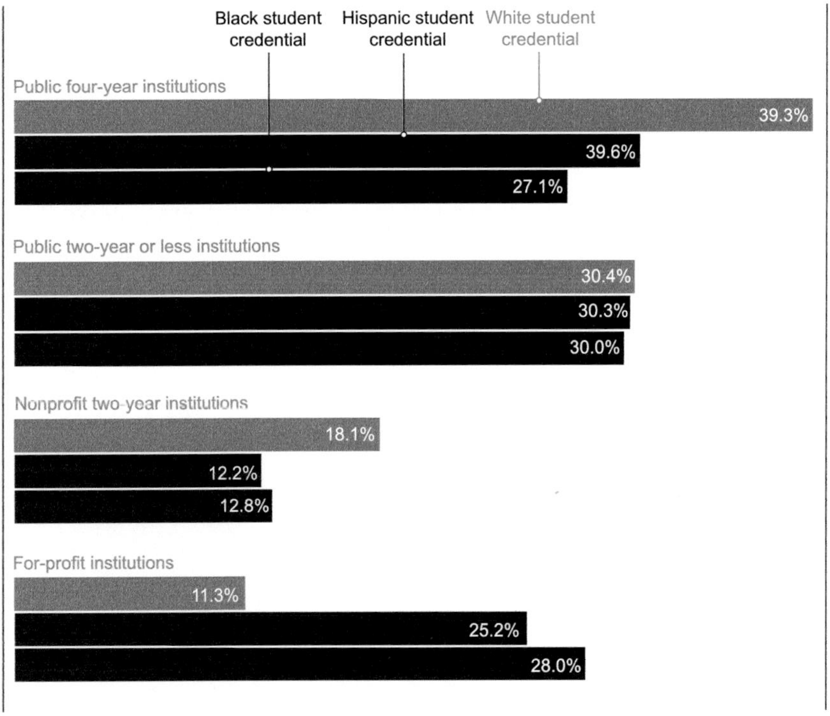

FIGURE 7.11 Share of Racial Group's Completions in Each Sector, 2013–2015.

Source: Adapted from Center for American Progress analysis of data from the Integrated Postsecondary Education Data System from 2013 through 2015. See National Center for Education Statistics, Integrated Postsecondary Education Data System, "Use the Data," available at https://nces.ed.gov/ipeds/use-the-data (last accessed April 2018)

Note: Bar chart includes all students completing a bachelor's degree or below

retention rates, enroll students with lower SAT scores, have faculty who earn lower salaries and have higher student-faculty ratios (Libassi, 2018).

Higher education student loan debt

Ultimately, students who attend for-profit institutions, (who are most commonly Black, Hispanic/Latine and students of color) are also more likely to incur student loan debt than those who attend public four-year institutions and even more likely than those who attend private nonprofit institutions (Wood, 2024). According to The Institute for College Access and Success (2019) in 2016, 66% of students who attended public four-year institutions incurred student loans, while 68% from private nonprofit colleges and 80% of students at for-profit institutions did.

Obviously, the amount of student loan debt is a key issue because students leaving with "minimal" debt are better situated financially than those leaving with moderate or substantial debt. So, what is a minimal amount of debt that a student is willing to accept upon their graduation? That is a difficult question to answer, in part, because many students choose majors based upon a field of study that they will enjoy rather than the amount of debt that it will cost them to obtain. What we do know is that graduates from for-profit colleges left those institutions with, on average, $39,900 in student debt (The Institute for College Access & Success, 2019).

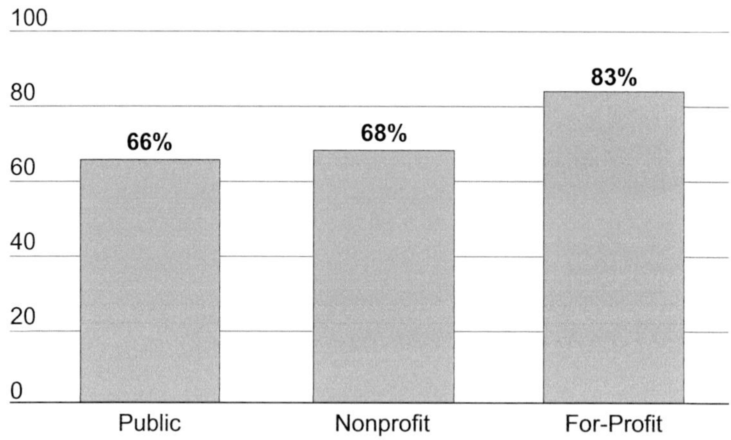

FIGURE 7.12 Share of Bachelor of Arts (BA) Recipients With Student Loan Debt, by College Type—2016.

Source: Adapted from The Institute for College Access & Success. 2019. Quick Facts about Student Debt. http://bit.ly/1lxjskr

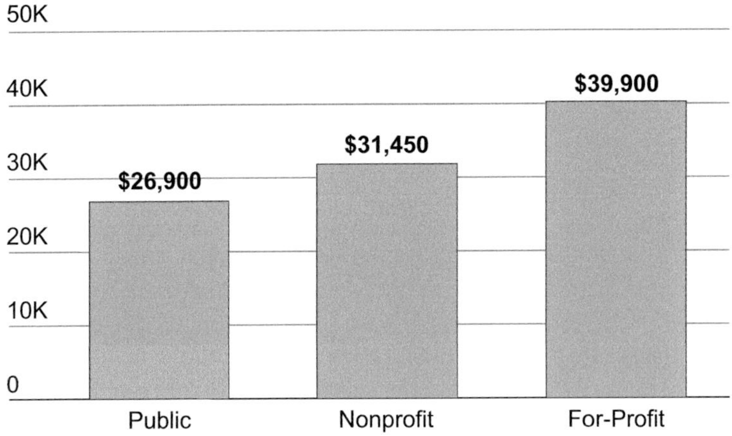

FIGURE 7.13 Average Student Loan Debt for Bachelor of Arts (BA) Recipients by College Type 2016.

Source: Adapted from The Institute for College Access & Success. 2019. Quick Facts about Student Debt. http://bit.ly/1lxjskr

In addition, students from public four-year institutions had, on average, $26,900 in student loan debt and students from nonprofit four-year institutions had $31,450 in student loan debt, on average (The Institute for College Access & Success, 2019). Not including interest on student loan debt, which can be anywhere between 5.5% for undergraduates and 8% for graduate school, students can expect to have around $30,000 in debt upon graduation (Calonia et al., 2023). Depending on the field they enter, this figure could amount to nearly one full year of salary.

While student loan debt is pervasive for all races and ethnicities, it is particularly acute for Black students. For example, as of 2016, the percentage of Black graduates who had student loan debt reached 85%. At the same time, the percentage of White students with student loan debt was 69%, and 66% for Hispanic/Latine students. The race/ethnicity with the lowest percentage of graduates with student loan debt was Asians (45%) but this still represents nearly *half* of all Asian graduates.

One of the most concerning statistics related to student loan debt is the average amount based upon race and ethnicity. As of 2016, Black students had the most student loan debt, on average, at $34,000, followed by White students ($30,000), Hispanics/Latines and Asian students (25,450) (Institute for College Access & Success, 2019).

The numbers demonstrate that Black and Hispanic/Latine students, who are more likely to attend for-profit four-year institutions that spend the

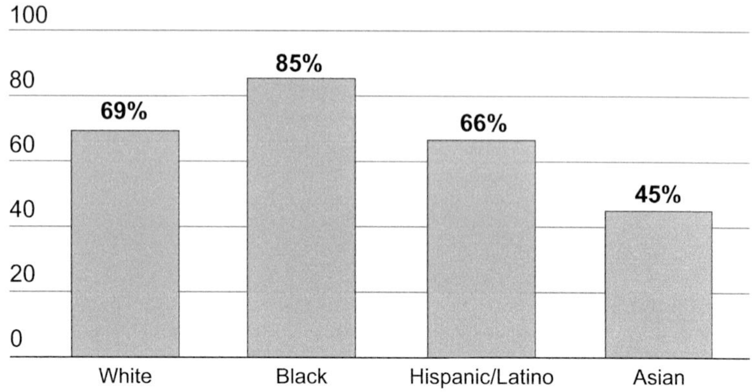

FIGURE 7.14 Share of Bachelor of Arts (BA) Recipients With Student Loan Debt in 2016, by Race/Ethnicity.

Source: Adapted from The Institute for College Access & Success. 2019. Quick Facts about Student Debt. http://bit.ly/1lxjskr

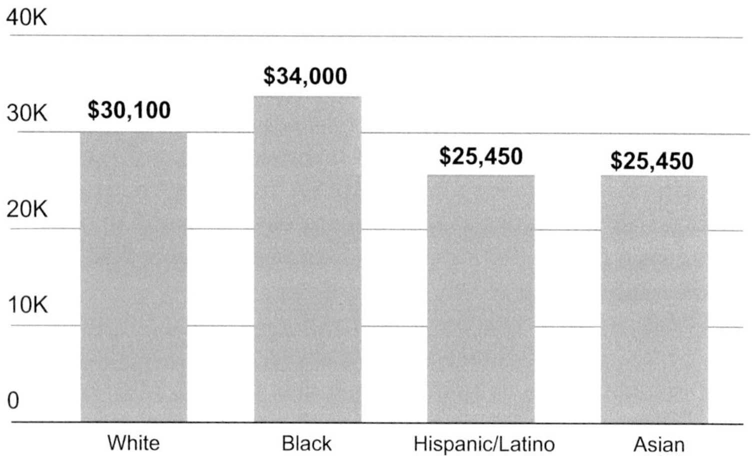

FIGURE 7.15 Average Debt for Bachelor of Arts (BA) Recipients With Loans in 2016, by Race/Ethnicity.

Source: Adapted from The Institute for College Access & Success. 2019. Quick Facts about Student Debt. http://bit.ly/1lxjskr

least per pupil, and have higher student-faculty ratios, leave school from lower-rated institutions with an enormous amount of student loan debt. The lower-ranking schools are important to note because they may hinder the type of job attained after graduating, and or the pay that is earned once in the workforce. Student loan debt continues to increase at a high rate and as a result, "the greatest concern should be confined to students with debt levels substantially above average, especially students who do not obtain their degree and therefore will have a lower average income to repay their debt" (Haskins et al., 2008, p. 32).

Opposition to eliminating student loan debt

During the Coronavirus Pandemic, unemployment rose significantly, economic output declined precipitously and the global economy shrank dramatically. Many individuals and families found it difficult to pay rent, mortgages and various bills and maintain the lifestyles they enjoyed prior to the pandemic. As a result, the US Department of Education allowed student loan borrowers to pause their payments for nearly years (2020–2023). Former President Biden declared the Coronavirus Pandemic to be a national emergency and ultimately he attempted to eliminate up to $10,000 of student loan debt for all borrowers. The Biden Administration believed that the Higher Education Relief Opportunities for Students Act (HEROES) allowed the US Secretary of Education the ability to waive or modify loan forgiveness, under the Higher Education Act and based upon a national emergency (Frederick, 2023). According to US Secretary of Education, Miguel Cardona, the Biden Administration's plan protects "students from unaffordable debt, make repayment more affordable, and ensure that investments in higher education pay off for students and working families" (U.S. Department of Education, 2023). As economically beneficial as Biden's plan would have been, it was met with staunch opposition. Louisiana Senator Bill Cassidy led efforts to oppose the debt relief plan indicating that the Biden Administration did not have the authority to eliminate over $400 billion in student debt (Figueroa, 2023). Another vocal critic of the plan was Representative Marjorie Taylor-Greene (GA) who exclaimed, "and taxpayers all over the country, taxpayers that never took out a student loan, taxpayers that pay their bills and maybe even never went to college and are just hardworking people, they shouldn't have to pay off the great big student loan debt for some college student that piled up massive debt going to some Ivy League school. That's not fair" (Richards, 2022). Despite their criticisms regarding student loan debt relief efforts, many of these same critics were notably silent when it came to the Paycheck Protection Program (PPP) loans they received and were ultimately *forgiven* by the federal government. For example, Congresswoman Greene had over $183,000 in PPP Loans forgiven. Representative Vern Buchanan of Florida, another vocal critic of Biden's student loan debt plan, also benefitted from having his PPP loans forgiven to the amount of $2.3 million. Other critics of Bidens plan, hypocritically did not feel as strongly when they were bailed out from repaying their own PPP loans. Representative Markwayne Mullin (OK) who stated that farmers, ranchers, small business owners and teachers in his state don't need to be "paying the debts of Ivy League lawyers and doctors across the U.S." had $1.4 million in PPP loans forgiven (Richards, 2022). Other members of Congress who were bailed out from paying their PPP loans included, Representative Kevin Hern (OK)—$1 million forgiven; Representative Mike Kelly (PA)—$987,000 forgiven and Representative Matt Gaetz (FL)—$482,300 forgiven. Arkansas, Iowa, Kansas, Missouri, Nebraska and South Carolina agreed with the critics who believed that student loan debt should not be forgiven, arguing that the loan forgiveness plan exceeded the secretary of education's authority which then brought the case to the Supreme Court (Frederick, 2023). Similar to the Supreme Court's ruling banning Affirmative Action in higher education, in *Biden v. Nebraska*, the Supreme Court ruled that the student loan forgiveness plan was an overreach of the administration's power even considering the Higher Education Relief Opportunities for Students Act (HEROES). In her dissent, Justice Kagan stated, "The statute provides the Secretary with broad authority to give emergency relief to student-loan borrowers, including by altering usual discharge rules. What the Secretary did fits comfortably within that delegation. But the Court forbids him to proceed. As in other cases, the rules of the game change when Congress enacts broad delegations allowing agencies to take substantial regulatory measures." (Frederick, 2023). She continued by stating, "the majority overrides the combined judgment of the legislative and executive branches, with the consequence of eliminating loan forgiveness for 43 million Americans" (Liptak, 2023). In eliminating loan forgiveness for millions of Americans, the students who are the most needy and who come from disadvantaged backgrounds, and those who would benefit the most are left behind. They are not asking for more than what the members of Congress were afforded when individually hundreds of thousands to millions of dollars in Paycheck Protection Program loans were forgiven. It is difficult to take the arguments against student loan forgiveness by members of Congress seriously when they themselves have had their own loans forgiven. And even beyond the obvious hypocrisy that exists in this case, from the perspective of improving the lives of individuals and the overall economy, loan forgiveness is the fiscally smart and prudent course of action. Student loan debt is the second highest source of debt for Americans, following only home mortgages and the debt represents over 40 million individuals who have amassed over 1.5 trillion dollars of debt (Council on Foreign Relations, 2023; Roosevelt Institute, 2021). The average borrower between the ages of 18 and 39 spends over 20% of their monthly income on student loan debt which not only impacts the individual but slows business growth and decreases consumer spending

(Miller et al., 2023; Roosevelt Institute, 2021). It may be reasonable to assume, therefore, that individuals who have student loan debt will find it more difficult to purchase a home and make other financial investments. Furthermore, and perhaps more importantly, eliminating or canceling student loan debt, altogether, will provide a stimulus to the economy whereby "increasing borrowers [financial] freedom, and mobility allowing them to change jobs, pay down debts, or move; and increasing average pay by $3,000 over a 10-year period" (Roosevelt Institute).

Equity implications

The equity implications are obvious. Student loan debt is a hindrance for borrowers who would like to purchase a home, pay off other debt and save for retirement or emergencies. The majority (nearly 60%) of borrowers have delayed important financial decisions because of the student loan debt they have accrued pursuing their degrees (Bareham, 2023). As we have stated, the vast majority of individuals who have student loans are Blacks and other people of color. Another deeper issue with student loan debt is that the most likely Black and people of color students who actually apply for them are the most needy from those groups. For example, Pell Grants are educational funds awarded to individuals from low-income families. Blacks (71%), Hispanic/Latine (65%) and Asian (72%) students comprise the overwhelming majority of Pell Grant recipients (Rivera & Smith, 2023). In comparison, White students comprise the lowest percentage of Pell Grant recipients at 60% (Rivera & Smith, 2023).

Hispanic/Latine students appear to be the most risk-adverse in terms of taking out student loans, representing only 15% of borrowers. The reasons for these figures are unclear (Rivera & Smith, 2023). What is also unclear is whether Hispanic/Latine individuals who decide not to take out student loans choose other options to finance their education or do not attend college, at all. If the latter is the case, then that means a large segment of would-be college students are forgoing this option to enter the workforce immediately after high school. As we have previously shown, the difference in annual income between a high school graduate and a college graduate is approximately $40,000. Further, the significantly lower annual income between high school and college graduates adversely impacts students', in this case Hispanic/Latine, ability to decrease the wealth gap with Whites.

Finally, the percentage of Black and Hispanic/Latine students who default on their student loans is significantly higher than White students (Nichols & Anthony, 2020).

Eliminating student loan debt would be a relatively easy and financially smart thing to do, but because of false assumptions, inaccurate information

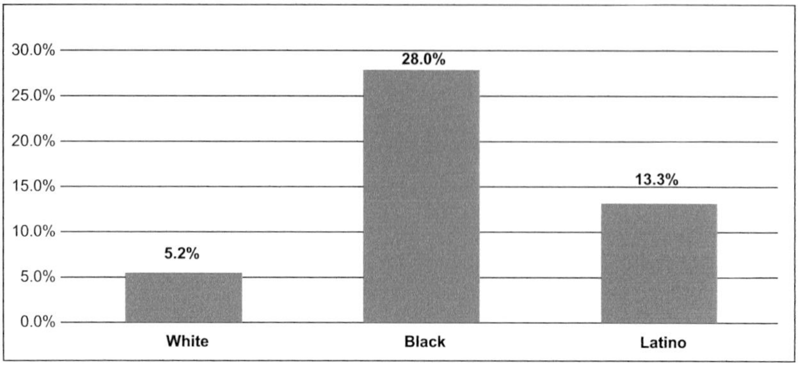

FIGURE 7.16 Twelve-Year Student Loan Default Rate by Race/Ethnicity 2003 and 2004.

Source: Adapted from Nichols and Anthony Jr. analysis of US Department of Education, National Center for Education Statistics, 2003–04 Beginning Postsecondary Students Longitudinal Study, Second Follow-Up (BPS:04/09)

and political gamesmanship, it has become a much larger issue than it should be. Only time will tell how the United States proceeds in dealing with this societal problem that has enormous equity implications.

References

Bareham, H. (2023). *Survey: Student loans have delayed wealth-building for Gen Z and millennial borrowers.* https://www.bankrate.com/loans/student-loans/financial-milestone-survey/

Baum, S., & Ma, J. (2008). *Trends in college pricing: 2008. Trends in higher education series.* College Board.

Blume, G. H., & Long M. C. (2014). Changes in levels of affirmative action in college admissions in response to statewide bans and judicial rulings. *Educational Evaluation and Policy Analysis*, *36*, 228–252.

Calonia, J., Wing, C., & Kantrovitz, M. (2023). *Student loan interest rates in December 2023.* Bankrate.com

Council on Foreign Relations. (2023). *Is rising student debt harming the U.S. economy?* https://www.cfr.org/backgrounder/us-student-loan-debt-trends-economic-impact

Czachor, E. M. (2023). What is affirmative action? History behind race-based college admissions practices Supreme Court overruled. https://www.cbsnews.com/news/what-is-affirmative-action-history-college-admissions-supreme-court/

The employees of the California State University. (2021). *California State University External Relations.* calstate.edu

Figueroa, A. (2023). *U.S. Senate votes to block student loan relief, White House will veto.* https://missouriindependent.com/2023/06/01/u-s-senate-votes-to-block-student-loan-relief-white-house-will-veto/

Frederick, S. (2023). *Supreme Court strikes down student loan forgiveness program.* National Council of State Legislatures. https://www.ncsl.org/state-legislatures-news/details/supreme-court-strikes-down-student-loan-forgiveness-program

Gibson, J. (2010). *K-12 school funding and resource allocation: The effect of white flight on education funding among public school districts in rust belt states*. Northern Illinois University ProQuest Dissertations & Theses.

Gordon, L. (2018). *Whites dominate California college faculties while students are diverse, study shows*. https://edsource.org/2018/whites-dominate-california-college-faculties-while-students-are-more-diverse-study-shows/594268

Grossman, J., & Wells, R. (1988). *Constitutional law and judicial policy making* (3rd ed.). Pitman Publishing, Inc.

Harper, S. (2023). *Black Harvard and Princeton students graduate at higher rates than classmates overall, equally at Yale*. https://www.forbes.com/sites/shaunharper/2023/07/03/graduation-rates-higher-for-black-collegians-than-for-students-overall-at-harvard-and-princeton-equal-at-yale/?sh=5a3b69e8208c

Haskins, R. (2008). Education and economic mobility. In J. Isaacs, I. Sawhill, & R. Haskins (Eds.), *Getting ahead or losing ground: Economic mobility in America* (pp. 91–104). Economic Mobility Project, an Initiative of the Pew Charitable Trusts. http://www.economicmobility.org/assets/pdfs/PEW_EMP_GETTING_AHEAD.pdf

Haskins, R., Holzer, H., & Lerman, R. (2009). *Promoting economic mobility by increasing postsecondary education*. Economic Mobility Project, an Initiative of the Pew Charitable Trusts.

The Institute for College Access & Success. (2019). *Quick facts about student debt*. http://bit.ly/1lxjskr

Integrated Postsecondary Education Data System. (2018). *National Center for Education Statistics*. https://nces.ed.gov/ipeds/search/viewtable?tableId=34516&returnUrl=%2Fsearch

Integrated Postsecondary Education Data System. (2019). *National Center for Education Statistics*. https://nces.ed.gov/ipeds/search/viewtable?tableId=34516&returnUrl=%2Fsearch

Jayapal, S. (1987). School desegregation and White flight: The unconstitutionality of integration maintenance plans. *University of Chicago Legal Forum*, *1987*(1), Article 16. http://chicagounbound.uchicago.edu/uclf/vol1987/iss1/16

Libassi, C. J. (2018). *The neglected college race gap: Racial disparities among college completers*. Center for American Progress.

Liptak, A. (2023). Student loan forgiveness Supreme Court rules 6-3 against Biden plan. *New York Times*. https://www.nytimes.com/live/2023/06/30/us/student-loans-supreme-court-biden

Maxwell, C., & Garcia, S. (2019). *5 reasons to support affirmative action in college admissions*. Center for American Progress. https://www.americanprogress.org/article/5-reasons-support-affirmative-action-college-admissions/

Miller, D., Smith, A., & Velasquez, V. (2023). *The impact of canceling student debt*. https://www.investopedia.com/the-impact-of-cancelling-student-debt-5101053#:~:text=Student%20loan%20debt%20both%20slows,borrowers%20to%20participate%20in%20it

National Archives, Office of Federal Register. (n.d.). *Executive orders*. https://www.archives.gov/federal-register/codification/executive-order/11246.html

Nichols, A. H., & Anthony, M., Jr. (2020). *Graduation rates don't tell the full story: Racial gaps in college success are larger than we think*. https://edtrust.org/resource/graduation-rates-dont-tell-the-full-story-racial-gaps-in-college-success-are-larger-than-we-think/

Peele, T., & Willis, D. (2020). Dropping affirmative action had huge impact on California's public universities—Proposition 16 would allow race and ethnicity to become factors in admissions, hiring and contracts. *EdSource*. https://edsource.org/2020/dropping-affirmative-action-had-huge-impact-on-californias-public-universities/642437

Reber, S., Goodman, G., & Nagashima, N. (2023). *Admissions at most colleges will be unaffected by Supreme Court ruling on Affirmative Action*. https://www.brookings.edu/articles/admissions-at-most-colleges-will-be-unaffected-by-supreme-court-ruling-on-affirmative-action/

Richards, Z. (2022). White House shines light on Republicans who are criticizing student debt cancellation after getting their PPP loans forgiven—The White House used its Twitter account to point the finger at a handful of GOP lawmakers. *NBC News*. https://www.nbcnews.com/politics/white-house/white-house-shines-light-republicans-are-criticizing-student-debt-canc-rcna44904

Rivera, H., & Smith, H. (2023), Average student loan debt by race. *Bankrate*. https://www.bankrate.com/loans/student-loans/student-loan-debt-statistics-by-race/

Roosevelt Institute. (2021). Unburdened: How canceling student debt can boost growth, equity, and innovation. *Roosevelt.org*

Rothstein, R. (2017). *The color of law: A forgotten history of how our government segregated America*. W. W. Norton & Co.

Schneider, J. (2008). Escape from Los Angeles—White flight from Los Angeles and its schools, 1960–1980. *Journal of Urban History*, *34*(6), 995–1012.

Totenberg, N. (2023). *Supreme Court guts affirmative action, effectively ending race-conscious admissions*. https://www.npr.org/2023/06/29/1181138066/affirmative-action-supreme-court-decision

United States Department of Education. (2023). *Biden-Harris administration announces an additional $9 billion in student debt relief*. https://www.ed.gov/news/press-releases/biden-harris-administration-announces-additional-9-billion-student-debt-relief

University of California Irvine, Office of Equal Opportunity and Diversity. (n.d.). *A brief history of affirmative action*. https://www.oeod.uci.edu/policies/aa_history.php

Wood, S. (2024). How much student loan debt does the average college graduate have? *U.S. News and World Report*. https://www.usnews.com/education/best-colleges/paying-for-college/articles/see-how-student-loan-borrowing-has-changed

Xie, Y. (2020). CSU and UC freshmen enrollment by race and ethnicity. *EdSource*. https://edsource.org/2020/freshmen-enrollment-csu-and-uc-by-race-and-ethnicity/642182

8

RACIAL WEALTH GAP

Over the course of a 24-year period, family wealth in the United States grew by over 16%, from $83,000 in 1992 to $97,000 in 2016 (Noel et al., 2019). The growth experienced during this time period is impressive, especially given the fact that it occurred across two recessions (2001 and 2007). While the United States was experiencing economic growth, the accumulation of wealth was concentrated and not shared by all groups of people. Countless studies (Mimbela & Duarte, 2023; Derenoncourt et al., 2022; Alesini et al., 2021; Weller & Figueroa, 2021; Noel et al., 2019; Hamilton & Darity, 2010; Chiteji & Hamilton, 2002) have not only shown the existence of the racial wealth gap in the United States since the end of slavery but research also shows that it has persisted over time and continues today. We see examples of the racial wealth gap in the United States in home ownership (in 2022, 45% of Black families owned a home compared to 75% of White families); mortgage loans (Blacks were 1.8 and Hispanics/Latines 1.4 times more likely to be denied a mortgage than Whites); and median income (Black median income was $33,000 less than Whites in 2018) (Mimbela & Duarte, 2023).

According to the Federal Reserve's Survey of Consumer Finances, the median wealth of White families was over $124,000 in 1992, while the median wealth of Black families stood at approximately $17,000 and $12,000 for Hispanics/Latines (Jee et al., 2023). By 2019, White wealth had grown to over $181,000 representing approximately a 46% increase (Jee et al., 2023). During the same time period, Black wealth increased by just $4,000 and Hispanic/Latine wealth increased by $24,000. While these groups increased their overall wealth, it still significantly paled in

DOI: 10.4324/9781032670850-9

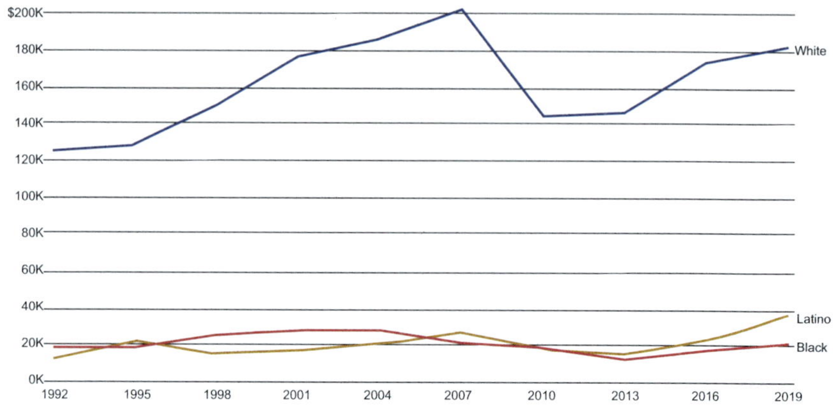

FIGURE 8.1 US Median Wealth by Race—1992–2019.

Source: Adapted from Institute for Economic and Racial Equity, Brandeis University Source: Survey of Consumer Finances (SCF)

Note: The United States. Dollar values in 2019 USD

comparison to Whites during the same time period. Figure 8.1 shows the median wealth by race in the United States between 1992 and 2019. What is obvious are the dramatic differences in wealth between Whites and Blacks and Hispanics/Latines.

The racial wealth gap seems as if it is a term that would be self-explanatory, but it is a complex and nuanced concept. Not to be confused with income, which includes wages earned by an individual or family, wealth refers to liquid and illiquid assets that are passed down from one generation to another. Wealth includes the value of assets such as stocks, bonds, savings accounts, a home and additional properties, minus debt that is owed. Racial wealth refers to the amount of wealth accumulated by an individual, or family, based upon their race. Thus, the racial wealth gap is the differences in wealth between various races.

When examined over time, we can see why the racial wealth gap began in the United States. Because Blacks were enslaved, the per capita White-Black wealth ratio was 56:1 in 1860 (Derenoncourt et al., 2022). Whereas this disparity could easily be explained due to the social conditions of the time, it is challenging to understand why the racial wealth gap has continued to be the largest of the economic gaps between Blacks and Whites today. What accounts for these great differences and disparities in wealth? Why have they continued to occur over time despite overall economic growth by society? To what extent can we attribute systemic racism as the cause of the racial wealth gap? What other factors contribute to the racial wealth gap? In what ways can these disparities be decreased? These are some of the questions that will be covered in this chapter as we examine the racial wealth gap in the United States.

Causes of racial wealth gap and implications

Racism in the area of education, that prevented Black, Hispanic/Latine, and other students of color from attending the same schools as White students has led to disparities in wealth and income (Mimbela & Duarte, 2023). But while a poor educational system obviously can lead to inadequate and otherwise failing results, it is not the sole cause of the racial wealth gap in the United States in the manner in which many think. Noting the impact slavery has had on contributing to the racial wealth gap is axiomatic. Derenoncourt et al.'s (2022) research examines the US racial wealth gap between 1870 and 2020 and illustrates the impact various policies have had on this issue over a 150-year period. For example, immediately after the Civil War and for decades after, Blacks were not permitted to have access to financial institutions, faced frequent violent and destructive attacks on their property and were denied equal access to education (Derenoncourt et al., 2022; McWhirter, 2011). Further, there are many other policy-related reasons leading to the gap, such as the National Labor Relations Act of 1935 not considering agricultural and domestic laborers, who were most commonly Black, as employees which ultimately excluded them from wealth-building sources such as unemployment compensation, worker's rights and old-age insurance (Katznelson, 2005). We have previously discussed in the Housing chapter the impact racially segregated housing and redlining, created by the Federal Housing Administration (FHA), has had on the racial wealth gap. There have been factors such as the vast majority of Black soldiers being excluded from G.I. Bill benefits that included low-cost mortgages, low-interest home and business loans, unemployment and tuition benefits which predominately benefitted Whites over Black veterans (Baker & Addo, 2023).

Even after the elimination of racist US policies, there has been minimal positive effects as we have seen the racial wealth gap diverging and unfortunately not converging. Over the past 40 years higher rates of capital gains, coupled with family savings, have had a pronounced impact on exacerbating the racial wealth gap (Derenoncourt et al., 2022). While past research shows the policies that were created immediately after the Civil War, through Reconstruction, led to the racial wealth gap (Derenoncourt et al., 2022; Miller, 2020; Spriggs, 1984), there have been other determinants leading to this inequity.

Discrimination and disparate treatment of racial minorities in housing, employment, education and banking are but a few of the factors research has shown influencing the racial wealth gap (Baker & Addo, 2023; Mimbela & Duarte, 2023; Derenoncourt et al., 2022; Faber & Friedline, 2018; Darity, 2005; Clements, 2016; Piketty, 2014). Another prominent factor influencing the racial wealth gap is mass incarceration of Blacks, Hispanics/Latines and other people of color. In the United States, more than 70 million people have a criminal record, over 8 million have been to prison and, at least, 14% (around 45 million) have been convicted of a misdemeanor (Grawert & Craigie, 2020). The impact mass incarceration, however, has on Blacks and Hispanics/Latines is more pronounced than it is for Whites. For example, White men and women who have been incarcerated lose approximately $270,000 in earnings over the course of their lifetimes. Conversely, Blacks lose approximately $360,000 ($90,000 less than Whites) and Hispanics/Latines lose $510,000 ($240,000 less than Whites) over the course of their lifetimes. These figures are staggering for the Black and Hispanic/Latine communities in the United States as they amount to wages that will never be recovered and continue to depress economic growth in these communities.

Most recently, we have seen how the Covid-19 pandemic exacerbated the racial wealth gap in the United States. Weller and Figureoa (2021) found that in 2020, "nearly 46.7 percent of unemployed White households could not come up with $400 in an emergency, while 65.2 percent of unemployed Black households lacked access to $400 in such situations" (p. 3). The lack of financial security is tied to the fact that Black workers receive lower average salaries while also having lower-income stability (Hardy & Logan, 2020).

According to a report by the Center for American Progress (CAP), Blacks own approximately one-tenth of the wealth as Whites, have fewer assets than whites, are less likely to be homeowners, to own their own business, or have a retirement account (Hanks et al., 2018). Debt comprises approximately 25% of total asset values for Black households compared to 10% for White households. Black households have 29% of their debt tied into their homes, compared with White households whose housing debt is approximately 21% (Derenoncourt et al., 2022). Further, Blacks typically own *more expensive* debt than Whites such as high-interest credit cards (Hanks et al., 2018). What this inevitably leads to is that Black households are more vulnerable to financial shocks, like the Great Recession or the Covid-19 pandemic, than White households.

Indeed, the racial wealth gap continues to persist and to be a problem for Blacks, Hispanics/Latines and other racial minorities as it depresses their economic power (Pattillo-McCoy, 1999). The negative issues associated with a poor economic situation also include, among others, less political mobility and influence, along with an inadequate representation in media,

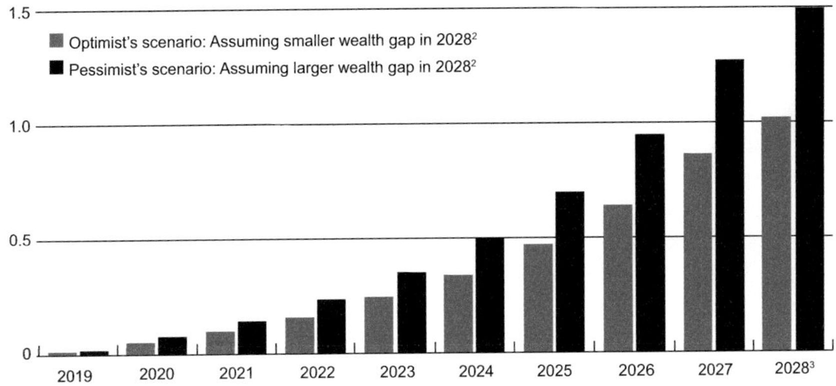

FIGURE 8.2 The Racial Wealth Gaps Impact on the US Economy: 2019–2028.

Source: Adapted from Noel et al. (2019)

which helps formulate public opinion. Some may see the racial wealth gap only as a problem for Blacks or other non-Whites, but there is more.

It is estimated that the racial wealth gap also adversely impacts the overall US economy. According to Noel et al. (2019), the racial wealth gap "will cost the US economy between $1 trillion and $1.5 trillion between 2019 and 2028–4 to 6 percent of the projected GDP in 2028" (p. 6).

Misconceptions about racial equality and equity

Blacks and Whites appear to have a general misunderstanding of the racial wealth gap in the United States, which ultimately leads to misperceptions about it and its impact as well. In a survey of measuring perceptions of racial gaps, along with their causes, White respondents were less likely to perceive the economic conditions for Blacks as worse off than their own, less likely to believe that racial gaps are due to current racism and discrimination, or that racial gaps are due to past slavery and discrimination (Alesini et al., 2021). Their study also found that teenagers' views on the racial wealth gap and policies designed to address racism were different based upon their own political party affiliation. For example, 39% of White Democratic teenagers and 71% of White Republican teenagers believed that Blacks were poor because of a lack of effort. Conversely, 91% of White Democratic teenagers and 51% of White Republican teenagers thought that discrimination was the cause of Blacks being worse off economically than Whites (Alesini et al., 2021). "Overall, it appears that parents' beliefs about individual responsibility, the role of effort, and race, which are at the core of the partisan divide, have already been absorbed (and even amplified) by their teen children" (Alesini et al., 2021, p. 7). It is assumed, therefore, that misperceptions by individuals, at least, related to the racial wealth gap but also likely in other related topics, will continue to persist.

Americans also misperceive the extent to which society has made progress towards achieving racial economic equality. Kraus et al. (2017) surveyed Americans regarding their perceptions of racial economic progress of Blacks compared to Whites in the areas of employee-provided benefits, hourly wages of college graduates, hourly wages of high school graduates, annual income and accumulated wealth. In each of the categories examined, respondents believed that significantly more progress had occurred than actually had. Even one of the researchers who conducted the study was surprised to see the results. Michael Kraus stated, "I'm a person who studies inequality, who should really know how inequality looks, and I look at the black-white gap, and I'm shocked at the magnitude" (Badger, 2017). Part of that reasoning may be because we have seen some progress in terms of racial equality over the past 20 years.

In 2008, the United States elected the first African-American President Barack Obama. In 2012, he was reelected and for many his election and subsequent reelection represented a "racial awakening" of the country. There was a belief that America could not be considered racist any longer since the majority of the nation's residents were not African-American or Black. In fact, Larry Kudlow, host of Kudlow on the Fox Business Network claimed, "Here's a thought: President Obama, the first Black president, was elected twice. And he got 79 million white votes, 79 million in two elections. Now therefore I find it hard to understand something called 'systemic racism'" (Panetta, 2020; Businessinsider.com). Further buoying Kudlow's claims has been the fact that between 2015 and 2020 there has been an increase in the percentage of African-Americans who earn over $125,000 annually. According to the Ipsos Affluent Study, African-Americans affluence increased 65% as compared with 53% of the general US population (Diverse Viewpoints: Exploiting Wealth in the Black/African-American Community, Merrill Lynch). While the increase in affluence among African-Americans is certainly a positive, along with the historical importance of electing an African-American US President are inarguable, believing that economic inequality does not exist is a fallacy. Believing in the fallacy of economic equality is fortified by the historical data presented here along with a closer inspection of the ability of poor children to overcome the economic situation they were born into. Alesini et al. (2021) analyzed intergenerational racial gap mobility between Whites and Blacks. The

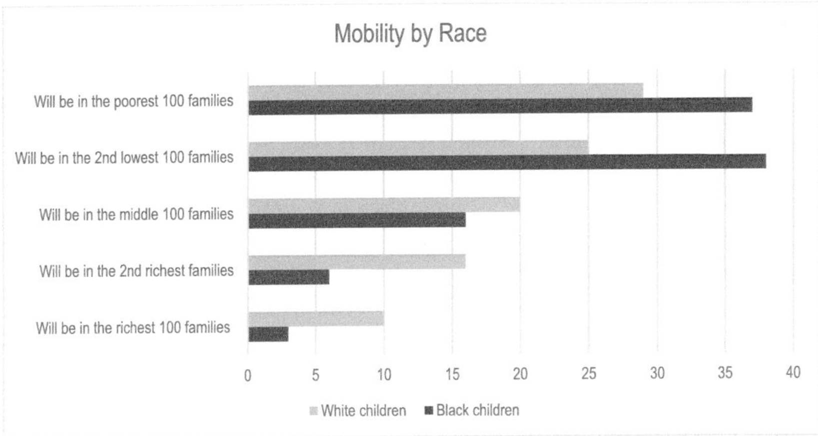

FIGURE 8.3 Racial Gap in Intergenerational Mobility—*A Comparison of How Black and White Children Born in One of the Poorest 100 Families Will Do When They Grow Up.*

Source: Adapted from Alesini et al. (2021)

results of their study shows that it is more than three times less likely that a Black child born to one of the poorest 100 families would ever be in a group of the 100 richest families.

Questioning the validity of racial wealth gap

Jennifer Richeson, a researcher who examined the misperception of racial economic equality reasoned, "It seems that we've convinced ourselves—and by 'we' I mean Americans writ large—that racial discrimination is a thing of the past. It's very difficult to consider the possibility that some of what we've achieved or gained is due to forces that aren't our own individual hard work. That's hard to grapple with, especially in American society. We really believe in egalitarianism and meritocracy" (Badger, 2017). This belief leads to the concept of systematic racism and further to the extent that individuals believe it exists. There is a great debate currently being waged in the United States over the existence of systemic racism. According to Alesini et al. (2021), 50% of Whites and 80% of Blacks believe that racism is a serious problem in the United States and the fact that these are not higher is interesting. There are many people who believe, while the United States affords many opportunities to all people, that racism exists in institutions and organizations which have led to and continue to lead to racist policies, laws, procedures, actions and attitudes. Another segment of the United States, including people like Larry Kudlow, acknowledges that "changes can be made" and there are some "bad apples." In 2024, Republican Presidential candidate, Nikki Haley, who is Indian-American and whose birth name is Nimarata Randhawa, said that America is not racist, nor has it ever been a racist country. She made these proclamations despite stating in her memoir that when her family bought its house in South Carolina, they could do so as long as they did not entertain Black people in it (Morrison, 2024).

The denial of the existence of racism in the United States is also a denial of the existence of systematic racism. The existence of systemic racism does not necessarily mean that there are not many good people in the United States who support equal rights and equity for all. When we fail to acknowledge that laws and policies such as the Federal Housing Authority's (FHA) refusal to insure home mortgages to African-Americans, while also prohibiting Whites from renting or selling their homes to African-Americans as anything other than a racist institutional policy with significant adverse consequences, then we are not dealing in reality. According to the Cambridge Dictionary, Systemic Racism refers to "policies and practices that exist throughout a whole society or organization, and that result in and support a continued unfair advantage to some people and unfair or harmful treatment of others based on race" (https://dictionary.cambridge.org/us/dictionary/english/systemic-racism). Banaji et al. (2021) say that systemic racism occurs when "racially unequal opportunities and outcomes are inbuilt or intrinsic to the operation of a society's structures" (Banaji, Fiske & Massey, p. 2). They go on to say that systemic racism "refers to the processes and outcomes of racial inequality and inequity in life opportunities and treatment. Systemic racism permeates a society's institutional structures (practices, policies, climate), social structures (state/federal programs, laws, culture), individual mental structures (e.g., learning, memory, attitudes, beliefs, values), and everyday interaction patterns (norms, scripts, habits). Systemic racism not only operates at multiple levels, but it can also emerge with or without animus or intention to harm and with or without awareness of its existence" (Banaji, Fiske & Massey, p. 2). The application and practice of systemic racism, therefore has, in part, led to the racial wealth gap in the United States. Acknowledging the existence of systematic racism in the United States disallows anyone from believing that if one Black, Latina or other person of color can become a high educational achiever and secure a well-paying job then all can. *If Obama was able to become President of the US, then any Black person can do the same!* How many times have we heard someone say, *my grandparents came to this country with only the clothes on their backs, and now look at them!* This line of thinking assumes that because one has been able to become president, or some have attained a high level of education and economic success that *all* can do so, only if they would work harder. To take this example yet a step further, this belief also assumes that the majority of Blacks, Hispanics/Latines and other people of color are lazy, dumb and have not worked as hard as Whites. *What else explains the differences?* Ultimately, adhering to these beliefs not only predisposes those individuals from supporting policies and practices that would likely decrease the racial wealth gap but also leads them to work *against* policies that would decrease the gap (Alesini et al., 2021). Discussing the existence of a racial wealth gap tends to make some feel as if Whites have not earned their place at the "top of the racial hierarchy". There is also a perception that non-Whites have an opportunity to decrease the gap simply by working harder and saving more (Alesini et al., 2021). Both ideas are based on a framework of racism and deny the vast amount of evidence that has led to disparities in the first place. One can see evidence of the belief that the racial wealth gap is not based on race, but caused by other factors, when we explore the subtle changes in how contemporary wording leads to a more politically palatable explanation. Darity (2005) highlights this shrewd altering in phraseology when he states, "the politically acceptable trope of cultural determinism progressively has displaced the impolite trope of biological determinism" (p. 144) when discussing the racial wealth gap.

Reinforcing these beliefs also, unfortunately, arrived from the United States' first and only Black president. In 2009, while then President Barack Obama spoke to the National Association for the Advancement of Colored People, he talked about discrimination of Black women, Hispanics/Latines, Muslims and the LGBTQ community (Politico, 2008), while simultaneously criticizing the Black community. "We need a new mindset, a new set of attitudes—because one of the most durable and destructive legacies of discrimination is the way that we have internalized a sense of limitation; how so many in our community have come to expect so little of ourselves" (retrieved from https://www.politico.com/story/2009/07/obamas-remarks-at-naacp-centennial-025053). He goes on to further state that Blacks need to ensure that they are "put[ting] away the Xbox and put[ting] our kids to bed at a reasonable hour." In Obama's Father's Day speech given to parishioners at the Apostolic Church of God in Chicago, he addresses the Black community: "We need fathers to realize that responsibility does not end at conception. We need them to realize that what makes you a man is not the ability to have a child—it's the courage to raise one" (Politico, retrieved from https://www.politico.com/story/2008/06/text-of-obamas-fatherhood-speech-011094). In both instances, Obama provides motivation to overcome obstacles, but also points the finger at the very same people he is attempting to inspire. Some of the content of these speeches creates and perpetuates the notion that Blacks and other minorities can do more to overcome their obstacles. Furthermore, it allows others, who also reason that these groups can "do more," to actually do more and stop blaming others who are usually Whites. *If the first US Black President says this, it must be true, right?* President Obama was a great leader for the United States, and certainly better than his immediate successor, but the tone in these sections of his speeches provided an ill-gotten opportunity for those who oppose equity. Relatedly, because the educational outcomes for Blacks and people of color, in general, are lower than those for Whites, there is a prevailing belief that Black and Hispanic/Latine families care less about education. Moreover, it is opined if they cared more about education then the results would be different.

A particularly interesting facet of the racial wealth gap explores the factors that impact individual families to save money for the future. Noel et al. (2019) found that the communities where families began to build wealth, family wealth, income and savings were all factors that impacted wealth accumulation. Similar to the racist tropes used to suggest Blacks should work harder to accumulate wealth, so too is the belief that Blacks and other racial minorities should spend and invest their income more wisely. They should make less purchases of high-end luxury items (expensive cars and clothes) that do not help in the accumulation of wealth and instead invest in stocks and bonds. Making assumptions such as these underscores misconceptions many have regarding this topic. Chiteji and Hamilton (2002) found that the propensity for Blacks to save and ultimately accumulate wealth is disproportionately influenced by their willingness to generously give and provide financial assistance to family members. Whereas White families are more likely to provide financial assistance to their children, Black and Hispanic/Latine families are more likely to provide that assistance to their relatives who are more likely to have less financial resources. Blacks are more than twice as likely to provide financial assistance to their parents than Whites, while Hispanics/Latines are five times more likely.

Whereas Black and Hispanic/Latine families provide the most financial assistance to their parents, we also find that White families *receive more* financial assistance from their parents than other groups of people. Under-examined data such as the above presents other compelling factors impacting the ability of Blacks and Hispanics/Latines from saving at the same rate as Whites.

"Families' ability to accumulate wealth is affected by constraints that some families experience because of the desperate circumstances of their relatives, and that black families are more likely to be in this position

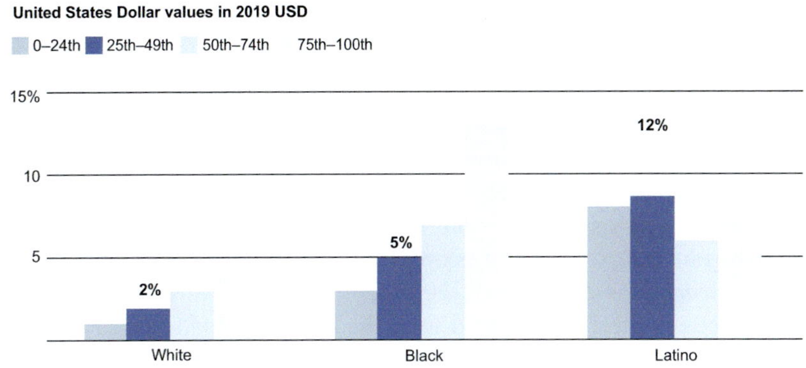

FIGURE 8.4 Percent of Households Providing Financial Support to Parents by Income Quartile: 2010–2019.

Source: Adapted from Chiteji and Hamilton (2002)

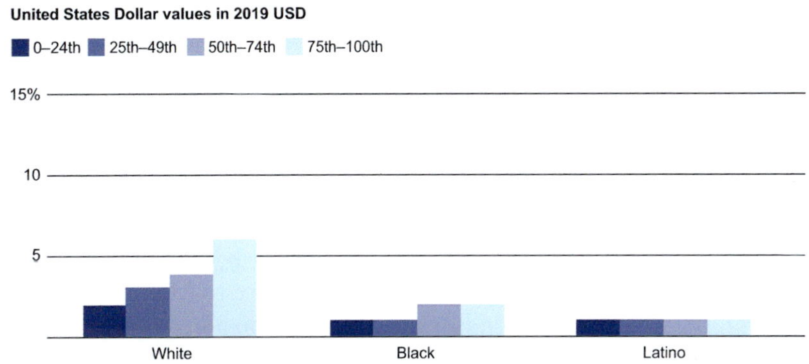

FIGURE 8.5 Percent of Households Receiving Financial Support from Parents by Income Quartile: 2010–2019.

Source: Adapted from Chiteji and Hamilton (2002)

than white families are" (Chiteji & Hamilton, 2002). They pose the question to ponder whether, or not, a connection exists between low levels of wealth accumulated by Blacks and relative poverty among their relatives (Chiteji & Hamilton, 2002). It is not often the case in the Black community where a father gifts $1,000,000, "a small amount of money" to their children to help them out.

What are the equity implications?

Bruce's Beach

In 1912, Willa Bruce bought a piece of property along the coast in what is now Manhattan Beach, California. Willa Bruce paid $1,225 for the parcel of land, which was considered high based upon the comparable lots sold at the time (L.A. Times, 1912). Soon, Willa and her husband, Charles, opened a beachfront resort where *all* people could visit and named the property *Bruce's Beach Front* (Lindwall, 2023). As one could imagine, no sooner than Bruce's Beach Front opened were the Bruces forced to face racist harassment by their neighbors. In addition, according to a LA Times report, Blacks who wanted to visit Bruce's Beach Front were blocked from accessing it because "No Trespassing" signs were placed around a ten-block strip of ocean frontage forcing them to walk a half-mile in order to put their feet in the water (L.A. Times, 1912). "White neighbors resented the resort's growing popularity and prosperity of its African American owners. By the early 1920s White neighbors were 'concerned' about a 'Negro invasion' and the impact it could have on property values" (Chappell, 2023). Despite all of the problems that they faced, Willa Bruce was determined to keep the property, as she stated at the time, "Wherever we have tried to buy land for a beach resort we have been refused, but I own this land and I am going to keep it" (Chappell, 2023). Yet, despite Bruce's determination, in 1924 and just 12 years since it opened, the city of Manhattan Beach, California, seized the property where Bruce's Beach Front stood under the guise of eminent domain. George Lindsey, a real estate agent at the time, led the charge towards condemning the property, largely because Whites feared that a large migration of Blacks were going to move to Manhattan Beach. In an interview years later, Lindsey said, "Education and co-operation will eventually solve the problem (of White's and Black's residing in close proximity to each other) perhaps in five hundred years or so" but until that time I was trying to peacefully put a stop to "negro invasion" (Chappell, 2023). City officials claimed that the property was going to be converted into a park, but it stood empty for more than 30 years.

Nearly 100 years later, a small form of amends was made to repair the damages the Bruce family incurred. In 2021, the Los Angeles County Board of Supervisors voted for the Los Angeles County Anti-Racism, Diversity and Inclusion (ARDI) Initiative to return Bruce's Beach to the Bruce family. On June 28, 2022, the L.A. County Board of Supervisors officially, and finally, returned the property to the heirs of Willa and Charles Bruce (LA County CEO, ARDI Initiative, 2023). Under the terms of the agreement, the Bruce family heirs have agreed to sell the property back to L.A. County for $20 million (Chappell, 2023). California Governor, Gavin Newsom, who signed the legislation that paved the way for the rightful return of the property back to the Bruce family stated, "I want to apologize to the Bruce family for the injustice that was done to them. We haven't always had a proud past." (Chappell, 2023).

While the eventual and rightful return of Bruce Beach to the Bruce family, which was long overdue, provided financial relief, one is left to wonder how much generational wealth was lost over the 97-year period that they did not own the property? If the Bruce's had been able to keep their property, they may have built a larger home, a restaurant, a hotel, or all of these, thus leading to structures that would be more valuable than $20 million.

As of 2024, homes that are within three to four blocks from Bruce's Beach Front, range in price from $3 million to $13 million with a picture of homes located just a few blocks from where Bruce's Beach was.

Baby Bonds

In 2021, the Child Tax Credit was revised under the American Rescue Plan. It increased the Child Tax Credit from $2,000 per child to $3,000 per child for children over the age of 6 and from $2,000 to $3,600 for children under the age of 6. It raised the age limit from 16 to 17 while simultaneously allowing all working families to earn the full credit if they make up to $150,000 for a couple or $112,500 for a family with a single parent. The revision was a step in the right direction to assist eligible families financially. What would be a greater step in the direction towards decreasing the racial wealth gap would be the utilization of Baby Bonds.

Prior to the enactment of the Child Tax Credit of 2021, current US Senator and then presidential candidate, Corey Booker, unveiled the American Opportunity Accounts proposal in 2020 which would provide bonds for every newborn baby in the United States. This version of "Baby Bonds" had previously been introduced in the United Kingdom in 2002 under former prime minister and then chancellor Gordon Brown. The Baby Bond program under Brown would provide a £250 endowment to every child born from September 1, 2002 to January 2, 2011. The program also allowed up to £500 for children from low-income families and permitted unmatched contributions of £1,200 annually from private companies or individuals. Recipients of the bonds would only be allowed to withdraw the funds when they turned 18 years of age (Curtis, 2010). Fortunately, Brown's Baby Bond program, or Child Trust Fund (CTF) as it is called, was implemented in 2005. In 2020, over 700,000 teenagers, who have now turned 18, were eligible to receive money from their CTFs. Depending on whether, or not, the children's parents made additional contributions and if the contributions were invested in the stock market, determines how much money would be available. Approximately, half of the now 18-year-olds will receive £5,000, more than a quarter will receive £20,000 and parents who had invested the most may receive up to £50,000 (Curtis, 2010).

Under Booker's proposal, every child would receive $1,000 annually and would be eligible for up to $2,000 annually based upon their family's income. The funds would be placed in an interest-bearing US Treasury Account and would be eligible for withdrawal, upon turning 18, for the specific purposes of education, purchasing a home or retirement. Booker's proposal would cost approximately $82 billion annually to fund, or less than 10% of the annual expenditure on Social Security (Cassidy et al., 2019).

Based upon Booker's proposal, the estimated value of a Black child's Baby Bond account in 18 years would be $29,038, whereas the average value of a White child's account would be $15,790 (Cassidy et al., 2019). These figures are likely where the "pushback" occurs because some may feel as if it is unfair that their children receive approximately half of what Black children would end up receiving. They may also likely be displeased by the perception of being "punished" for the racial wealth gap, something that they had no part of creating yet have benefitted from tremendously.

It is exceptionally important to note, as we have thoroughly discussed in this chapter, that the racial wealth gap is not only significant but that it

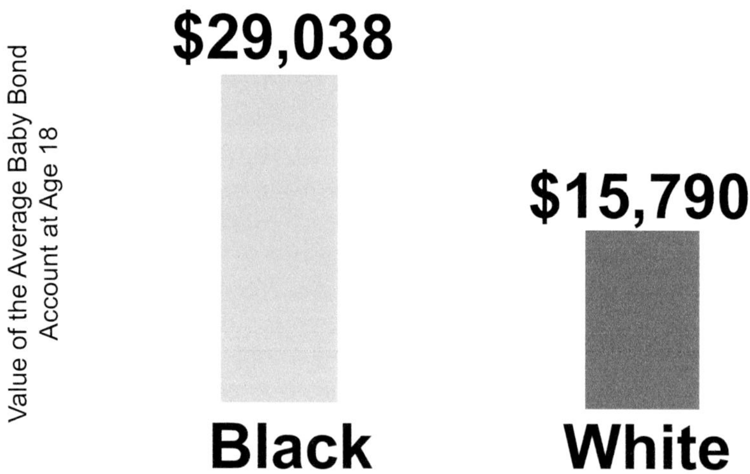

FIGURE 8.6 Estimated Value of Average Baby Bond Account at the Age of 18 by Race—2019 Dollars.

Source: Adapted from Cassidy et al. (2019)

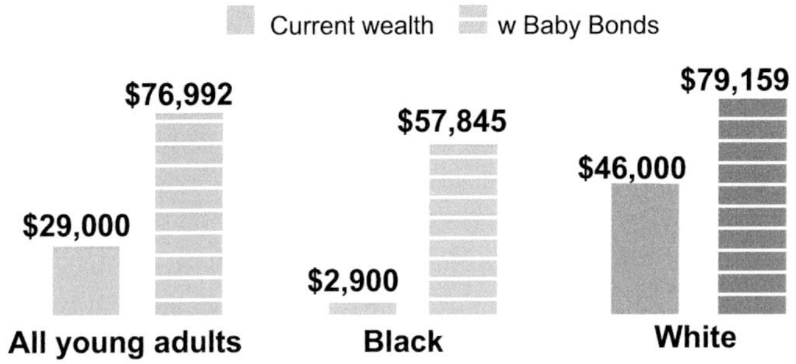

FIGURE 8.7 Universal Baby Bonds Reduce Median Racial Wealth Gap.

Source: Adapted from Cassidy et al. (2019)

is also persistent and the implementation and utilization of a Baby Bond program has the ability to significantly decrease the gap. This continues to be a critical issue of our time as Black median wealth is predicted to fall to *zero* by 2053, while simultaneously, White median wealth is expected to climb to $137,000 (Asante-Muhammad et al., 2017). "If current trends continue, Black households stand to lose nearly 18% of the wealth they held in 2013, and the median white household will own 86 times more wealth than its Black counterpart" (Cassidy et al., 2019, p. 1). These statistics have led many to surmise that Baby Bonds would have the single greatest effect on reducing the racial wealth gap (Darity, 2019).

Unfortunately, Booker's bill was never passed and this method of achieving equity and thus lowering the racial wealth gap never came to fruition.

Potential remedies

We have seen evidence of convergence of the racial wealth gap between 1930 and 1960, where wealth converged at an annual rate of around 1% but between 1960 and 1980, wealth convergence increased to 1.5% (Derenoncourt et al., 2022). What factors led to wealth gap decreasing? The implementation of several key policies during the 20-year period (1960–1980), coincides with the racial wealth gap decreasing at the highest rate since the emancipation of the enslaved. Such policies included the Civil Rights Act of 1964, the Voting Rights Act of 1965 and minimum wage legislation in the 1960s (Derenoncourt et al., 2022). In the future, more policies that specifically address the racial wealth gap should be proposed and implemented.

One such area for policy reform to assist in decreasing the racial wealth gap would be the creation of more banks and financial institutions in Black and Hispanic/Latine communities (Darity, 2019). As we have discussed, the ability to save money over time influences the accumulation of wealth. But what happens when access to commercial banks is not readily available, thus prohibiting the ability to save money in the first place? (Noel et al., 2019; Clements, 2016). Studies have consistently shown that access to traditional financial institutions is a significant contributor to the amount of money individuals and families can save (Cohen et al., 2019; Love, 2016). Clements (2016) found that US counties that were more than 50% White had 40.6 banks for every 100,000 people. Conversely, counties where more than 50% of their residents were Black, Hispanic/Latine, or non-White had 27.1 banks for every 100,000 people.

What is more, between 2013 and 2018, banks in urban communities closed at a higher rate than they did elsewhere, and Black-owned minority depository institutions (MDIs) declined from 41 in 2001 to just 19 in 2021 (US Department of Treasury, 2022). Between 2010 and 2021, in majority-Black Census tracts, bank branches declined 14.6% compared to a 9.7% decline in all other communities (US Department of Treasury, 2022). While we have seen the continuous decline in the number of financial institutions in non-White communities, we have simultaneously witnessed

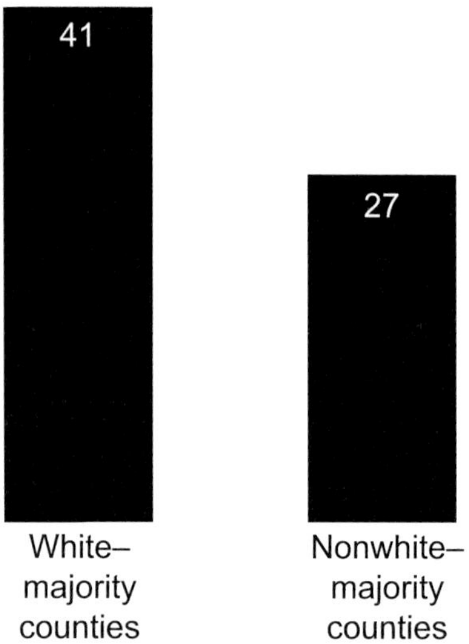

FIGURE 8.8 Financial Institutions per 100,000 People.

Source: Adapted from Parker Cohen, Stephanie Landry, and Santiago Sueiro, "Analyzing the landscape of saving solutions for low-income families *part 1*: The savings crisis and the need for holistic solutions," Prosperity Now, April 2019, prosperitynow.org; Jacob Faber and Terri Friedline, "The racialized costs of banking," New America, June 21, 2018, newamerica.org

predatory lending practices in Black and Hispanic/Latine communities. Faber and Friedline (2018) found that banks charge more for opening and maintaining checking accounts in Black communities compared to White communities and that it is cheaper to maintain a checking account in a White community in comparison to a Black community. Moreover, what is more perplexing according to Faber and Friedline (2018) is that the average White needs to deposit approximately 3% of a paycheck to open an account and maintain 28% of their paycheck to avoid fees or an account closure. On the other hand, Blacks need to deposit approximately 6% of their paycheck and keep 60 of it unused to prevent fees or account closure. Comparatively, Hispanics/Latines need 6% of paycheck and 54 unused, while Asians need 3% and 22% unused. Stricter enforcement of regulations and consumer protections could address this dilemma. The Federal Deposit Insurance Corporation (FDIC) Model Safe Accounts and the Cities for Financial Empowerment (CFE) Fund's Bank on National Account Standards suggest standards such as an opening deposit of $10 to $25, a monthly maintenance fee between $3 and $10, no overdraft or insufficient funds fees, and free online and mobile banking (Faber & Friedline, 2018). At issue, however, is that the vast majority of financial institutions do not adhere to these recommendations. Another recommendation posed by Faber and Friedline (2018) is a higher level of scrutiny of the Community Reinvestment Act (CRA). The CRA came into existence to address banks' racially discriminatory lending practices and was passed in 1977. FDIC-insured banks receive ratings from "substantial non-compliance," to "outstanding" from the CRA which could impact the financial capabilities of the institutions, if the ratings were accurate. Despite significant evidence of racial discrimination in lending practices, CRA awards "outstanding" to 97% of banks (Faber & Friedline, 2018). "Thus, the CRA inadequately redresses banks' racially discriminatory practices by conflating income and race and underestimates discriminatory practices in checking and transaction accounts by emphasizing lending" (p. 18). Finally, according to Noel et al. (2019), increasing banking access could save many Blacks up to $40,000 over the course of their lives. These are but a few of the ideas to minimize and ultimately eliminate the racial wealth gap. More strategies and recommendations are suggested in the next chapter.

References

Alesini, A., Ferroni, M., & Stantcheva, S. (2021). *Perceptions of racial gaps, their causes and ways to reduce them* (National Bureau of Economic Research working paper series). http://www.nber.org/papers/w29245

Anti-Racism, Diversity and Inclusion Initiative (2023). *Bruce's Beach*. https://ceo.lacounty.gov/ardi/bruces-beach/

Asante-Muhammad, D., Collins, C., Hoxie, J., & Nieves, E. (2017). *The road to zero wealth: How the racial wealth divide is hollowing out America's Middle Class*. Institute for Policy Studies. https://ips-dc.org/wp-content/uploads/2017/09/The-Road-to-Zero-Wealth_FINAL.pdf

Badger, E. (2017). Whites have huge wealth edge over Blacks (but don't know it). *New York Times*. https://www.nytimes.com/interactive/2017/09/18/upshot/black-white-wealth-gap-perceptions.html

Baker, R., & Addo, F. (2023). Barriers to racial wealth equality. *Human Rights; Chicago, 48*(2), 2–3, 5.

Banaji, M. R., Fiske, S. T., & Massey, D. S. (2021). Systemic racism: Individuals and interactions, institutions and society. *Cognitive Research*, *6*, 82. https://doi.org/10.1186/s41235-021-00349-3

Cassidy, C., Heydemann, R., Price, A., Unah, N., & Darity, W., Jr. (2019). *Baby bonds: A universal path to ensure the next generation has the capital to survive*. The Samuel Dubois Cook Center on Social Equity.

Chappell, B. (2023). *The Black family who won the return of Bruce's Beach will sell it back to LA County*. https://www.npr.org/2023/01/04/1146879302/bruces-beach-la-county-california

Chiteji, N. S., & Hamilton, D. (2002). Family connections and the Black-White wealth gap among middle-class families. *The Review of Black Political Economy*, *30*(1), 9–28.

Clements, N. (2016). Research on bank branch penetration. *Magnify Money*. https://www.magnifymoney.com/resource/market-data/research-on-bank-branch-penetration/

Cohen, P., Landry, S., & Sueiro, S. (2019). Analyzing the landscape of saving solutions for low-income families, part 1: The savings crisis and the need for holistic solutions. *Prosperity Now*. propseritynow.org

Curtis, P. (2010). Osborne's Åí6.25bn savings plan hits baby bonds and students. *The Guardian*. https://www.theguardian.com/politics/2010/may/24/george-osborne-spending-cuts-6bn

Darity, W., Jr. (2005). Stratification economics: The role of intergroup inequality. *Journal of Economics and Finance*, *29*(2), 144–153.

Darity, W., Jr. (2019). *A new agenda for eliminating racial inequality in the United States: The research we need*. William T. Grant Foundation.

Derenoncourt, E., Kim, C. H., Kuhn, M., & Schularick, M. (2022). *Wealth of two nations: The U.S. racial wealth gap, 1860–2020*. Federal Reserve Bank-Minneapolis, Opportunity and Growth Institute.

Faber, J., & Friedline, T. (2018). *The racialized costs of banking*. Newamerica.org

Grawert, A., & Craigie, T. (2020). Mass incarceration has been a driving force of economic inequality. *Brennan Center for Justice*. https://www.brennancenter.org/our-work/analysis-opinion/mass-incarceration-has-been-driving-force-economic-inequality

Hamilton, D., & Darity, W. (2010). Can 'Baby Bonds' eliminate the racial wealth gap in putative post-racial America? *The Review of Black Political Economy*, *37*(3–4), 207–216.

Hanks, A., Solomon, D., & Weller, C. (2018). Systematic inequality—How America's structural racism helped create the Black-White wealth gap. *Center for American Progress*. https://www.americanprogress.org/article/systematic-inequality/

Hardy, B., & Logan, T. (2020). *Racial economic inequality amid the Covid-19 crisis*. The Hamilton Project.

Jee, E., Meschede, T. Stewart, S., Ciurczak, P., & Schuster, L. (2023). *Racial equity wealth chartbook—National trends and the challenge of local data*. Institute for Economic and Racial Equity & Boston Indicators.

Katznelson, I. (2005). *When affirmative action was white: An untold history of racial inequality in twentieth-century America*. W.W. Norton & Company.
Kraus, M., Rucker, J., & Richeson, J. (2017). Americans misperceive racial economic equality. *Proceedings of the National Academy of Sciences, 114*(39), 10324–10331. https://doi.org/10.1073/pnas.1707719114
Lindwall, C. (2023). *A once-thriving black-owned beach is returned to its rightful owners*. National Resources Defense Council. https://www.nrdc.org/stories/once-thriving-black-owned-beach-returned-its-rightful-owners
Los Angeles County, Chief Executive Officer. (2023). Anti-racism, diversity and inclusion (ARDI) initiative. https://ceo.lacounty.gov/ardi/bruces-beach/
Los Angeles Times. (1912, June 27). Colored people's resort meets with opposition, p. I15. latimes.com
Love, D. (2016). *Bank deserts: Study finds banks are concentrated in majority white communities, scarce in Black communities*. https://atlantablackstar.com/2016/02/20/bank-deserts-study-finds-banks-concentrated-majority-white-communities-scarce-black-neighborhoods/
McWhirter, C. (2011). *Red summer – The summer of 1919 and the awakening of Black America*. St. Martin's Griffin.
Miller, M. (2020). The righteous and reasonable ambition to become a landholder: Land and racial inequality in the postbellum south. *Review of Economics and Statistics, 102*(2), 381–394.
Mimbela, R., & Duarte, K. (2023). *Visualizing the racial wealth gap—From homeownership to income, systemic inequities perpetuate disparities in wealth*. American Civil Liberties Union (ACLU). https://www.aclu.org/news/racial-justice/visualizing-the-racial-wealth-gap
Noel, N., Pinder, D., Stewart, S., & Wright, J. (2019). *The economic impact of closing the racial wealth gap*. McKinsey and Company.
Panetta, G. (2020). Larry Kudlow argues systemic racism doesn't exist because Barack Obama won '79 million white votes' in his 2 presidential runs. *Business Insider*. https://www.businessinsider.com/kudlow-systemic-racism-isnt-real-because-obama-won-79-million-white-votes-2020-6
Pattillo-McCoy, M. (1999). *Black picket fences: Privilege and peril in the Black Middle Class neighborhood*. University of Chicago Press.
Piketty, T. (2014). *Capital – In the twenty-first century*. The Belkap Press of Harvard University Press.
Politico. (2008). *Text of Obama's fatherhood speech*. https://www.politico.com/story/2008/06/text-of-obamas-fatherhood-speech-011094
Spriggs, W. (1984). *W. Afro-American Wealth Accumulation, Virginia 1900–1914*. Dissertation, University of Wisconsin-Madison.
Systemic racism. https://dictionary.cambridge.org/us/dictionary/english/systemic-racism
U.S. Department of Treasury. (2022). *Assessing the impact of new entrant non-bank firms on competition in consumer finance markets*. U.S. Department of the Treasury Report to the White House Competition Council.
Weller, C., & Figueroa, R. (2021). *Wealth matters—The Black-White wealth gap before and during the pandemic*. Center for American Progress.

9

ADVANCING THE EQUITY NEEDLE FORWARD

Throughout the course of this book, we have discussed various topics such as education, healthcare, housing, voting and how communities of color have been adversely affected through racist policies and legislation in each of these areas. More than simply an adverse effect, but a perverse and perpetually harming impact on Blacks, Hispanics/Latines, Indigenous and other people of color, has persisted for many years. We have discussed, in depth, these issues and, perhaps most importantly, illuminated how these inequities and injustices have had a significant financial impact on non-White communities, leading to the racial wealth gap we currently see in the United States today.

Housing policy and inequity

A significant component contributing to the racial wealth gap in the United States, as we previously stated, is related to racist housing policies. As of 2018, the percentage of areas with HOLC grades (Best, Desirable, Declining and Hazardous) remain highly segregated by race. In fact, areas viewed by HOLC as "best" are 86% White, while areas deemed to be "hazardous" have a 64% minority population (Mitchell & Franco, 2018).

Sood et al. (2021) found that in Minneapolis, MN, the percentage of racially covenanted homes in a neighborhood significantly increased the value of homes in the surrounding area. Specifically, increasing the share of covenanted homes by 1% in a one-third of a mile radius around the home, increased house values by 40%, and 45%, respectively. The results

DOI: 10.4324/9781032670850-10

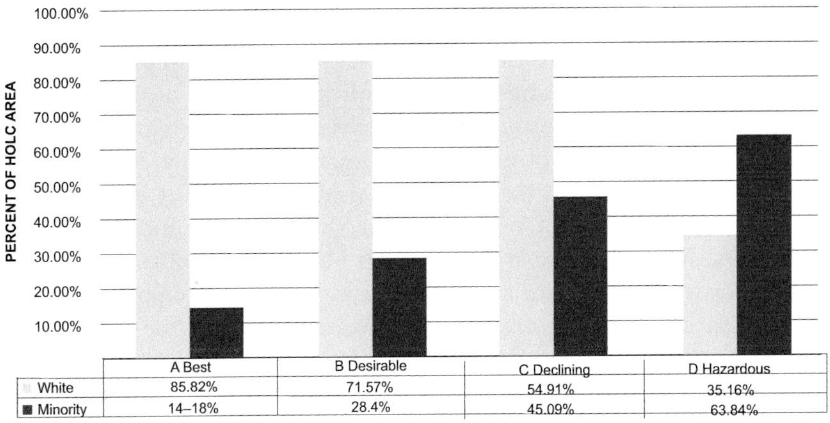

FIGURE 9.1 National HOLC Grades and Race. Percentage of Areas With HOLC Grades That Are Currently Majority Non-Hispanic White, or Majority-Minority Nationally

Source: Adapted from Original 1935–1940 HOLC maps and 2016 FFIEC Census data

of their study indicate the impact of racial covenants on the value of homes in segregated neighborhoods. Unfortunately, these and other similar racist housing policies took precedence over data that would prove otherwise. According to Laurenti (1952), a study of the San Francisco Bay area prepared for the FHA found that the introduction of Black residents into predominantly White neighborhoods did not have a statistically significant impact on the values of homes. Yet, we continuously here racist tropes stating, as if statistically significant, that as the percentage of minorities moving into a community increases, property values decrease.

Supreme Court Chief Justice Vinson, who is not considered the greatest ally of racial minorities in the fight for equal justice and equity, in terms of racially restrictive covenants stated, "We have no doubt that there has been state action in these cases in the full and complete sense of the phrase. The undisputed facts disclose that petitioners were willing sellers, and contract of sale were accordingly consummated. It is clear that but for the active intervention of state courts, supported the full panoply of state power, petitioners would have been free to occupy the properties in question without restraint" (Grossman & Wells, 1988, p. 337).

The push for legislation and stricter enforcement of policies that penalize racially motivated segregation should be ongoing because we continue to see evidence where racial minorities consistently have to fight to overcome centuries of racist housing policies today.

Education policy and inequity

Similarly in the area of education, Blacks and other minorities have faced years of unfair treatment, racist policies and open hostility leading to poorer outcomes. At a time when Blacks were not permitted to attend predominately white institutions (PWIs), schools of higher education for Blacks emerged. Built on the ashes of racism and prejudice in the United States, the impact of HBCUs has been an overwhelming success for over 100 years. Further, the role that HBCUs play has shown to be a viable option for students to earn a college degree, find gainful employment traditional in and growing areas, and ultimately decrease the wealth gap. While the amount of funding HBCUs receive in endowments is significantly less than non-HBCUs, the economic mobility rate of HBCU graduates is greater than graduates from non-HBCUs.

The share of HBCU students in the lowest US income quintile who eventually reach the highest US income quintile is nearly twice as large as students from non-HBCUs who reach the highest quintile. Moreover, the share of HBCU graduates in the lowest two US income quintiles, who eventually reach the two highest US income quintiles, is nearly twice as large as students from non-HBCUs (Espinosa et al., 2018).

In terms of financing higher education, we have seen strong evidence stating the tremendous growth of student loan debt over recent years. Student loan debt is an extremely cumbersome financial burden that suppresses income and wealth accumulation.

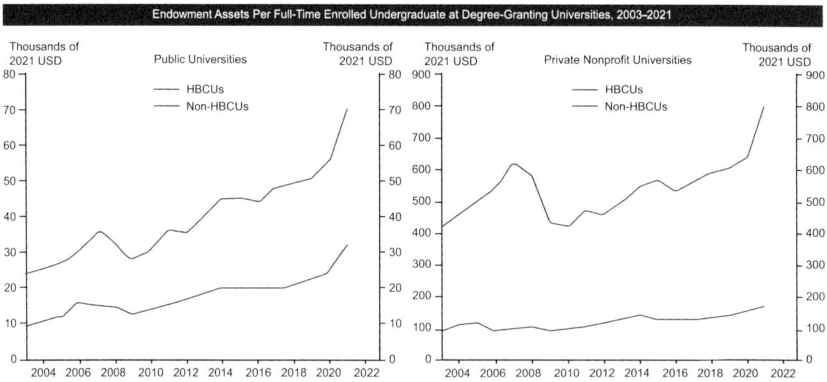

FIGURE 9.2 The Endowment Gap Between HBCUs and Non-HBCUs Is Extensive.

Source: Adapted from National Center for Education Statistics, IPEDS, Goldman Sachs Global Investment Research

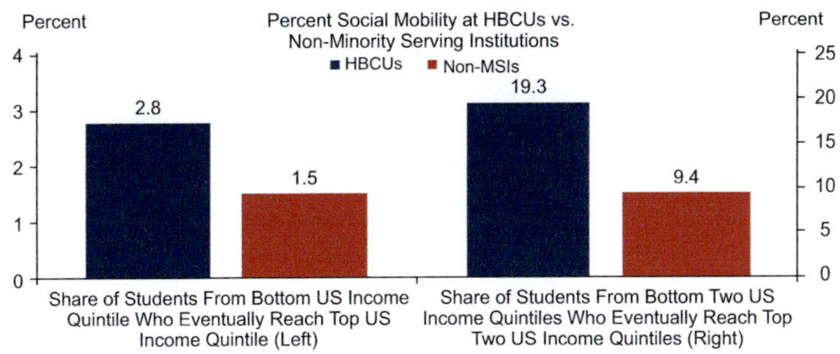

FIGURE 9.3 The Extended Mobility Rate at Four-Year HBCUs Is More Than Double That of Non-Minority Serving Institutions.

Source: Adapted from Espinosa et al. (2018), Goldman Sachs Global Investment Research

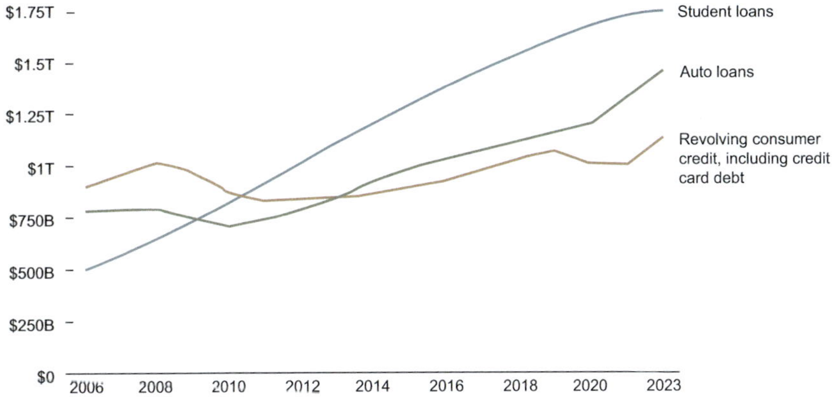

FIGURE 9.4 US Student Loan Debt Has Grown Tremendously.

Source: Adapted from https://www.cfr.org/backgrounder/us-student-loan-debt-trends-economic-impact

One strategy that we have discussed here is to eliminate student loan debt completely. The drain student loan debt has on the US economy is substantial and only exemplified by data that indicates poor children are less likely to enroll in college and less likely to graduate than nonpoor children (Haskins, 2008). It is also the case that the impact student loan debt has on Blacks, Hispanics/Latines, Indigenous and people of color is greater than it is for Whites. Twenty years after beginning college, the median White borrowers' debt has been reduced by 94%, while median Black borrowers still owe 95% of their balance (Federal Reserve, St. Louis). "This hardship creates immense problems for the wider economy, holding back

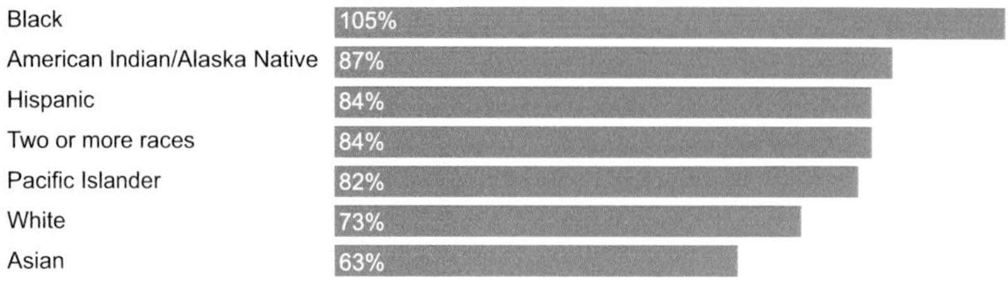

FIGURE 9.5 Racial Disparities in Student Debt.

Source: Council on Foreign Relations (2024)

Average Amount Owed as a Percentage of Amount Borrowed Among Federal Student Loan Borrowers Four Years After Undergraduate Graduation, *2020*

Source: Adapted from National Center for Education Statistics

economic growth, increasing racial inequality, and slowing innovation and entrepreneurship" (Federal Reserve, St. Louis).

Healthcare policy and inequity

Other ways to improve equity while simultaneously reducing the racial wealth gap can be seen in the area of healthcare. To improve healthcare equity in the United States, Cui et al. (2023) suggest making equity a non-negotiable object in every aspect of the process, developing health equity goals and measurements, embracing new ways of working, empowering top-down reform, and importantly to do what you say you are going to do, "walk the talk." There is ample data and evidence to assist hospitals and healthcare organizations to take the necessary and appropriate steps to decrease healthcare inequities. An example of an organization that has been walking the talk is the Boston Medical Center and their Health Equity Accelerator, whose goal is to eliminate disparities in health outcomes across different races and ethnicities (retrieved from https://www.bmc.org/health-equity-accelerator/our-goal). Some of the areas they address are life expectancy, premature mortality rate, infant mortality rate, homelessness, food insecurity and maternal health justice. According to Patrina Martin Cherry, Vice-President of Community Engagement & External Affairs, "economic mobility is a true social determinant of health." They have created health equity fellowships to assist individuals interested in the field of healthcare and medicine in an effort to open pathways and professional development opportunities for those in the community. "The Health Equity Fellowship reflects our commitment to creating change across the entire healthcare delivery spectrum including the people who will lead the next generation" (Cherry, retrieved from https://www.bmc.org/health-equity-accelerator/our-goal).

Repair, remedy, reparations or whatever you want to call it

While many acknowledge that the US economy was largely built upon the backs of enslaved Africans, and that racist policies and laws only perpetuated inequity and inequality between Whites and Blacks and other people of color, agreement on a form, if any, of remedying those past atrocities has not occurred. There appears to be a sentiment that America has done enough through school desegregation after the Brown v. Board of Education (BOE) case in 1954, the Civil Rights Act of 1964 followed by the creation of the Equal Employment Opportunity Commission (EEOC) in the same year, the Voting Act of 1965, Affirmative Action and other legislation, and that more action is unnecessary. We often here, *I had nothing to do with slavery, so why am I paying or being punished for it?* Disparities and equities in education, income, wealth, employment, healthcare, voting and many other aspects of American society tell us otherwise. And while all Whites certainly have not been directly responsible for slavery, they have very often benefitted from its existence.

Part of any plan to move equity to the forefront of public policies must also include reparations. After George Floyd was killed by Minneapolis Police Officers in 2020, former President Biden and former Vice-President Harris acknowledged America's long and enduring history of systemic racism which has been a stain on our nation's soul (Remarks by President Biden on the Verdict in the Derek Chauvin Trial for the Death of George Floyd, 2021).

What are reparations?

The term reparations conjures up a broad array of feelings and sentiments typically in favor or against the idea altogether. Arriving at a general consensus, however, likely first begins by understanding what reparations refer to and in what context the term should be placed in when discussing different groups of people and situations. The International Center for Transitional Justice (ICTJ) defines reparations as something that is "meant to acknowledge and repair the causes and consequences of human rights violations and inequality in countries emerging from dictatorship, armed conflict, and political violence, as well as in societies dealing with racial injustice and legacies of colonization" (ICTJ, n.d.). Reparations, as defined by Merriam-Webster, is the act of making amends, offering expiation, or giving satisfaction for a wrong or injury (Merriam-Webster, retrieved from https://www.merriam-webster.com/dictionary/reparation). According to the United Nations (UN), "victims of gross violations of international human rights law and serious violations of international humanitarian law should, as appropriate and proportional to the gravity of the violation and the circumstances of each case, be provided with full and effective reparation, which: restitution, compensation, rehabilitation, satisfaction and guarantees of non-repetition" (UN General Assembly, Basic Principles and Guidelines on the Right to a Remedy and Reparation for Victims of Gross Violations of International Human Rights Law and Serious Violations of International Humanitarian Law, 2005). In their call for reparations, Ray and Perry (2020) define it as "a system of redress for egregious injustices" (p. 2).

> *There has not been a single year since the founding of the United States when Black people in this country have not been sicker and died younger than White people.*
>
> —*Bassett and Galea, 2020*

Calls for reparations began immediately after the US Civil War that ended in 1865. While portrayed as a "states-rights" issue, the War really was about southern states viewing themselves as having the right to indenture Blacks into involuntary servitude simply because of the color of their skin. As southern states sought to secede from the Union, a war between northern and southern states ensued. After the Civil War, General William Sherman signed Field Order 15 which would allocate 40 acres of land to each Black family, totaling 400,000 acres of confiscated Confederate land, along with any mules left over from the war. When Abraham Lincoln was assassinated, however, President Andrew Johnson reversed the order and gave the land back to the former slaveholders (Ray & Perry, 2020). Furthermore, many former slave owners in states and territories, including Washington, DC, were given *reparations* from the loss of slave property and the earnings yielded (Ray & Perry, 2020). Since that time, countless scholars, such as W.E.B. DuBois, Martin Luther King, Jr., William Darity Jr., Nora Derenoncourt, Ta-Nehisi Coates, Kirsten Mullen, Franklin Obeng-Odom and Evelyn McDowell, along with various commissions, and organizations have made pleas for reparations due to the harm perpetuated against Blacks in the United States.

Not just about slavery

One of the issues associated with detractors of reparations is that they aim to tie it *only* to slavery. In addition to the cataclysmic repercussions from the unnatural events of slavery in the United States, and as we have thoroughly discussed throughout this book, there are many other reasons why reparations for Blacks are appropriate. These reasons include segregation in housing, employment and education; continuous, unceasing examples of discriminatory and racist policies towards Blacks; and the resultant effects of the racial wealth gap that has historically and perpetually depressed income and generational wealth opportunities for Blacks. Darity (2001) found that employment and education discrimination faced by Blacks between 1890 and 1910 had a significant impact on the occupational attainment of their descendants in 1980 and 1990, over 100 years later (Darity & Frank, 2003). Some have even referred to the disparate treatment of Blacks in America as a public health crisis (Bassett & Galea, 2020). Moreover, examples of extreme brutality against Blacks are pervasive as thousands of lynchings and race-related murders have occurred throughout history including those chronicled in the late 19th and early 20th centuries. Just between April and November of 1919, a period referred to as the Red Summer, hundreds of Blacks were killed across the United States in places such as Washington, DC, Chicago, IL, Montgomery, AL, Charleston, SC and Elaine, AR. Also, race riots followed in other areas, most notably in Tulsa, OK, where Blacks had their homes and businesses burned to the ground by racist Whites (Brown, 2020; McWhirter, 2011; Gibson, 1979). Figure 9.6 shows lynchings of Blacks in the United States between 1889 and 1921, by state.

Opposition to reparations

It is obvious that there is a belief that Blacks do not deserve reparations, for a variety of reasons. Some say, "Slavery was a long time ago," while others ask, "Why should they receive money from something that occurred well over 100 years ago, and which I was not responsible?" Another group pointedly asks, "How would it work, and who has a right to make a claim?"

In response to Ta-Nehisi Coates' *The Case for Reparations*, Frum (2014) asks, if Blacks are provided with reparations because of slavery and subjugation, what does that mean for "Native Americans," Mexican-Americans, Japanese Americans, Chinese Americans and any other group that feels as if they were maltreated? He says that Coates' case, and presumably others who make similar proposals, are "built on an unstated assumption that America's racial composition is essentially binary, a white majority that inflicts inequality; a black minority that suffers inequality" (Frum, 2014). Frum, and others who think in this manner seem to be saying that America may be less inclined to open up the reparations "can of worms" for fear that other groups of people will seek similar resolutions. While examining reparations for non-Blacks is not scope of this book, it is likely that we all should examine the issue much more closely. These examples, and

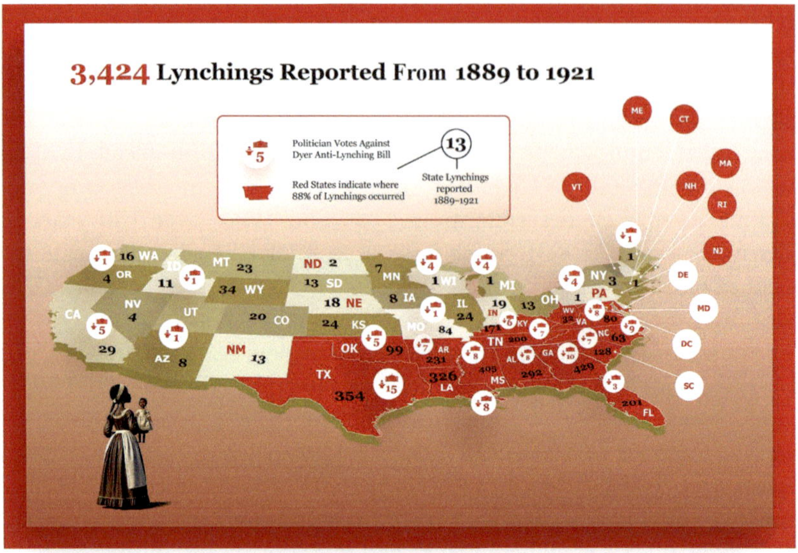

Northern State Congressman That Voted Against the Dyer Anti-Lynching Bill

Congressman	State	Congressman	State
Stafford	Wisconsin	Sinnott	Oregon
Barbour	California	Hayden	Arizona
Curry	California	Kelley	Michigan
Lea	California	Jones	Pennsylvania
Nolan	California	Luce	Massachusettes
Raner	California	Hersey	Maine
French	Idaho	Parker	New Jersey
		Hawes	Missouri

FIGURE 9.6 The Number of Blacks Lynched in the United States: 1889–1921.
Source: Adapted from National Archives Catalog, NAID: 149268727

countless others, cement the case for reparations to Blacks in the United States.

When examined over racial lines, we find mixed support of cash payments as a form of reparations by Blacks. In a Pew Research Center study, in 2021, 77% of Blacks and 18% of Whites supported reparations for descendants of enslaved people (Blazina & Cox, 2022). In a different poll, we see indications that the appetite of Whites in favor of supporting cash payments, as a form of reparations from descendants of slaves, has improved over recent years. In 2014, 68% of Whites opposed cash payments to Blacks for slavery, while 15% were in favor, but by 2021, White opposition had declined to 62% while those in favor had increased to 38% of respondents (Reichelmann & Hunt, 2021). As continued examples of Blacks being murdered at the hands of racists continues (George Floyd, Sandra Bland, Tyre Nichols, Akira Ross, the ten Black Buffalo residents murdered while shopping and countless others), the appeal towards reparations may soften.

H.R.40

Any worthwhile endeavor to study reparations should begin by legislation that supports such a study. In 2017, Representative John Conyers, Maryland, introduced H.R.40—*Commission to Study and Develop Reparation Proposals for African Americans Act.* It would later be reintroduced in 2021, by Congresswoman Shelia Jackson Lee (Texas) and again in 2023 by Senator Corey Booker (New Jersey). The bill would establish a commission "To address the fundamental injustice, cruelty, brutality, and inhumanity of slavery in the United States and the 13 American colonies between 1619 and 1865 and to establish a commission to study and consider a national apology and proposal for reparations for the institution of slavery, its subsequent de jure and de facto racial and economic discrimination against African Americans, and the impact of these forces on living African Americans, to make recommendations to the Congress on appropriate remedies, and for other purposes" (Commission to Study and Develop Reparation Proposals for African Americans Act, retrieved from Congress.gov). It is important to note that the bill would simply create a commission to *study* and *consider a national apology* and a *proposal for reparations for the institution of slavery.* In other words, the commission would study the implications that slavery had on African-Americans and based upon our research here, there are many. As with other initiatives, policy proposals or requests made on behalf of Blacks and people of color, H.R.40 has met with an unsurprising amount of opposition. Ohio Congressman Jim Jordan said that H.R.40 would spend millions of dollars on a commission to take money away from people who were never involved with slavery and give it to Blacks today even though they were never slaves. Senator, Mitch McConnell (Kentucky) has expressed similar views. The fact that Jordan, McConnell and many others are opposed to even studying and more closely examining the topic is evidence enough of the value they place on Black people in the United States today. Conversely, the California State Assembly enacted Assembly Bill 3121 (AB 3121) and established the Task Force to Study and Develop Reparation Proposals for African Americans in 2020. Researching additional information to see what the implications are, seems as if it would be a logical first step, but for those who oppose equity, they would rather leave society as it is with all of the disparities, inequities and injustices we have witnessed for over the past 400 years.

US history is wrought with examples of reparations being paid to groups of individuals for previous harms committed against them. For example, Japanese who were put in internment camps during World War II and Indigenous people in the United States were afforded reparations. While it can be argued that they should have received even larger financial payments due to the harm they incurred, the fact remains that they have been provided with a measure of "relief" (Blakemore, 2023; Ray & Perry, 2020; Darity, 2019; Darity & Frank, 2003, US Department of the Interior, 2022). In fact, we have even learned of White slaveholders being paid reparations for the loss of income as a result of having slaves. Thus, they were paid when slavery was abolished and they could no longer earn income off of their work. In 2025, the city of Tulsa, OK, where one of the bloodiest massacres of Black people occurred, plan to allocate $105 million dollars in reparations towards community redevelopment, housing and cultural preservation (Drenon, 2025). We have also seen examples of US colleges and universities paying some form of reparations for past harms, including Harvard, Georgetown and the University of Virginia (Brooks, 2020; Moscufo, 2020, Forson, 2020). Internationally, many countries have paid for the ills and harm they have caused individuals, such as West Germany paying Holocaust survivors 3.5 Deutsche Marks (Ray & Perry, 2020).

What reparations could look like

The National African American Reparations Committee (NAARC, n.d.) suggests, among other ideas, the establishment of an African Holocaust Institute, education for community development and empowerment, affordable housing for healthy Black communities and wealth generation, funds for cooperative enterprises and socially responsible entrepreneurial development, repairing the damages of the "criminal injustice system," resources for the health, wellness and healing of Black families and communities, and a formal apology by the US Federal Government (NAARC, n.d.).

For those that do support the idea of reparations for Blacks, 82% support educational scholarships, 75 % support the idea of financial assistance for starting or improving a business, 73% think financial assistance for buying or remodeling a home would be appropriate and 57% support the idea of cash payments (Blazina & Cox, 2022).

There are numerous studies that have examined the impact slavery and the resultant fiscal effects it has had on Blacks in the United States. In terms of studies of this kind, calculations can include the amount in loss earnings that Blacks gave up because of being enslaved, estimating how much revenue each slave earned for the economy, monetizing earnings as present values, along with other types of calculations. Ranson and Sutch (2001) estimate the profit of slavery enjoyed by White slave owners between 1806 and 1860, compounded to 2018 at 5% interest to be $19.7 billion (Darity & Mullen, 2022; Ranson & Sutch, 1990). Economist, Larry Neal (1990) calculated the total amount of reparations to be $8.1 trillion at 5% interest in 2019 (Darity & Mullen, 2020). Others have developed similar studies, using different criteria, and in each case suggest a substantial sum of money (Craemer, 2015; Marketti, 1990). Similarly, Miller (2020) found that as a result of land and capital redistribution to those formerly enslaved in the Cherokee Nation, racial wealth gaps reduced and educational outcomes improved correlative to other southern states. In *From Here to Equality—Reparations for Black Americans in the Twenty-First Century*, Darity and Mullen (2022) estimate an outlay of $10.7 trillion, or approximately $267,000 per Black person. They also suggest establishing a trust fund Blacks could apply to for grants related to asset-building projects, homeownership, education, business development and creation, and money set aside for Historically Black Colleges and Universities (HBCUs) (Darity & Mullen, 2020). Ultimately, the cost to repair the harm inflicted upon Black's, in this case, would be extraordinarily high, but so too has the damage that has been done. As we carefully articulate, the high cost should not be a reason to ignore all that has been done, however. The responsibility first falls on the American government to begin earnestly studying the effects of their racist policies and then take the necessary steps to address their atrocities.

In what can only fall in the category of *better late than never*, CitiGroup has been active in funding initiatives to decrease fiscal inequities. They are providing financial opportunities to close the racial wealth gap, such as their pledge to invest $1 billion in Black and brown communities. CitiGroup, along with other large financial institutions like J.P. Morgan, Bank of America, FleetBoston Financial, Wachovia and later Wells Fargo have been complicit in creating economic disparities, particularly as a result of directly benefitting from the slave trade (Flitter, 2022). Despite Citi's involvement in the slave trade, they have begun to make amends in communities all across the United States by investing in distressed neighborhoods. CitiGroup (2022) has stated that it is important to become an anti-racist institution because "Advancing racial equity requires a more intentional focus on the challenges faced by communities of color and a commitment to becoming an anti-racist institution. Citi is taking a hard look at its own policies and practices to actively identify potential bias to help level the playing field for communities of color." For example, Citi has invested over $1 billion in areas to support homeownership for people of color, Black-owned business suppliers, Minority Depository Institutions (MDIs) and economic development (CitiGroup, 2022).

Conclusion and action steps

Throughout the course of this book, we have outlined inequity in the areas including education and healthcare along with several others. For example, the Federal Housing Authority was complicit in creating segregated neighborhoods across the United States. Without their intervention, it is likely that our communities would look significantly different than they currently do. Various forms of racism, including "blockbusting," forced many Blacks and other racial minorities to move to hyper-segregated inner cities, they were excluded from the housing, educational and employment benefits enjoyed by Whites in suburban America, while they simultaneously lived in environments characterized by poverty, crime, and other indices of social disorganization (Fishman, 2000). We have seen inequity in many areas of employment, including paying non-Whites and women lower salaries. "In fact, the Blacker an occupation is, the less employers tend to pay workers, and the more female-dominated an occupation is, the more underpaid that work is, especially care work. This is our nation's default policy, a continuing legacy of chattel slavery and Jim Crow" (Dixon, 2021, p. 3). Each of the topics uncovered has led to the racial wealth gap in the United States. Examining the relationship between public budgeting, finance and equity has allowed us to explore and critically analyze examples where Blacks, Hispanics/Latines, Native American, Indigenous, Asians and other people of color experienced disparate treatment simply because of their race. Unfortunately, there are many more such examples that exist and will continue to plague our society unless strategic interventions in policy begin. Addressing inequities will also require a concerted effort by all races of people who view inequity as a problem and not simply a nuisance or an unfortunate inconvenience. The US economy could be significantly stronger, which would benefit **all** groups of people, if we could simply move past insignificant differences. It is currently popular to state the polarization that currently exists in America is at its zenith. America is not more politically or socially polarized today as opposed to other times in its history. Only those who have forgotten about slavery, the Trail of Tears, Japanese Internment Camps, Jim Crow, and segregation, among other examples, would say such a thing. What we see now, as we have always seen throughout history, is political polarization which is tied to issues of race and ethnicity. When racial minorities try to level the playing field through legislation (H.R.40), within institutions of higher education

(Critical Race Theory), or in companies and organizations (Diversity, Equity, Inclusion and Accessibility initiatives), they are portrayed as being divisive, anti-American, Woke, or racists themselves. This example of gaslighting exemplifies the hypocritical and historically ignorant attitudes of those who fight to oppose equity and equality. "Make no mistake, the linking of discussions of systemic oppression, race, gender expression, and sexual orientation with 'anti-American' sentiments is intentional. It's an attempt to redefine and reclassify who gets to call themselves American, regardless of their relationship to the country" (DeVenny, 2023).

When one examines hiring, elections or admission to a university/college from the perspective of equity, it is statistically impossible that over the course of history, White men are the only ones qualified to be in positions of leadership. The belief that the overwhelmingly high rate of White men's ascension into positions of power and leadership as normal leads one to assume that this result is expected and that it is satisfactory. It is also statistically impossible that the vast majority of organizations, businesses and schools would be led by White men but for the fact of some type of intervention. Another term confidently bandied about by those who fail to examine issues like these closely is "identity politics." Identity politics typically refers to inappropriately placing a racial minority, or a woman, into a position of leadership who is not qualified for that position. According to Merriam-Webster, identity politics refers to "politics in which groups of people having a particular racial, religious, ethnic, social, or cultural identity tend to promote their own specific interests or concerns without regard to the interests or concerns of any larger political group" (Merriam-Webster, retrieved from https://www.merriam webster.com/dictionary/identity%20politics). Real identity politics occurs when we assume that only White men are qualified for positions of leadership. When this occurs, we assume that the natural and right condition for society to exist and be measured against only happens when White men are in charge. The fact of the matter remains that unless a White man is hired for a particular position, or another position of leadership, the assumption by many is that it is an example of identity politics.

While data since the 2016 election (that Donald Trump won) shows hate crimes have increased by 20%, recent studies have also shown that more than 50% of Whites feel as if they have replaced Blacks as the primary victims of discrimination (Chua, 2018). While positions of power in elected politics are beginning to shift, it has been a slow process. Hispanic/Latine women comprise 9.3% of the US population, yet of the 100 most populous US cities, only 3% of mayors identify as Latina (Rutgers Eagleton Institute of Politics, 2023). Are there not Hispanic/Latine women who are more than qualified to become mayors of the US cities? When representative racial and ethnic samples of the population begin mirroring representation in elected positions along with positions of leadership, calls of "reverse discrimination," fear of replacement quickly emerges. These are the sentiments of people from various races or ethnicities because it has been indoctrinated into our way of thinking. "For those looking to entrench the white, patriarchal power structure that has built America, this growing diversity represents a destabilization of the status quo" (DeVenny, 2023).

Table 9.1 provides action steps to be taken to achieve equity in the areas of taxation, voting, healthcare, housing, education and addressing the

TABLE 9.1 Improving Equity through Fiscal Policy

Equity Areas	*Action Steps*
Taxation	• Reform the Tax Cuts and Jobs Act so that a greater share of tax cuts benefit households earning <$100,000 • Create equitable taxation of pass-through entities by eliminating or reducing provision that allows PTEs to report income based upon individual tax returns • Reduce income requirement eligible for the AMT • Implement tax breaks for filers who rent/lease their residences • Provide funding for states and local governments to establish taxation equity metrics
Voting	• Support legislation that aims to eliminate racist redistricting maps • Enact into law the John Lewis Voting Rights Advancement Act • Enact into law the Freedom to Vote Act • Expand early voting opportunities at the state and local government level • Expand voting by mail options at the state and local government level • Provide funding for states and local governments to establish voting equity metrics • Make election day and federal holiday
Healthcare	• Increase the percentage of healthcare facilities in rural communities • Provide funding for states and local governments to establish health equity metrics • Provide federal funding to increase the number of health equity fellowships • Provide funding for hospitals to improve methods to assess financial conditions • Create federal government financial incentives for ACA Medicaid expansion • Make equity a nonnegotiable object in every aspect of healthcare

(*Continued*)

TABLE 9.1 (Continued)

Equity Areas	*Action Steps*
Housing	• Provide federal government financial assistance for first time home buyers to include 5–7% of loan • FHA-backed deferred loans for low-income home buyers • Improve Department of Justice enforcement of housing discrimination claims • Provide funding for states and local governments to establish housing equity metrics • Increase enforcement efforts of predatory lending practices
Education	• Increase federal government financial investment in public schools in non-White communities • Increase federal government funding for afterschool tutoring • Increase federal government funding to support K-12 digital learning platforms • Increase federal government funding to Historically Black Colleges and Universities (HBCUs) and Hispanic-Serving Institutions (HSIs) • Provide federal funding to increase workforce development, research and community-based partnerships in emerging technologies • Provide funding for states and local governments to establish education equity metrics • Provide student loan forgiveness for all borrowers
Racial Wealth Gap	• Create a trust fund of grants that recipients can apply to for asset-building projects such as housing and education assistance • Creation of "Baby Bonds" ($1,000) for all children at birth • Federal government funding to increase entrepreneurship through community-based professional development opportunities • Federal government economic development initiative that provides funding for minority-owned businesses • Federal government financial assistance to increase the percentage of financial institutions in Black, Latina and rural communities by 2–3% annually • Provide funding for states and local governments to establish racial wealth gap equity metrics • Greater scrutiny of Community Reinvestment Act (CRA)

racial wealth gap. The list is not exhaustive but is meant to be a starting point from where policy makers, elected officials, organizations and firms can begin work as we aim to improve equity through fiscal policy.

Achieving equity through fiscal policy is expected to be exceptionally challenging. One of the greatest calamities in American history is the continuous appropriation of wealth accumulation from Blacks, Latinas and other people of color in favor of Whites. Through racist taxation, voting, healthcare, housing and education policies, non-Whites have been relegated to living in a society where they have to compete against a historical assailant who has cornered nearly all areas of economic growth. This assailant is none other than racist American policies that have led to the enormous and almost insurmountable racial wealth gap. To decrease this gap, a similar herculean effort must be undertaken where fiscal policies are created to undue years of maltreatment.

We are currently in the midst of Trump 2.0 and Americans can expect more oppressive acts towards those who embrace diversity, inclusion and who seek equity. His obstreperous and puerile personality relies upon extreme, authoritarian actions towards those who make opprobrious remarks in opposition to him, and who speak freely against atrocities in America and abroad. Working towards equity, in an environment like this, while difficult, is still attainable. It is often the case in politics that immediately after one administration leaves office that the subsequent administration favors policies diametrically different than the preceding one.

The road to equity will continue to be a long and arduous trip that only the brave, morally upright and righteous will continue to travel with hopes of seeing a better result for future generations.

References

Bassett, M., & Galea, S. (2020). Reparations as a public health priority – A strategy for ending Black-White health disparities. *New England Journal of Medicine, 383*(22).

Blakemore, E. (2023). The thorny history of reparations in the US. *History*. https://www.history.com/news/reparations-slavery-native-americans-japanese-internment

Blazina, C., & Cox, K. (2022). Black and White Americans are far apart in their views of reparations for slavery. *Pew Research Center*. https://www.pewresearch.org/short-reads/2022/11/28/black-and-white-americans-are-far-apart-in-their-views-of-reparations-for-slavery/

Booker. (2010). https://www.congress.gov/bill/115th-congress/senate-bill/3766/text

Brooks, T. (2020). Enslaved labor built these universities. Now they are starting to repay the debt. *USA Today*. https://www.usatoday.com/story/news/education/2020/02/12/colleges-slavery-offering-atonement-reparations/2612821001/

Brown, D. (2020). Remembering 'Red Summer,' when White mobs massacred Blacks from Tulsa to D.C. *National Geographic*. https://www.nationalgeographic.com/history/article/remembering-red-summer-white-mobs-massacred-blacks-tulsa-dc

Chua, A. (2018). How America's politics went from inclusion to division. *The Guardian*. https://www.theguardian.com/society/2018/mar/01/how-americas-identity-politics-went-from-inclusion-to-division

CitiGroup Financial. (2022). *Action for racial equity two year progress report*. citi.com/racialequity

Council on Foreign Relations. (2024). *Is rising student debt harming the US economy?* https://www.cfr.org/backgrounder/us-student-loan-debt-trends-economic-impact

Craemer, T. (2015). Estimating slavery reparations: Present value comparisons of historical multigenerational reparations policies. *Social Science Quarterly*, *96*(2), 639–655.

Cui, A., Feehan, E., Julien, J. P., & Nagarajan, N. (2023). *Reimagining public health programs to deliver equitable impact*. McKinsey & Company.

Darity, W., Jr. (2019). *A new agenda for eliminating racial inequality in the United States: The research we need*. William T. Grant Foundation.

Darity, W., Jr., & Frank, D. (2003). The political economy of ending racism and the WCAR—The economics of reparations. *American Economic Review*, *93*(2), 326–329.

Darity, W. & Mullen, K. (2022). *From here to equality – reparation for Black Americans in the twenty-first century* (2nd ed.). University of North Carolina Press.

Darity, W. A., Jr. (2001). Why did black relative earnings surge in the early 1990s? *Journal of Economic Issues*, *35*(2), 533–542.

DeVenny, K. (2023). American, redefined—how language is weaponized to oppress and marginalize. *Legal Defense Fund*. https://www.naacpldf.org/white-supremacy-what-it-means-to-be-american/

Dixon, R. (2021). From excluded to essential: Tracing the racist exclusion of farmworkers, domestic workers, and tipped workers from the Fair Labor Standards Act. Hearing before the U.S. House of Representatives Education and Labor Committee, Workforce Protections Subcommittee. *National Employment Law Project*.

Drenon, B. (2025). Tulsa plans $105m in reparations for America's hidden massacre. *BBC.com*. https://www.bbc.com/news/articles/c9dqnz37v1wo

Espinosa, L., Kelchen, R., & Taylor, M. (2018). *Minority serving institutions as engines of upward mobility*. American Council on Education, Center for Policy Research & Strategy.

Fishman, R. (2000). The American Metropolis at century's end: Past and future influences. *Housing Policy Debate*, *11*(1), 199–213.

Flitter, E. (2022). *At Wells Fargo, a quest to increase diversity leads to fake job interviews*. https://www.nytimes.com/2022/05/19/business/wells-fargo-fake-interviews.html

Forson, T. S. (2020). Enslaved labor built these universities. Now they are starting to repay the debt. *USA Today*. https://www.usatoday.com/story/news/education/2020/02/12/colleges-slavery-offering-atonement-reparations/2612821001/

Frum, D. (2014). The impossibility of reparations: Considering the single most important question about racial restitution: How would it work? *The Atlantic*. https://www.theatlantic.com/business/archive/2014/06/the-impossibility-of-reparations/372041/

Gibson, R. (1979). *The Negro Holocaust: Lynching and race riots in the United States, 1880–1950*. Yale-New Haven Teachers Institute, Curricular Resources.

Grossman, J., & Wells, R. (1988). *Constitutional law and judicial policy making* (3rd ed.). Longman Inc.

Haskins, R. (2008). Education and economic mobility. In J. Isaacs, I. Sawhill, & R. Haskins (Eds.), *Getting ahead or losing ground: Economic mobility in America* (pp. 91–104). Economic Mobility Project, an Initiative of the Pew Charitable Trusts. http://www.economicmobility.org/assets/pdfs/PEW_EMP_GETTING_AHEAD.pdf

International Center for Transitional Justice (ICTJ). (n.d.) *Reparations definition*. https://www.ictj.org/reparations

Laurenti, L. (1952). Effects of nonwhite purchases on market prices. *The Appraisal Journal*, *3*(20).
Marketti, J. (1990). Estimated present value of income diverted during slavery. In R. F. America (Ed.), *The wealth of races: The present value of benefits from past injustices* (pp. 107–112). Greenwood Press.
McWhirter, C. (2011). *Red summer – The summer of 1919 and the awakening of Black America*. St. Martin's Griffin.
Miller, M. (2020). The righteous and reasonable ambition to become a landholder: Land and racial inequality in the postbellum south. *Review of Economics and Statistics*, *102*(2), 381–394.
Mitchell, B., & Franco, J. (2018). *HOLC "redlining" maps: The persistent structure of segregation and economic inequality*. National Community Reinvestment Coalition. https://ncrc.org/holc/
Moscufo, M. (2020). Harvard sets up $100 million endowment fund for slavery reparations. *Reuters*. https://www.reuters.com/world/us/harvard-sets-up-100-million-endowment-fund-slavery-reparations-2022-04-26/
National African American Reparations Committee. (n.d.). *10-Point reparations plan*. https://reparationscomm.org/
National Archives Catalog, NAID 149268727. https://catalog.archives.gov/id/149268727
Neal, L. (1990). A calculation and comparison of the current benefits of slavery and an analysis of who benefits. In R. F. America (Ed.), *The wealth of races: The present value of benefits from past injustices*. Greenwood Press.
Ranson, R., & Sutch, R. (2001). *One kind of freedom – The economic consequences of emancipation* (2nd ed.). Cambridge University Press.
Ray, R., & Perry, A. (2020). *Why we need reparations for Black Americans*. Brookings. https://www.brookings.edu/wp content/uploads/2020/04/BigIdeas_Ray_Perry_Reparations-1.pdf
Reichelmann, A., & Hunt, M. (2021). How we repair it: White Americans' attitudes toward reparations. *Brookings*. https://www.brookings.edu/articles/how-we-repair-it-white-americans-attitudes-toward-reparations/
"Remarks by President Biden on the Verdict in the Derek Chauvin Trial for the Death of George Floyd". (2021, April 29). https://www.whitehouse.gov/briefing-room/speeches-remarks/2021/04/20/remarks-bypresident-biden-on-the-verdict-in-the-derek-chauvin-trial-for-the-death-of-george-floyd/
Rutgers-Eagleton Institute on Politics. (2023). *Women Mayors in U.S. Cities 2023*. https://cawp.rutgers.edu/facts/levels-office/local/women-mayors-us-cities-2023
Sood, A., Speagle, W., & Ehrman-Solberg, K. (2021). *Long shadow of racial discrimination: Evidence from housing racial covenants*. Social Science Research Network (SSRN).
UN General Assembly, Basic Principles and Guidelines on the Right to a Remedy and Reparation for Victims of Gross Violations of International Human Rights Law and Serious Violations of International Humanitarian Law. (2005). Retrieved June 10, 2025, from https://www.refworld.org/legal/resolution/unga/2006/en/12095
US Department of the Interior. (2022). Tribes to receive $1.7 billion from President Biden's Bipartisan Infrastructure Law to fulfill Indian Water Rights Settlements. https://www.doi.gov/pressreleases/tribes-receive-17-billion-president-bidens-bipartisan-infrastructure-law-fulfill

INDEX

Note: Page numbers in *italics* indicate figures, and page numbers in **bold** indicate tables in the text.

For Product Safety Concerns and Information please contact our
EU representative GPSR@taylorandfrancis.com Taylor & Francis
Verlag GmbH, Kaufingerstraße 24, 80331 München, Germany